Comeast
1936 university
103

BOATBUILDING WITH PLYWOOD

THIRD EDITION

by

GLEN L. WITT, NAVAL ARCHITECT

(WITH 2ND EDITION REVISIONS by KEN HANKINSON)

PUBLISHED BY
GLEN-L MARINE DESIGNS

TO THE SKIPPER . . .
A. E. WITT
ever patient, understanding, helpful, and guiding.

TABLE OF CONTENTS

PREFACE

My brother, Elbert Witt, and I started building boats when I was still in high school. Plywood was virtually unknown in those days, we rabbeted stems, spiled planks, and used what we thought were proper building procedures. The plans available in those days didn't take into account the amateur builder. It was more of a "here-it-is, now-build-it" approach. We couldn't afford to build boats (these were Depression times, after all), but we somehow did it, anyway.

Frame lumber — white oak — was scrounged from old table leaves, obtained for virtually nothing from junk furniture stores. It took a long time to get that old finish off. Then again, time we had, money we didn't. Planking had to be natural mahogany (didn't it?) and took lots of mowing lawns and delivering papers to procure. Each plank was fitted with care. The seams were spaced oh so uniformly. The screw holes were plugged or blind-fastened, and spaced so precisely, from the edges and each other. The filled and stained mahogany planks were given numerous coats of varnish, then hand-rubbed with pumice, and finished with rotten rock and rubbing oil. How else did you properly finish a boat?

Eventually plywood was "discovered." But you couldn't find a plan that showed how to use it, or many people who even believed it COULD be used to build a boat. Perhaps ignorance proved to be the best teacher after all. As there were no guidelines on the "right way" to use plywood, we had to discover them for ourselves, or make them up. We went through a learning curve, using "proven" or "accepted" methods of conventional boatbuilding. Most of them didn't work, as we found out, more often than not the hard way.

By this time, a cadre of pioneer plywood boatbuilders had begun to form. We all built boats, shared our experiences (both good and bad), and used the craft we had labored so hard to make. Having taken up naval architecture, I seemed the logical one to compile just what this plywood stuff would (and WOULDN'T) do. Years later, the first edition of this book was published.

This is the Third Edition of "BOATBUILDING WITH PLYWOOD." And yes, we're still learning and compiling information about the subject. Epoxy resins and adhesives have opened up new and different building methods. Stitch-and-glue and cold-molded plywood boatbuilding are accepted, and even common. Yet, many basic methods have not changed. They have been modified or perhaps improved, but remain essentially the same.

Obviously, one person does not write a book like this all by himself. It has been my good fortune over the years to have had some fine associates. Among plywood boatbuilders, Don Ruffa (retired), the handsome curly-headed fellow in many of the construction photos, stands alone. Allyn Perry, shown in the stitch-and-glue section, is a very meticulous craftsman, who assisted in the development of many new ideas. A special thanks to Ken Hankinson, for rewriting the second edition so ably. All these people helped make this book. Thanks, people.

My hobby is (and has been for many years) building boats and playing with them. Oddly enough, that's exactly what I do for a living, too. It has been my pleasure to be the founder of Glen-L Marine Designs, a company specializing in creating boat plans for the amateur builder. My business is designing boats and talking to people about how they are built (the boats, that is).

It's fun working with people who have just started their first boat, just as it is talking to experienced builders. The questions they bring up are often provocative, and the suggestions they have offered have been very useful. They have often helped to pinpoint problem areas in plywood boatbuilding that need clarification or simplification. That's what we've tried to do here and I would like to express my gratitude to these many builders for their input. In some ways, it's their book, too. As a fellow craftsman, I thank them and trust that this book will help make boatbuilding a more enjoyable hobby both for them and for all those who will discover it in the future.

Glen L. Witt
Bellflower, CA

FOREWORD

The amateur built boat is a tangible, usable by-product of enjoyment. Boatbuilding is not only a pleasure, but also a hobby that the whole family can join in. The resultant craft, be it a dinghy, sailboat, runabout, or cruiser, provides a lasting source of entertainment for both the builder's family and friends. There is no finer feeling of pride of accomplishment than that which occurs when a boat owner can proudly state, "I built her myself".

Before the advent of reliable waterproof glues used to make today's plywood, boatbuilders were looked upon as rare "nuts" who carved lumber into little pieces with more than average ability. Conventional planking was and still is time consuming besides being beyond the abilities and pocketbooks of most amateurs. Plywood, on the other hand, is the obvious material for the great majority of amateur builders, and has brought the hobby of boatbuilding within the abilities and budget of the average home workshop "do-it-yourselfer".

Most texts on boatbuilding discuss plywood and its application to boatbuilding in a short paragraph, or at best in a single chapter. This book, however, will show in detail the "how-to" of boat construction with the emphasis on the use of plywood. All aspects of the plywood boatbuilding process will be covered whenever possible in three ways; written text, illustrations, and by photos. With these three methods, the various processes of construction will be covered in such a manner as to make boatbuilding more easily understood and thus more enjoyable. If the reader absorbs all the information contained herein, there is no reason why his boat will not equal or exceed the quality of a comparable stock boat and represent an outstanding value.

CHAPTER 1 — WHY BUILD A PLYWOOD BOAT?

As anyone with any boating experience knows, there are many different materials that can be used to build a boat. There are wood boats, steel boats, aluminum boats, plastic boats, fiberglass boats, fabric boats, ferrocement boats, and even rubber boats! If one has the money, he can buy a ready-made boat of just about any of these materials if a suitable craft can be found. But, from the standpoint of the person who wants to build his own boat, the practical choices narrow down quickly, especially where limited pocketbooks and ease of construction are important.

Few amateurs have the welding abilities together with the knowledge of handling corrosion problems associated with metal boats to turn out a decent boat in steel or aluminum. The boat of ferrocement also requires some welding skills as well as professional plastering skills to make a decent looking and enduring craft. And while there are "one-off" fiberglass boatbuilding methods suitable for many amateurs, such processes are not the most economical or simple methods of building a boat. As noted in the foreword, the conventional wood boatbuilding methods using planking require a lot of woodworking ability as well as patience that few amateurs possess. As for the other materials used to build boats, these are, for the most part, relegated to the factory production line and not really adaptable to the home builder who may want to build just a single boat.

Since low cost and ease of construction are the most important factors in building a boat as far as the do-it-yourselfer is concerned, this narrows the scope of materials down to the point where the plywood boat really shines. However, there are many other reasons why plywood makes a good boat regardless of who builds the boat. For example, pound for pound, plywood is stronger than steel. It does not rust, corrode, or deteriorate like metal and ferrocement boats can. The plywood boat can be made to be as light or lighter in weight commensurate with strength as any material (as is witnessed by the many record breaking competition craft which are made using this material). When the plywood boat is sheathed with a covering of fiberglass and resin or equivalent materials, it has all the so-called "no-maintenance" advantages of a fiberglass hull. Such a covering can give the same cosmetic appearance, reduced maintenance, and leak-proof qualities just like those found in stock boats.

But one fact must be brought up at this point: There is no such thing as a "maintenance-free" boat. All boats need care if they are to look as good as when new, and be reliable and safe vessels. The man who claims he has never painted his fiberglass boat probably doesn't mention that it requires a good,

FIG. 1-1—This striking craft is an excellent example of the high quality craftsmanship that amateur boatbuilders can achieve using plywood. One would be hard-pressed to tell the difference between this boat and one built by professionals. The individual who built this boat had never built a boat before.

thorough waxing at least once a year if normally exposed. And anybody who has ever spent a good amount of "elbow grease" doing a job like this will probably agree that moving a paint brush along may be easier. In fact, sooner or later, all boats require a fresh coat of paint for appearance's sake if nothing else.

A common statement that comes up from the novice is, if plywood boats are so good, how come factories don't build them? While it is true that the production line factory probably does not build plywood hulled boats, this does not mean that the material is not used. It is true that there are many numerous small yards throughout the world that do turn out plywood boats, usually on a high-quality custom basis, however. The reason for this is that plywood simply does not lend itself to the mass production unskilled labor techniques required for the stock boat where high profits are important (and low quality is often a by-product as well).

But on the other side of the same coin, one must realize that regardless of the material used to build a hull, just about all boats employ plywood to some degree. And when one realizes the unique qualities of this versatile material it is little wonder. For example, what other material can span such a large distance with so little support, so much stiffness, and so little expense and labor? It is nothing unusual to find plywood panels well hidden between fiberglass laminates on so-called "all-fiberglass" boats making up for the inherent weaknesses in panels of fiberglass and the high cost of the raw materials that a fiberglass laminate requires for an equal amount of strength. Transoms, sandwiched bottom panels, motor stringers, cabin sides and tops, decking, bulkheads, and an endless list of structural members of plywood are used throughout the boatbuilding industry not only in fiberglass boats, but in boats built of other materials as well. Why? Simply because plywood is the most suitable material for the given application.

Because of the waterproof glues used in the manufacture of plywood, it is a "trusted" material by all who are familiar with boatbuilding procedures. They know of its reliable engineering qualities and its proven consistency. While plywood panels can still check and crack on the surface when exposed to the elements and not protected by suitable coatings, steel, aluminum, and ferro-cement will rust, corrode, and abrade; and fiberglass structures will craze, blister, and bubble when similarly abused. Nevertheless, failures with any of these materials usually are not the fault of the material, but rather the builder and/or the designer who didn't realize the full potentials and drawbacks of the materials involved. Luckily, failures are far and few between regardless of the material, but there still is yet no perfect boatbuilding material.

Probably one of the most compelling reasons for building your own boat out of plywood is simply that it is a familiar material. Just about everyone knows the "feel" of plywood. It's a warm material, easy to handle and work, and doesn't require any really "exotic" tools and equipment. Its mass availability makes it low in cost at least on a square foot basis when compared to comparable materials. Grading standards let the buyer know the quality of the material before it's put into the boat. Plus it possesses no "quirks" that may tend to discourage the beginner. In short, it's a nice material, and still the most suitable for the amateur boatbuilder for the majority of craft. It's the task of this book to tell you how to use the material to its best advantages so that you can turn out the "boat-of-your-dreams" with the least amount of work, mistakes, and money, but still with the pride of accomplishment that everyone hopes to have in the completed craft.

CHAPTER 2 — CAN YOU BUILD YOUR OWN BOAT?

Can you build your own boat? In all honesty, no one can answer this question but you. It does take certain abilities and personal qualifications that will be discussed in the following. But with plywood, the chances of a successful boatbuilding project are much more likely for the majority of amateurs, regardless of their abilities and qualifications. Hence the popularity of this material.

Building your own boat is one of the most satisfying and rewarding of experiences. Those who have built a piece of furniture or constructed an addition to their home realize the feeling of pride of craftsmanship that is second to none. In building a boat, the pleasures are even greater since the craft is a usable product intended to increase the pleasure and enjoyment of life not only for the builder, but for his friends and family. As one boatbuilding advocate stated, "Noah did it once, so probably you can too".

The type and size boat that the amateur should attempt depends on his ability for the most part. Unless the individual is an experienced craftsman, it is preferable for him to start on a smaller-sized boat. The reason for this is that everything will occur much more quickly and give that needed confidence so important for the beginner to avoid discouragement. It also is a good way to gain the necessary experience that one should have before he attempts that "world-cruiser" or "live-aboard" retirement vessel that seems to be the dream of so many people. Although the "crawl-before-you-walk" approach of starting with the small boat is advocated, it must be admitted that many people who have never built a boat before often jump in head first and build a much bigger boat than is recommended. Most will succeed, with perseverance though some will not, but if this is your inclination, only you can make the judgement.

Regardless of the size of boat that you intend to build, start off with a good set of plans from a known designer or design firm. Don't attempt to go "creative" and design your own! The value of a good set of plans will be repaid many times over by the savings in time and work that they will provide. Why take a chance on questionable results when you are going to put in your own labor and hard-earned bucks on the completed project? A hashed-up mess is worth very little, if anything, except by the cord as firewood. On the other hand, a craft built to a good design with care and per the designer's recommendations can prove to be worth many times its original cost of materials over the years. The choice is up to you, the builder.

Consider carefully the type of boat you desire. When you have selected the plans, stick to them. Follow the recommendations of the designer as closely as

FIG. 2-1—Could you build this plywood boat? Only you can honestly answer this question. The amateur who built this boat took about 3 months of spare time work. Could you do it faster? Or would you require more time? This depends on many variables. But remember, boatbuilding is a pleasurable hobby where time often becomes secondary to the rewards of personal satisfaction.

possible. Usually the chief cause of an inferior home-built boat is failing to follow the design and branching out "on your own" so to speak. It must be admitted that making minor changes is one of the reasons for building your own boat. It could be the only way to get the boat that you want. However, always check with the designer first to make sure that such a modification is feasible and will not structurally damage the boat or otherwise affect the safety of the crew. A seemingly minor change could affect the performance of the boat and make the results questionable.

Beware of the advice of "backyard experts", or perhaps we should say "backyard wreckers"? These self-appointed "advisors" are constantly giving "expert" advice. If they want to give advice, suggest that they build their own boat and use the thoughts themselves. While building a boat, you will probably hear a lot of advice that generally begins as follows: "Cousin Charlie had a boat just exactly like this one, only it was six feet longer and had quite a bit more beam. His was an inboard and this one is an outboard, but boy what he did to make that thing go! Now take my advice . . .". Don't you believe it! If you have a strong will, such a person can be ignored. If not, be polite, hand him a beer, a chaw of tobacco, a cigarette — do anything to shut him up. Again, when using a set of plans prepared by a professional, follow his advice.

You're probably asking at this point just what makes for a good set of plans? How does one tell a good set of plans, especially since most plans are purchased through the mail? Well, this is admittedly a "buyer beware" situation, but here are some tips. The easiest plans to build by will provide full size patterns or at least offer these so that no lofting of the hull is required. Of course, there are good plans that do not offer patterns, but these require that the builder must lay out the lines from a table of offsets provided by the designer, and this is difficult and time consuming for most amateurs. The topic of lofting will be discussed in Chapter 8.

Find out if the plans come with some sort of instructions, which should preferably be of the sequential or step-by-step type. These instructions are preferably more than just the call-outs on the drawings. In some cases, such instructions may be substituted with a written set of specifications (especially on larger boats) that are acceptable if they cover all aspects of the construction. Another aid that is often furnished is a bill of materials that provides a listing of the members used to build the basic hull. Such a listing can be used to estimate the costs to build the boat as they will apply to your area. Designers are often asked how much it will cost to

build a given boat. Since he may be a long ways from where you plan on building the boat, the use of the material listings will give you, the builder, a better idea of what you will have to spend than a "ball park" figure guessed at by the designer. After all, he probably has many designs active and it would be impossible for him to keep up on the costs to build them all, let alone cost variations from one part of the country to the next.

Of course, if you have a chance, take a look at the set of plans you are interested in. Just about anybody can tell a good set of drawings from a poor set. Then too, ask around about the designer or firm you are considering, especially if you can find someone who is or has built from the same plans or those from the same designer or firm. Don't be too impressed by advertising claims seen in the boating magazines about plans that claim to have many, many sheets of drawings. It doesn't matter much how many sheets there are, but instead how much information is on the sheets. Don't be too impressed with price either. Some of the best boat plans are inexpensive, while some of the poorest may cost a fortune. Note that we said "inexpensive" and not cheap. If the plans seem too cheap, you probably will not get all the information you will require to do a complete job. Consider if the price asked for the plans could possibly cover the cost of mailing, the cost of printing, and the designer's profit for the size craft in question.

Best of all, contact the designer by mail or talk to him about the design and your requirements. In the event of problems during the construction, will he make himself available to you? While many designers charge a fee for such consultations, many will answer questions you may have about building problems at no cost. However, realize that their time is valuable and that their obligation ends where the construction of the boat ends. The fact that your wife gets seasick aboard the boat in a gale, or you want to sleep 10 aboard a 20′ express cruiser is not his problem, so don't expect him to be too cordial at hearing a one hour dissertation of your problems.

How long does it take to build a boat? No one can honestly answer that question, although some suppliers of plans will readily toss up any figure that sounds good. But how can anyone know what your abilities are? Or how fast you work? Or what tools and equipment you have that will speed up the process? Each individual has his own working speed, and any attempt at guessing at the time involved in building a boat would necessarily be based on what one particular individual could do. As an example, a professional, with knowledge and tools, can turn out a good custom plywood boat in the 16′ range, throughout the basic woodworking and ready for painting, in about 40 man-hours. The amateur would take perhaps three or four times as long. Some amateur builders try to keep track of the time involved in building. The boat illustrated in Fig. 2-1 was built in a little over three months of spare time, but the builder didn't keep exact hourly records, so just how many "manhours" were involved is a moot question. How long would it take you? In all probability you will spend more time than you think you will, and when you are finished, you will not know how many hours you have actually spent. Very few of us keep time on enjoyment, and the hobby of boatbuilding is certainly en-

joyable.

How much does it cost to build a boat? And how much can you save by doing it yourself? Again these are questions that cannot be answered exactly. While there are "rules-of-thumb" that are often bandied about regarding the percentage of the building cost as it applies to the construction of the hull-only, in relation to the entire boat, obviously this will vary considerably with the type of boat in question. This is why a copy of the bill of materials is the best guide, since the costs for this portion of the project can be determined more accurately by checking current prices in your area. As far as the cost of fitting out and equipping the boat, it all depends on how "deluxe" you want to go, and how much "scrounging" ability you have and use in locating the best prices. A common mistake in shopping for marine equipment is to start looking in the spring. Coincidentally, this is just the time when everyone else is looking for the same items you want so they can get their boats in the water and in operation. Consequently, there are no "deals" to be found. A better approach would be to go "bargain hunting" in the off-season when merchants may be willing to discount goods that they want to get out of their inventories.

As will be covered later in the chapter on lumber the cost of building the hull can vary considerably on how you buy your materials. And when comparing the cost of building your boat with the cost of another, you must take care that you are comparing "likes-with-likes" and not "apples with oranges". With careful shopping, however, there is nothing unusual about a builder saving 50% or more over the cost of a comparable stock boat. How much you save, of

FIG. 2-2—This plywood cruiser shows what can result when a builder can "scrounge" for materials. For example, much of the wood came from imported crating material which just happened to be a suitable boatbuilding lumber. The stainless handrails came from a demolished rest home, while dismantled bleacher seats and beams of oak were used for the joinerywork. After completion, this boat was valued by survey at well over twice its original cost. That's quite an accomplishment when one considers that the builders had never built a boat before.

course, may vary.

If you have the desire to build a boat, you probably wonder about the necessary personal qualifications. These can probably be enumerated as follows: (1) Perseverance, (2) Ability, (3) Following Instructions, (4) Scrounging, and (5) Money. These are not necessarily listed in order. The following paragraphs will discuss each of these qualifications.

(1) **Perseverance:** This is probably the most important character trait required for building a boat. A stubborn individual, who simply won't give up, can lack many other personal attributes and still get by. Building a boat is going

to take time, and is often tedious and even exasperating. The desire to stick to the job until it is completed is imperative. Don't take short cuts either; do it the right way, not the "quick-and-dirty" way.

(2) **Ability:** At least some mechanical ability is necessary in building your own boat. The person who considers building his own boat usually is a "do-it-yourselfer". He has a selection of hand tools and the ability to use them. If you are one of those individuals who does not like working with his hands, or getting his hands dirty, or has no particular aptitude for working with tools, the construction of a boat should not be contemplated. If you have doubts about your physical strength or endurance, however, just remember that many people with physical handicaps (including amputees and even blind people) have built and do build boats.

(3) **Following Instructions:** This is very important when building a boat. The drawings as prepared by the designer will need to be studied and reviewed PRIOR to the construction, and the instructions religiously followed to complete a successful boat. A general knowledge of blueprint reading is not absolutely necessary with most good plans, but the builder should at least understand the drawings before commencing the construction. Remember that famous saying, "When all else fails, read the instructions".

(4) **Scrounging:** This may not be considered a personal qualification, but some are better at it than others, and those who can do it, save the most and get better deals (see Fig. 2-2). Scrounging may consist of getting materials at slightly less than you would normally pay for them, or it may involve someone's cooperation in doing some welding, using someone's power tools, or even having a friend give a hand in the project. Remember that bartering for goods and services is sometimes as effective as using money.

(5) **Money:** Obviously you will probably save a considerable amount by building your own boat. The prices of ready-made boats today are staggering, what with the cost of labor, materials, overhead, distributor and dealer mark-ups, and the like. But this does not mean that you can start out your boatbuilding project with "peanuts". It will cost money, even though you will control the pursestrings and allot the funds as you can afford it. Try to determine what the total cost will be before you start, even though you will not need all the money at once. Don't get into the middle of something that you cannot afford. Consider what the costs will be AFTER completion as well, and be honest with yourself and your budget.

After appraising these qualifications and you react with a positive attitude to them, you will probably be successful in building your own boat and you will no doubt derive pleasure and satisfaction from the project. As many people discover, they like the activity so much that they may eventually build another one. Remember, many professional builders were once amateurs.

CHAPTER 3 — TOOLS & EQUIPMENT

If you want to build a boat but don't have much experience with tools, or don't know a thing about tools, then do two things. First, get a copy of a book showing woodworking tools and how they are used, and read it over. If you can't find such a book, then at least find a catalog that shows what woodworking tools look like and what they are called. Second, sign up for a class in woodworking such as those offered in adult education programs. Build a small project of anything you like, but make sure that it includes the use of as many woodworking tools from the list included in this chapter together with as many woodworking joints and procedures as possible. This will quickly familiarize you with the tools and methods of use. If you fit into this category, the one thing NOT to do is to splurge on a complete shop or brand new tools of every type. This will be a pure waste of money.

The prospective boatbuilder will wonder about the tools that are required regardless of his familiarity with woodworking tools. Many amateurs have built very fine boats with hand tools alone, and with a limited number of these. Most people already have a fair amount of handtools before they contemplate building a boat. The beauty of plywood boatbuilding is the fact that only ordinary common tools, whether of the hand-type or power-type, are required. Unlike conventional planking methods of wood boatbuilding, specialized tools and equipment are seldom necessary.

However, tools are a personal matter. What one individual prefers in the way of a certain tool, may not be to another's liking. Each chapter in this book shows various operations in plywood boatbuilding. The tools used are those that would be used most ordinarily for the particular job at hand. However, the builder will often come up with his own favorite type of tool for doing a certain job, and it is not uncommon for an ingenious person to invent or improvise his own tool or device for handling a particular operation.

While power tools are not an absolute necessity, they can make the job faster and easier, especially as the size of the boat increases. While power tools can be expensive, remember that most of these can be rented, and this may be the preferable route if your use of the tool will be limited. Or you may have a friend who can loan you the tool for a certain period.

Since getting the lumber to the required size is a basic boatbuilding operation, probably the most useful and versatile power tool you can have is a stationary power saw, either of the table or radial arm type. While a portable circular saw or even a band saw can be used as a substitute for many of the procedures done with a table or radial arm saws, these are not nearly as fast, simple, and accurate.

Another advantage of having access to a table or radial arm saw is that you can re-saw your own lumber to size instead of having the lumberyard do it. This not only gives you more leeway in the construction project, but can make for a considerable savings since you won't have to pay for custom milling. Because you can do many operations on saws of these types, such as pre-beveling, cutting grooves, and making wood joints, you can save a tremendous amount of time as opposed to hand operations. In working with saws, remember to pick blades that are suitable for the task. A ripping blade should not be used for cross cut work, or vice versa. Panel-type blades should be used for clean cuts on plywood, or better yet, use a carbide tipped blade with plenty of teeth for smooth, joiner-like edges on just about any cut with any type of wood or plywood.

Sawing out the frames can admittedly be done by hand with a keyhole saw or coping saw. But this would be an extremely tedious task, especially with thick hardwood stock used on bigger boats. A power portable saber saw would be much more suitable, or better yet, a band saw. Of course, if there is a frame kit offered for the design you are building, the frames will already be cut out and the use of the band saw may not be needed. Such a frame kit could amount to a considerable savings in work as well as money, too. However, on larger boats, a band saw is still often necessary.

A virtual "must" tool on any size boatbuilding project is a portable power drill. The most versatile type is the variable speed-type which can also be used for driving screws. In fact, the luxury of having two of these (one for drilling, the other for driving screws) will save a lot of time, If you don't have a variable speed type, then by all means get one of the power screw driver attachments available for standard power drills. There are power screwdrivers that can be used in lieu of drills, for driving screws, but you would still need a power drill, too.

In boatbuilding, with the exception of the stationary saws, it is generally required that the tools be brought to the work, as opposed to the work being brought to the tools. Consequently, hand and portable power tools are preferable for many of the procedures. Sawing various members to length is often easier, safer, and just about as fast with a hand saw as dragging around a power circular saw. The same goes for some of the fairing operations in tight places. An electric power plane is an excellent work-saving tool for fairing long sweeps, but a hand plane, or wood rasp is indispensable in many areas.

The builder should note that many tools are available of different shapes and configurations that will perform similar functions. As noted previously, much depends on the builder's preferences. Also note that new tools are constantly being introduced. A few gain acceptance, but many more die a quick death in the marketplace. Many of these tools are proprietary in nature, being patented and offered by only one company. About the most that can be said about these tools is to give them a try if you think they are of interest. But remember, there already may be standard tools that are proven and cheaper, and that may do the same job.

One thing in boatbuilding that you never seem to have enough of is clamps, especially "C"-clamps. The more you

Boatbuilding With Plywood

—MINIMUM—

HAND	PORTABLE POWER	STATIONARY POWER

Claw hammer
Nail set
Saws, rip and cross cut
Back saw
Keyhole saw
Ratchet screwdriver (e.g. "Yankee"-
  type)
Planes, block and jack types
Wood rasp
Wood chisel, ½"
Builders square
Adjustable square or try square
Chalk line
Plumb bob
Spirit level
Pliers, slip joint or adjustable
Measuring tape, steel
"C"-clamps, 6 @ 3" size or more
Pipe clamps, at least one
Drill bits, set ¹⁄₁₆" to ¼"
Mallet

Electric drill, ¼" min.
Saber saw

Table or radial arm saw, 8" min. (*)
Band saw, 12" (*)
(*) NOTE: For boatbuilding when material can be purchased to size, especially
with smaller boats, or where a frame kit
is available, these may not be required.

—BETTER—
(In addition to above)

Ball peen hammer
Coping saw w/replacement blades
Smooth plane
Files, bastard half-round, round, and
  flat
Expansive bit
Punch
Chisel set, ¼" to 1"
Countersink drill set (e.g. "Screw
  Mates")
Scratch awl
Wood boring or spade bits, ¼" to 1"
Wood rasps (e.g. "SurForm" types)

Variable speed drill, ⅜", or
Screwdriver attachment for electric
  drill
Portable circular saw

—BEST—
(In addition to above)

Sledge hammer, short handle
Selected set of screw drivers, all types
Selected set of punches and nail sets
Cold chisel set
Hack saw w/replacement blades
Miter box w/back saw to suit
Diagonal cutters or wire cutters
Needle nose pliers
Rabbet plane
Spokeshave
Draw knife
Assorted wood rasps and files
Assorted "C"-clamps, pipe clamps,
  and gluing clamps
Hole saw set w/mandrel for electric drill
Mechanics wrenches, box and open end
  set
Screwdriver bits for electric driver
Plug cutters to suit
Brace w/auger bits to suit

Power plane
Disc sander, heavy duty
Belt sander
Orbital or straight line sanders
Router w/attachments to suit
Variable speed drill, ⅜"
Shop vacuum

Table or radial arm saw, 10"
  (in place of 8")
Band saw, 16" (in place of 12")
Jointer, 6" or larger
Drill press
Shaper
Bench grinder
Thickness planer or surfacer
Spray paint outfit
Stationary disc sander

PLATE 3—Tool Listing Chart

12

Tools & Equipment

have, the better; and the larger the variety of sizes, the easier your job will be. You can get by with a limited number and can even devise your own clamping tools, but this is not usually as fast or as convenient. A wide variety of clamp types, including some pipe clamps, will make work easier due to the many clamping situations required in building a boat. While not listed in the tool listing, you'll want to have a work bench or work area where you can set tools, mark members, and so forth. This can be as rudimentary as a couple of saw horses with some heavy planks spanning them, or an elaborate workbench as exists in some shops, but which should be near the work area for convenience. Another piece of equipment that many workers like to have is a comfortable chair where one can take a break, look over the work, and contemplate the next steps.

The tool listing (see Plate 3) is divided into three categories. The first part is the MINIMUM selection in each group: HAND, HAND/POWER, and STATIONARY POWER. The second portion is the BETTER selection, and the third or BEST portion would be for the serious or professional builder. Note that these listings are not meant to be all-inclusive or comprehensive, but rather representative of the tools that could do all the operations required to build a boat using plywood. You can vary the lists to suit your own personal preferences if you like. Also, much will depend on the size of boat being built.

Whether using hand or power tools, proper safety and use of the tool should be exercised. All cutting tools should be kept sharp, not only for proper use, but for safety as well. Treat your tools with the care that they deserve and use them only for their intended function. If you are not sure how to use a certain tool or how to care for it, make it a point to learn. This is especially important with power tools such as saws. Always wear eye protection when operating power equipment, and be sure that such tools are properly grounded or double insulated if electric powered.

13

CHAPTER 4 — PLYWOOD

The advent of reliable waterproof glues and plywood grades suitable for continual exposure to the elements has put boatbuilding within the reach of everyone. A plywood boat is lightweight and waterproof. It is strong, has relatively few seams, and yet makes construction quick and economical. Plywoods in use are tough and seldom crack or fail, but have enough flexibility to absorb the shocks and extremes of use in a marine environment. However, to be used properly and to realize plywood's maximum potential, the boat should be specifically designed for the material, and by people or firms experienced with its capabilities and limitations.

Plywood planking in sheet form cannot be used on all boat contours. The contours must be either convex or straight, since plywood can only be applied on surfaces which have been developed from segments of a cylinder or cone (see Plate 4-A). It is virtually impossible to apply sheet plywood over concaved or double curved surfaces. This "conical development" process used for designing plywood boats is quite complicated, and the designer must know the limits of the material in order to select the proper thicknesses of plywood for given curvatures.

To better understand this limitation of plywood planking, compare the sheet of plywood with that of a piece of paper or thin cardboard. Any shape that you can normally bend this sheet of paper or cardboard to without crinkling or folding can be accomplished with a sheet of plywood (assuming it is of the proper thickness to make the bend). Looking through any section of a sheet plywood boat, the lines must be either convex, or in some cases, they can be straight as in those areas of the hull where the lines are generally parallel. Compound surfaces and concave sections can be obtained only if the plywood is cut up into strips and laid in alternating diagonal layers. This alternate method of plywood construction will be covered in Chapter 19.

In any plywood boat it must be considered that when a panel is bent in a convex shape, the outer surface or ply of the panel is in tension or "stretching", while the inner surface or ply is in compression or being "crushed". With excessive bends, the plywood may be extremely difficult to apply, and in some cases may fracture if pushed beyond its limits. To get around such a problem, double thicknesses of thinner plywood panels are often used. Practical experience is the best teacher for knowing the amount that a plywood panel can be bent. Of course bending ability can vary somewhat from panel to panel even if of the same species. But for practical purposes on a flat sheet, certain recommended radii can be prescribed to which ordinary Douglas fir plywood may be bent, as indicated on Plate 4B.

14

The modern plywood panel as used for boatbuilding is an engineered wood board or panel consisting of an odd number of veneers placed in layers at 90° or right angles to one another. Waterproof glues are used between the layers and then the composite layers are bonded under heat and pressure. After curing the panel, it is sanded to thickness and trimmed to size. The waterproof glues used are actually stronger than the wood itself, and will tolerate all conditions of exposure without failure of the panel. The ply construction of the panel eliminates almost completely, if not entirely, certain in-

herent weaknesses of normal lumber. Shrinkage, for example is reduced to the point that it is negligible for most uses. Splitting as in ordinary lumber is virtually impossible in any direction. Bending strength and stiffness is reduced somewhat lengthwise, but generally increased crosswise, depending on the number and thickness of the plies. The greater number of plies, the greater the utilization of strength in the two directions. Warping, cupping, and twisting are no longer a problem. Because of these strength qualities, the designer is able to considerably reduce the weight of the craft over comparably sized craft

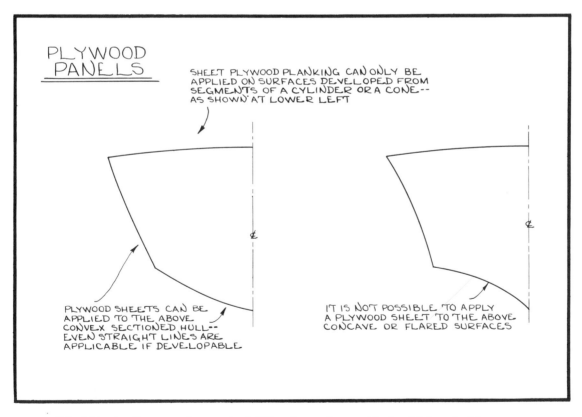

PLATE 4-A—Because sheet material like plywood cannot be bent into a double curvature or "compounded", the lines of the hull must be developed from segments of cylinders or cones. This means that boats intended to be planked with sheet plywood must be specifically designed for this material. Boats intended for planking with non-sheet materials cannot usually be adapted to sheet plywood for planking without extensive redesigning.

WEIGHTS OF DOUGLAS FIR PLYWOOD		
Thickness (Nominal)	Weight in Pounds per Square Foot	With Fiberglass
¼″ (6mm)	.80	.92
⁵⁄₁₆″ (7mm)	.95	1.07
⅜″ (9mm)	1.13	1.25
½″ (12mm)	1.53	1.65
⅝″ (16mm)	1.83	1.95
¾″ (19mm)	2.23	2.35
1″ (25mm)	3.00	3.12

RECOMMENDED MINIMUM RADIUS TO WHICH FIR PLYWOOD SHOULD BE BENT:		
Thickness	Radius when bent lengthwise	Radius when bent crosswise
¼″	5′	2′
⅜″	8′	3′
½″	12′	6′
⅝″	16′	8′
¾″	20′	12′

PLATE 4-B—The chart above is given for reference purposes. Bending ability can vary somewhat from panel to panel as can the weight per square foot. The weights given with fiberglass assume a covering on one side of 10 oz. fiberglass cloth saturated with polyester resin.

of conventional wood construction, and in most cases make a considerably stronger craft. In fact, there are few boats built, regardless of material, that cannot or do not utilize the advantages of plywood in some or many portions of their structure. As already noted, on a per pound basis, plywood is stronger than steel.

PLYWOOD TYPES

The most common type of plywood for boatbuilding in the United States and Canada use is made from Douglas fir, although Western larch can be substituted and for all practical purposes, cannot be distinguished from Douglas fir. The material comes from the Pacific Northwest and is available in a number of grades, thicknesses, and sizes. The American Plywood Association (A.P.A.) sets voluntary standards for their member-mills specifying the acceptable wood species, veneer grades, glue bonds, panel construction and workmanship, dimensions and tolerances, grade marking, moisture content variations, and packaging requirements for the manufacture of Douglas fir plywood. While the standards are voluntary and subject to change and modification, they are generally accepted throughout the country.

There are basically two types of Douglas fir plywood; Interior (INT), and Exterior (EXT). The two types are classed by exposure capability, adhesive dura-

16

bility, and veneer grade or quality. Interior-grade panels can be made with several glue types including interior glue (for strict interior use only), intermediate glues (for protected exterior conditions of limited exposure), and exterior glues (for protected exterior use). (The term "protected" means that the panel is not directly exposed to the elements such as sun, water, or similar conditions.) As a general rule, Interior-grade plywood should not be used in boats even though the panels may be made using exterior glues which are waterproof and the same as those used in the Exterior panels. It is true that this rule may be stretched in certain cases, such as for interior nonstructural joinerywork which will not be subjected to moisture or exposure, or in other special situations. But it seems a rather under-handed way of cutting costs, especially when the boat may be for one's own personal use.

Exterior-grade plywood is a panel that will retain its glue bond and structural integrity even when repeatedly wetted and dried, or exposed to weather permanently. A further expansion of the Exterior-grade panel is Marine-grade plywood. Basically, a Marine-grade panel is made the same way an Exterior panel is made (same glues, same wood species), except that the inner and outer plies are of higher quality. For example, while inner plies can be in more than one piece, the edges are jointed and the plies virtually void-free. Crossband gaps and edge splits are minimal and can't be filled. Outer plies, even though of the same grade as an Exterior panel, will be of higher quality.

The question frequently arises about substituting Exterior plywood for Marine-grade, and there is no simple answer. There is no question that the Marine panel is superior and more costly. However, on a per square foot basis and in terms of the entire cost of the boat, considering the investment over time and resale advantage, is it really worth not using the Marine grade if available? This, of course, can only be answered by the builder. In general, the Exterior panel can be used in place of a Marine panel wherever such a panel will be used flat without bending. However, if the panel must be bent, such as in planking, the Exterior panel may have voids in the inner cores not visible to the eye which may tend to fracture the panel during installation. Even if such a panel when in place on the hull does not fracture during installation, there still may be voids in the inner plies that may cause such a panel to fail in use, either through rough use (pounding), or on impact with an object. In short, the use of Exterior panels as a substitute for Marine panels is questionable, especially in the forward areas of a hull where bending will occur, and strength and integrity of the panel may be important.

Besides the Exterior and Marine-grade of Douglas fir plywood suitable for use in boatbuilding, there are other specialty types of plywood often used. These include the medium density overlay (MDO) Douglas fir plywood, and a variety of hardwood veneer plywoods often made from various types of mahoganies or hardwoods similar to mahogany. The MDO panel is just like an Exterior-grade panel except one or both of the surfaces have been covered with a resin-treated fiber overlay that is fused to the wood under heat and pressure. Such a surface is ideal for paint finishing and requires no other treatment (such as covering with fiberglass) to increase its durability. However, if panels are butt joined, such joints must be considered if it is desired to conceal these joints. Another difficulty is sanding over putty filled fastenings to avoid sanding through the overlay.

The hardwood plywood panel can be made using hardwood or softwood cores. As noted, the outer plies are often a type of mahogany which can be either ribbon grain or rotary grain. The ribbon grain is a more deluxe panel that is frequently used for naturally finished joinery work, where appearance is important. Usually hardwood plywood panels have very good face veneers which make excellent bases for the application of paint or clear finishes. However, such panels are frequently imported where grading standards for the manufacture of plywood may vary or be non-existent. If the panels do not have the stamping of a recognized standards making body, then you must put yourself at the mercy of the supplier. If the supplier has a good reputation and will guarantee the panel, it may be suitable for the intended use. However, beware of plywood panels not grade stamped. They could be only for interior use.

PLYWOOD PANEL GRADES

The quality of a plywood panel is rated by the quality of the exterior plies, which is basically determined by the number, size, and type of defects as well as how such defects may be repaired during the manufacture of the panel. For softwood plywood such as Douglas fir, the standards for grading the outer

plies are set forth by the A.P.A. The following grades describe the veneers that can be used for the outer plies for panels manufactured by their member-mills. Note, however, that such standards are subject to change or modification, and that these standards are voluntary.

N-GRADE: Highest veneer classification and is primarily intended for plywood that will be naturally finished such as cabinet wood used for joinery work. Veneers must be select all-heartwood or all-sapwood free from knots, knot holes, pitch pockets, open splits, open defects, and stains. Outer plies should not have more than 2 pieces which are well matched and tightly jointed. Some small defects can be filled and patched. Generally, this veneer grade does not apply to the Exterior or Marine grade Douglas fir plywood panel since such a panel is not intended for "natural finish" work.

A-GRADE: This panel will be smooth, paintable, free of knots, pitch pockets, open splits, and other open defects. If of more than one piece on a ply, they will be well-jointed. Small defects can be filled, patched, or plugged. This grade is the best Douglas fir veneer.

B-GRADE: This panel has solid surfaces free of defects. Slightly rough grain is permitted together with tight knots of limited size. Defects must be filled and patched.

C-PLUGGED GRADE: This is an improved "C"-GRADE veneer which may be sanded or not. The grade allows for small knotholes, open defects, splits, sound and tight knots, broken grain, plugs, patches, and shims.

C-GRADE: This is generally the lowest grade of full Exterior-grade plywood. It permits sanding defects, more and bigger defects than the "C"-PLUGGED grade, but is otherwise similar.

D-GRADE: This veneer can contain knots, knotholes, splits, and other open defects. While limited to Interior grades, some "D" grade and "C" grade panels are frequently called an "exterior" panel because they are glued with exterior glue. However, such plywood under the standards is an Interior quality panel, and has no place in boatbuilding.

From the above, it can be seen that when using Douglas fir plywood there is a limited selection of veneer types and combinations for the use of outer plies of plywood panels. Below are listed the most common selections of panel grade combinations available:

STANDARD EXTERIOR
GRADE:	"A-A" EXT
	"A-B" EXT
	"A-C" EXT
	"B-B" EXT
	"B-C" EXT
	"MDO" EXT
MARINE GRADES:	"A-A" MAR
	"A-B" MAR
	"B-B" MAR

Panel construction should consist of at least three plies for thicknesses up to ⅜", at least five plies for panels between ⅜" and ¾", and at least seven plies for panels over ¾". In all cases, the more

plies, the better. Marine-grades must be "B"-grade or better inner plies with jointed edges. All panels made by A.P.A. member-mills will be grade stamped for ready identification on the edge of each panel. Beware of any plywood panel not so stamped by a recognized standards organization. Note that while a panel with more plies may be more rigid and stronger, such a panel will be harder to bend for a given thickness.

The standard plywood panel size is 4' x 8' (1.22M x 2.44M), with the 4' x 10' (1.22M x 3.05M) sometimes available. However, plywood can be made in virtually any size, being limited only by the equipment available. Such non-standard sizes, however, may be difficult to find or be available on special order only. Usually plywood is available in the standard 4' widths in special order lengths of 12', 14', 16', and 20'. Such panels are usually scarf-joined by machine using shorter panels, and the price paid includes the price-per-square-foot plus the scarfing charge. Making your own long panels will be covered in Chapter 19. The following lists the standard plywood nominal thicknesses available for Douglas fir types:

¼" =	.250" =	6.350 mm
5/16" =	.3125" =	7.938 mm
⅜" =	.375" =	9.525 mm
½" =	.500" =	12.700 mm
⅝" =	.625" =	15.875 mm
¾" =	1.000" =	25.400 mm

In addition to this, hardwood plywoods are frequently available in similar thicknesses plus the addition of thinner 3mm (⅛") and 5mm (3/16") thicknesses for special applications.

Always shop carefully for plywood, looking over each panel in order to pick one with the fewest possible defects or patches. Consider where the plywood will be used in the boat. For example, plywood graded "A-A" or "A-B" is best for planking or where appearance on both sides is important. The "B"-grade veneer in a planking panel, however, may have patches that could tend to "pop-out" if bent severely, but under most circumstances can be suitably used. A "C"-grade veneer may have open knots and other defects, and therefore is not recommended for planking. However, such a panel can be used where it will be concealed and will not be bent, for example in bulkheads, decking, and transoms.

TIPS ON SELECTING & USING PLYWOOD

Always store plywood in a protected location before it is used. Exposure to the elements such as rain and sunlight will tend to weather the panel, making it more difficult to work and finish later. Also, be sure to keep the panels clean and free of oil or grease. Avoid excess sanding of Douglas fir plywood. This type of plywood is usually made by rotary cutting which exposes alternating soft and hard areas of the grain. When sanding, there is a tendency to remove more soft wood than hard wood, thereby leaving obvious "hills" and "valleys" which just become more accentuated with more sanding.

Plywood edges should always be sealed. Open defects and knotholes which will be visible, exposed to the elements, or otherwise located where

rot and decay could be promoted should be filled. However, such defects and knotholes that will not be visible (such as on the concealed face of a bulkhead), or will not be subject to exposure (such as on the underside of floorboards) need not be necessarily filled. Sealing edges and filling open defects is usually done after the panel has been sawn to shape or in place in the boat to prevent leaks, moisture absorption, and rot. Where voids occur along the edges of plywood, these should be filled with glue-coated scraps of wood if the void is of any size. Open defects and knotholes on the surfaces should be filled with a hard-setting putty. If the surfaces will subsequently be covered with fiberglass and resin, or other similar sheathing processes where a positive bond is critical, the sealing or filling materials must be compatible with the resin used. Of course, edges which are covered with the sheathing process are automatically sealed. A mixture of glue and sawdust or wood chips also makes a good edge sealing treatment that is compatible with most resins, as are most of the plastic wood fillers. In other cases, the edges and surfaces of plywood can be sealed with a wood preservative or rot preventative, clear wood sealers, paints, and/or varnishes.

When sawing plywood, especially Douglas fir types, take care to avoid splintering along the cut edge. One technique is to apply a strip of masking tape along the area to be cut. A better method is to clamp a piece of solid wood (usually on the underside) where this is practical. Cutting plywood is best done with a fine-toothed panel blade, or better yet, with carbide tipped blades.

A topic which frequently comes up, especially with would-be boatbuilders, is the idea of reducing the thickness of the plywood planking and making up the thickness with a build-up of fiberglass materials and resin. There are many reasons why this should not be done, and the "reasoning" behind this idea is based on some myths and fallacies about fiberglass. First, the novice has been led to believe that by using more fiberglass instead of plywood, his boat will not only be lighter, but stronger as well. However, this just isn't so. For a given thickness of hull, the plywood will ALWAYS be much lighter in weight, plus by itself, MUCH stiffer than fiberglass panels of comparable thickness. To make a fiberglass panel rigid would require additional stiffening in the form of sandwich cores, stringers, and other reinforcing probably not required for the plywood panel. Reducing the plywood panel thickness will also reduce its stiffness which will not be made up with a heavy build-up of fiberglass material. Such a procedure is not only more expensive, but more difficult to build and finish. The purposes of a fiberglass covering or "sheathing" over a plywood hull are to protect the plywood surface from checking, make for watertight joints, reduce maintenance, and provide a more durable finish. The fiberglass covering is NOT provided for additional strength in a well-designed and well-built plywood boat. In fact, common practice with fiberglass boat manufacturers is to use plywood as a reinforcing member where fiberglass alone is not sufficient.

CHAPTER 5 — LUMBER

It would take a good sized book to adequately cover all aspects of lumber as it applies to boatbuilding alone. However, a chapter devoted to lumber covering the basics that the average amateur will need to know is probably just as valuable, since the boring technicalities and scientific aspects that tend to confuse more than to clarify can be dispensed with. After all, the point in discussing lumber is to provide knowledge to help the builder select, buy, and use the proper types of lumber for the particular boat that is being built; not to provide a scientific or technical foundation. With a little practical information, the novice will be better equipped to go to his lumber dealer, know how to ask and receive exactly what he will need for the best possible price, and rest assured that his boat will be built with the most suitable materials for his special application.

It is impossible to cover all types of lumber that are available for boat construction. Each part of the country not only has certain woods that will be common to the area, but there usually will be several imported lumbers available as well. When in doubt about what type of lumber to use, a general rule to follow is that any lumber that has been proven successful in similar boats in the locale can be used. However, if the designer of the boat specifies certain types of lumber, especially where light weight, or high strength, or decay resis-

tance characteristics may be important, try to substitute woods that will be equally matched to such requirements. For example, on a high speed runabout where a designer might specify the use of Sitka spruce because of its light weight, it would be foolish to substitute with a wood such as white oak which weighs nearly 65% more than Sitka spruce, even though both woods are suitable boatbuilding lumbers. Such a substitution would not only make the boat much heavier, but performance could be disappointing. From an economy standpoint it is usually less costly to buy those lumbers that are readily available in the general area even though the designer of the boat may have specified another type of lumber not available. Here again, woods of similar weight and strength characteristics which have been proven in use in the area can always be substituted. After all, the designer cannot be expected to specify all the suitable alternatives, especially when he may be located in another part of the country where such woods may be unfamiliar to him.

BUYING LUMBER

Probably no aspect of the boatbuilding project causes more initial confusion for the novice than that of attempting to buy lumber. And yet, with the understanding of a few basic concepts, the process can not only be simplified, but can even be interesting. The first mistake to avoid is to grab the plans for the boat or a copy of the bill of materials, immediately rush to the nearest lumberyard, and then give the listing to the man at the lumberyard for a quotation. This is a sure way to waste money.

First, understand how lumber is measured and sold. Lumber is usually sold by the "board foot". A board foot is a measure of size equal to 12″ x 12″ x 1″ thick, or 144 cubic inches of wood. With every board foot of lumber charged, you will be paying for this amount of material. However, this does not mean that you will actually receive this much material. This is because that when the tree is cut down and sawn up, the lumber will be in a rather rough form. To make the lumber suitable for use, this rough board (which may be 1″ in actual thickness at this point) is decreased by the milling or surfacing process to where it will be less than the initial rough thickness. Usually such milling will remove from ⅛″ to ¼″ from the board, but the customer still pays for the "sawdust" lost through milling even though each board foot he pays for will actually be less than the 144 cubic inches that was there when the tree was cut up into lumber.

Almost all hardwoods are sold as "random-random" material in the rough. This means that lengths and widths will vary. Thickness of such material is specified in "quarters", with each quarter being ¼″. Thus, "four-quarters" material is 1″ in the rough state, "five-quarters" stock would be 1¼″, etc. Commonly available rough thicknesses are 4/4, 5/4, 6/4, 8/4, and 12/4 stock, or 1″, 1¼″. 1½″, 2″, and 3″ respectively. After the rough lumber has been milled or surface planed to be smooth on two sides, it is given the designation "S-2-S", or surfaced-two-sides. In cases where completely milled lumber is available, it is given the designation "S-4-S" to show that not only have the two surfaces been milled, but the edges have been jointed square and smooth as well. Normally, S-4-S lumber will be more costly than S-2-S lumber for the same species. Lumber with the S-4-S designation will often be less in the width dimension as well, due to the fact that some material will be lost when jointing the edge. Hence, not only in such lumber more costly than the same type in the S-2-S grade, but the result will be even less wood per board foot paid for.

A deviation to the above lumber measuring system comes with softwood lumbers such as Douglas fir. These types are commonly sold only in S-4-S grade, with both dimensions actually less than that which they are designated by. For example, a Douglas fir member that is specified as 2″ x 6″ will actually net less in both dimensions by virtue of the grading standard under which softwood lumbers are measured. It would be common to find the actual net size of such a 2″ x 6″ member to be 1½″ x 5½″. This variation with softwood species is common for all standard size designations and should be allowed for when purchasing softwood lumber types. These lumber types are also commonly sold by the lineal foot for convenience in some lumberyards which can increase the buyer's difficulty in determining the cost per board foot in order to compare costs with hardwood lumbers. For example, a 2″ x

4″ Douglas fir member priced per lineal foot contains only ⅔ board foot.

In buying lumber for the boatbuilding project, the builder must first determine just what thicknesses of materials will be required. When the designer notes that a given member should be 1″ material, does he mean that the material will actually NET 1″? Or does he mean for the builder to purchase "four-quarters" stock? The designer should note somewhere on the plans or material listing just what is meant by the noted lumber thickness. The lumber thickness is usually the first dimension noted for a given member and is often called the "sided" dimension. From a practical standpoint, as well as making the purchasing easier, the designer should preferably specify standard lumberyard dimensions. That is, 1″ material will actually refer to "four quarters" stock that will be milled or "sided" as full or thick as possible. In this case, the stock could range from ¾″ to ⅞″ in actual milled thickness, and the designer would have made allowances for this variation in his scantling decisions. If the lumberyard is in a position to mill all stock on order, specify that milling should be as thick as possible AND that it should be uniform. It can prove exasperating to work with, say 1″ stock, that varies in net thickness by several fractions of an inch. If the lumber has already been milled, check the thicknesses when buying to assure that there is little or no variation in milled thickness.

If, on the other hand, the designer means for such 1″ material to actually be 1″ NET in thickness, this would mean that the lumberyard would have to take the next thickest material (in this case "five quarters" rough stock) and then mill it to the 1″ NET thickness. As anyone can quickly see, this would amount to 25% more lumber (1¼″ as opposed to 1″ stock) paid for, that would be wasted as sawdust. Plus the additional cost of custom milling the thicker stock to the specified net thickness. So unless the designer specifically notes that material will be to "NET" size, assume that lumber is purchased in the standard lumberyard thickness, and specifically note this to your lumber dealer when seeking a quotation.

Another important element for saving money in buying lumber is to group similar thickness members together into larger boards and then resaw or rip them to size using your own equipment. In other words, if the designer has specified three-1″ x 2″ members, group these together and purchase just one board that is 1″ x 6″ wide (plus a little extra allowance for the saw kerf), resawing them to the widths and number of pieces required. If the lumberyard does this for you, it will cost considerably more in most cases. Naturally, to resaw such material will require a power saw, preferably a table or radial arm saw, although a portable circular saw or band saw can also be used if they have a suitable guide or "fence".

In the matter of widths of materials, usually the designer will specify the actual NET or "molded" width unless otherwise stated. This is because widths can be varied with hardwoods to virtually any dimension. Softwoods, however, are an exception to this rule. As previously noted, the width of a softwood member will be actually less than the noted size, as in the 2″ x 6″ member example which will net about 1½″ thick x 5½″ wide. If given a choice of widths of stock, a general rule is to purchase stock in as wide of widths as possible. In many hardwoods, widths up to and exceeding 18″ are sometimes found. Not only is it possible to resaw such a member into more pieces, but it will allow greater versatility in the laying out of frame members. For example, a sawn frame member which is 4″ in width taken from a 6″ wide board could make for considerable waste. However, if a board a little over 8″ in width could be obtained, then two such members could be taken from one length. Also, when wide deeply contoured frame members are necessary, it is possible to "nest" several such frame members

within one width resulting in less scrap and lower material costs (see Plate 5-A). Obviously, some planning on the part of the builder will be required to take advantage of all these variations, but the savings in costs can be considerable. Once the builder has grouped all his lumber together and has carefully analyzed his bill of materials, or has determined what materials will be required, if the designer has not provided a bill of materials, he can go shopping. The first rule in shopping for lumber is to shop around for the best value. Note that we did NOT say shop for the best

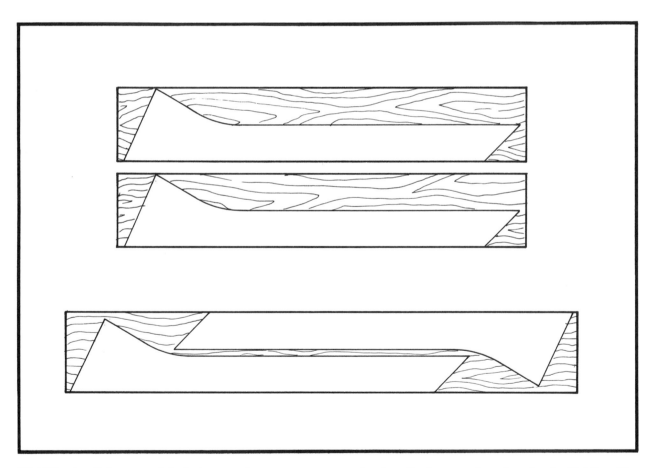

PLATE 5-A—Using material wisely can reduce costs considerably. For example, "nesting" of frame members with deep contours using wide stock will result in far less waste than using widths of stock that allow only one member from a given length of lumber. In the example, a board only slightly wider and longer than a board above yielding just one frame member, results in two frame members with much less waste and lumber.

"price", since there is no such thing as a good "cheap" boatbuilding lumber. In other words, lumber that might be half the price of other similar lumber, but that is full of defects, could wind up costing twice as much by virtue of wasted stock. This does not mean that special "close-outs" at favorable prices cannot be found and utilized, but the novice should be especially aware to avoid comparing lumber like "apples" with "oranges". He may end up with "lemons" instead.

Many boatbuilding woods cannot be found in ordinary lumberyards. Then too, some lumberyards are more adept at merchandising lumber for boatbuilding than others. The tendency, of course, is to find boatbuilding lumber in areas where boatbuilding is done. However, this does not mean that suitable sources cannot be found in other areas, even those that are far inland. This is because many boatbuilding woods are often used for other purposes. It is not uncommon, however, for lumberyards to ship lumber a considerable distance and to work on a custom-order basis, even with individuals building their own boats. When suitable sources cannot be found by utilizing the "yellow pages" or through local channels, a check with the advertising sections of the national boating magazines will usually reveal sources of boatbuilding lumbers and related materials. However, in selecting any sources of lumber, be sure that you understand all of the cost figures, including any "hidden extras" like shipping the delivery, milling charges, bundling fees, etc., before purchasing. Experience has shown that through careful purchasing, a difference of as much as 50% in the total material cost of the hull can be realized.

SELECTING LUMBER

Once a source of lumber has been found, and a type of lumber has been decided on, the next step is the selection of the lumber or actual boards that will be used. As previously stated, wide widths are usually preferable, especially if facilities are available for resawing or ripping to size. Also, long lengths are desirable. But what do you do when the plans call for a member 20' long and the longest member available is 12'? As will be covered in forthcoming chapters, such long members can usually be formed from two shorter lengths by means of a scarf joint or butt joint. However, the builder must check against his plans to assure that such a joint will be located at the most opportune location. For example, while two 10' lengths could be used to make a 20' member utilizing a butt joint and butt block (assuming material is available for the butt block), it is possible that the joint would be located in an area of the hull with severe curvature which would make the joint more difficult to make. On the other hand, a 12' and an 8' length, which would also make up the 20' member, could be utilized that might locate the joint beyond the curvature thereby simplifying the joint. In other words, the builder should check all options against the plans in order to select the most suitable material, considering all such joints and lengths that may be required.

All lumber used in boatbuilding must be seasoned, which means that the moisture from the green wood has to be removed in order to improve its serviceability. Air drying and kiln drying are the two methods used for lumber seasoning, and generally speaking, the air dried process is the best for boatbuilding woods. However, air drying can require a year or more depending on the thickness and wood species, and consequently is seldom done. Most of the lumber available is kiln dried, which is acceptable if done properly. However, there is a tendency in the kiln drying process to either rush the lumber through the kiln too quickly (leaving too much moisture in the wood), or "cooking" the lumber too long or at too high a temperature, (thereby removing too much of the moisture and making the wood brittle). For most boatbuilding lumber, the ideal moisture content ratio to lumber weight after drying (regardless of the process) is approximately 15%, with a range of from 12% to 16% being acceptable. When the wood is seasoned, it shrinks to some degree (see Plate 5-B), and if during drying too much moisture is removed, the wood will later absorb moisture and swell excessively once in use in the boat. On the other hand, if the wood is "green" or contains too much moisture after seasoning, the wood will tend to shrink and check or split while the boat is being built.

But how does the average person detect lumber that has been properly seasoned and is within the range of suitable moisture content? Here it is largely a matter of depending on the integrity of the lumber dealer. However, there are tell-tale signs that one can look for when it comes to selecting suitable boards. Lumber which is "green" or unseasoned will often actually be "wet", with moisture apparent especially between boards when one is lifted. Of course, such lumber will be considerably heavier than comparable seasoned wood. Conversely, lumber that has too little moisture content may appear to be dry or even "weathered" as well as brittle. Lumber that has been kiln dried too "hot" or quickly will often be warped, cupped, or wind severely along its length. These boards should be avoided even though the defects may only appear to a minor degree. When such boards are resawn after purchase, the problems are often magnified and can make it unusable.

Whenever possible, boards should be selected that have prevalent vertical grain (also known as "edge grain" or "rift sawn" stock). Such boards will tend to expand and contract uniformly without undue distortion. When a lumberman cuts a tree, he has two ways available that he can cut the log up into

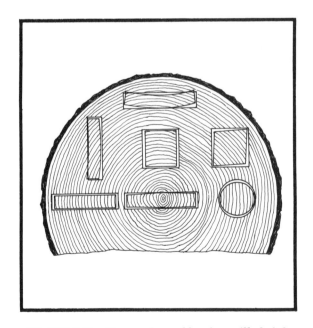

PLATE 5-B—How a piece of lumber will shrink with seasoning depends on how it is shaped in section and where it is cut from the tree. Tangential shrinkage (in the direction of the annual growth rings) is about twice as great as radial shrinkage (along the grain). The flat board at the lower left features the ideal vertical grain which makes such shrinkage uniform on all faces.

boards. The easy and quick way is to simply slice up the log or "plain saw" it (see Plate 5-C). With this method, only a few of the boards will have the ideal vertical grain pattern, while most of the boards will be of flat grain (the terms "plain sawn", "slash grain", and "flat grain" are synonymous). Such flat grain boards tend to "cup" or distort, and therefore can split or check more easily.

If the lumberman wants to take more care, he can cut the logs by what is called the "quarter sawn" (see Plate 5-C) method. This method results in many more boards of desirable vertical grain, however, the widths will vary. Because good vertical grain wood is more desirable and quarter sawing takes more effort on the part of the lumberman, besides wasting more lumber,

it is more costly. With most woods it is relatively easy for the buyer to look at the freshly cut end of a board to detect the prevalent grain structure and decide if a given board is of suitable vertical grain. While a board of obvious flat grain may look suitable in the lumberyard (otherwise flat and true), it could cup severely later, especially if not seasoned properly, and hence it is best to stick to vertical grain wood if at all possible.

LUMBER DEFECTS

Once lumber of suitable grain structure has been selected, look for defects. Some people confuse defects with blemishes. A blemish as such does not affect the serviceability of the wood, but merely mars the appearance. A blemish can be important, however, where the natural grain appearance of the wood is desired, such as with joinerywork. A defect, however, is an irregularity in or on the wood that may lower its strength. It is often difficult for the novice to detect defects or to understand their consequences. In many cases, a defect will be limited in area and can be worked around so that it can be cut away, or will otherwise end up in a member or area where a decrease in strength is not important. So depending on the defect and its extent, don't rule out an entire board simply because of a limited defect. It is often possible to get a discounted price on such a board.

Defects usually are of two types; those caused by seasoning, and those that are caused by the way the tree grows. Seasoning defects are usually the result of shrinkage caused as the moisture is re-

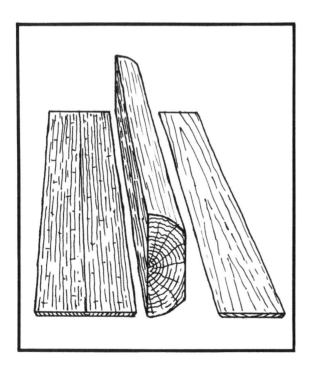

PLATE 5-C—Quarter sawed lumber results in ideal vertical or edge grained boards (at left of log), while plain sawed lumber provides boards of flat grain (to right of log) which are not as desirable for most uses in boatbuilding.

moved. Checking is a common seasoning defect, and it is a tension failure causing a split either along the surface of the board, or at the ends. An actual split in the wood is more severe than checking and is usually caused where an end check and a surface check meet. Warping is said to occur when the faces of the boards are no longer true planes. Warp defects include bows (lumber bowing along its length), crooks (distortion of the edges of a board so they appear concave or convex), cupping (a concave or convex appearance when viewed on the end edge), and twisting (when the four corners of a board are no longer in the same plane). A major problem with bows and twists is that while the warp may be minor in the board, the problem tends to magnify when the board is resawn. On the other hand, cupping can be reduced if the board is resawn into narrower widths. Likewise, on a board warped lengthwise, shorter lengths of the same board can minimize the problem. While there are other seasoning defects, checking, splits, and warping are the ones that are most common and easily detected by the novice.

Natural defects which are a part of the lumber caused by growth can vary considerably with the species of lumber. For example, Sitka spruce is a very straight grained wood with few natural defects. However, Douglas fir frequently contains knots to one degree or another, and it is often difficult to find the desirable dense, vertical grain type free of excessive knots. Knots are probably the most common natural defect, however, a knot in itself may be acceptable if it is minor in size in relation to the rest of the piece of wood and is tight or intergrown with the surrounding wood. Whether a knot can be accepted in a given board depends not only on the soundness and size of the knot, but what the board will be used for. For example, if the board will be used for a bending member such as a sheer clamp or chine log, a knot along the length of such a member will often be unacceptable. Such a member if it does not break during installation, may fail in use at the knot.

Cross grain in wood occurs when the fibers are not parallel with the major axis of the piece of lumber. Two types of cross grain include diagonal grain and spiral grain. Cross grained wood is not too commonly seen where boatbuilding lumber is sold, partly because such wood is difficult to machine or season properly. Cross grain wood should be avoided because such wood will fail under stress at the point of the cross grain.

A shake is somewhat like a check or split except that shakes do not develop in seasoning or handling, but originate in the green timber. They may, however, become more apparent during seasoning. Depending on the location of the shakes, they may weaken the member. However, in boatbuilding lumber, shakes are not too common because they occur mainly in lower grades of lumber that are not located near the heartwood of the tree.

Decay and rot can exist in wood before it has been installed in the boat, and it is almost always caused by fungi that grow in the wood. The decay and rot of wood after it is in the boat, its causes, and prevention are discussed later in the chapter, even though they are similar. An unusual fact of decay in wood is that all tree species are subject to heartwood decay in the living tree. However, once the heartwood lumber has been cut and seasoned, its decay resistance tends to increase, and in some cases, increases significantly depending on the species. On the other hand, rotting of sapwood in living trees is rare, but cut and seasoned, the resistance to rot is low. Therefore, decay that develops after the tree has been cut, and before use of the lumber, is likely to be found in the sapwood. Such decay is usually easily seen, and is often white or brown in color, with the surrounding wood greatly softened, punky, pocketed, brittle, collapsed, or cracked. Luckily such lumber is not commonly seen in a reputable lumberyard.

A common mistake by the novice is to confuse decay with insect damage. Insect damage is recognizable as holes in the wood and are classified as pin holes (or "pinwormy" in some species), grub holes, and powder post holes. All these insects are normally killed with kiln drying, or by wood preservative treatments. Insect damaged wood should not necessarily be automatically rejected. Much depends on the extent of the damage and where the wood will be used. Powder post damage (usually found in the seasoned sapwood of such woods as oak or ash) can destroy most of the interior of a piece of wood while the surface shows only minor holes, thereby reducing considerably the strength of the member. The other types of insect holes show up on the surface and the extent of damage thereby can be more easily determined.

ROT & WORM PROTECTION

On one hand, there seems to be a lot of talk bandied about by so-called "experts" about worm and rot "dangers" on wood boats. Yet on the other hand, finding a wood boat that is 50 years old or even older in sound condition is easy. In many cases such venerable craft seem to be unscathed by these purported "villains". Why is this so? The simple answers include using proper materials in the construction, proper construction techniques that will make the boat suitable for the conditions where it will be used, and proper maintenance.

To go into the technical aspects of this subject would not only be beyond the scope of this book, but would also be boring to the average boatbuilder. All that is important from the viewpoint of the average do-it-yourselfer is how to protect his craft from possible damage from rot or worms.

Protection from worms is relatively easy on most plywood boats and is seldom a problem at all. First of all, marine wood borers (the worms that can cause damage to wood) are not found in all waters. They are usually limited to the warmer waters common to tropical areas. If worms are common to the boating area where you are located, this will usually not be a well-kept secret; the boaters in the area will know if they are there.

Wood borers tend to invade some woods and not others, so in selecting woods that will be exposed underwater, those woods which are less subject to attack should be used. If such woods are not available, they should be treated with a suitable wood preservative or pressure treating technique. However, on a plywood boat, there is usually not much solid lumber below water with the exception of skegs or deadwood keels. Unlike solid lumbers, marine borers do not seem to like plywood nearly as much as some solid lumbers. One reason that this may be so is the glue line between plies which is distasteful or even toxic to them. Another aspect is that the edge grain is more susceptible than the surface of a panel, and sealing the edge grain for protection is easy.

Of course, a plywood boat that is entirely sheathed with fiberglass or equivalent material and resin is virtually immune from worm attack, and hence this is probably the easiest method of protection where attack by worms can be expected. Worms do not seem to like or be able to penetrate surfaces covered with the resins (either polyesters or epoxies) used with these sheathings.

There are different kinds of rot and reasons for their spread, but to keep things simple, rot requires moisture, lack of air circulation, and the proper temperature to spread and grow to cause any damage. Remove any one of these factors and rot will usually not be a problem in any wood boat. As with worms, using a rot resistant wood will be the first step in rot prevention.

Most boats tend to accumulate some water in the bilge. If the boat is used in salt water, it is a common mistake to assume that this bilge water will cause rot. The rot fungi cannot grow in salt water; they need fresh water to be promoted, and consequently most rot tends to occur along the deck and cabin areas where fresh water or moisture (from rain, condensation, etc.) tends to penetrate into the structural members.

With conventionally built wood boats this is more of a problem than with plywood boats since the deck and cabin areas are likely to be covered with fiberglass or equal sheathing on the plywood boat. Nevertheless, a positive

and adequate flow of air should be provided to all below-decks spaces, especially in the ends of the boat, This is notably important when the boat is not in use. Remember that rot can occur whether the boat is kept in the water at a mooring, or in the backyard on a trailer. So if it is kept covered regardless of where, take into consideration that air must flow inside. (Note that this rule applies to ALL boats regardless of the material used in the construction.) Temperatures should be kept down also since rot spores are not active at lower temperatures.

In building a plywood boat, the recommended technique for rot prevention, besides using suitable materials and proper maintenance, is to liberally apply wood preservative to all surfaces inside the hull. If the hull is to be sheathed with fiberglass or equal material and resin, this treatment should not be done until after the exterior of the hull has been covered since the resin will not bond to any areas where the preservative has been applied. For example, if the wood preservative liquid happens to penetrate through a joint, say along the chine, and gets onto the outside of the hull, the resin will not form a bond at this point. So apply the preservative after the hull is righted and the fiberglass covering has been completed.

There are several types of wood preservatives available under many brand names from paint dealers. Two common types are pentachlorophenol and copper napthanate, and these ingredients are usually noted on the fine print of the label. Follow the manufacturer's instructions carefully for proper protection. With most of these treatments, painting of the surfaces can be done after, but be sure to check the label.

A common mistake often is made by the amateur in assuming that if a fiberglass covering will protect the outside of the hull, why won't it do the same for the inside? The problem is not the theory in this case, but with the application. It is virtually impractical to properly apply the fiberglass coth around all the many corners and junctions within the hull so that it will bond 100% at all areas and not lift thereby forming air bubbles. If any air bubbles at all form in such a covering and go unnoticed, they will eventually form perfect moisture traps that could lead to rot. Since the bubble where the rot will start will be a small area, it won't be noticed on the surface, but the rot could spread under the covering and do a tremendous amount of damage before it is detected. By this time it could be too late and quite a repair operation would be necessary. In short, such a procedure is not recommended; let the interior of the hull "breathe" instead, using the recommended preservative treatment and later painting the hull interior areas if desired. Note that fiberglass laminates are hygroscopic, that is, they will absorb moisture to some extent (contrary to popular belief).

SAPWOODS & HEARTWOODS

Basically, the heartwood is the middle of the tree, while the sapwood is the layer surrounding the heartwood. Actually, the heartwood consists of dead cells, and year by year the tree increases in diameter by the addition of new layers of sapwood under the bark. As the outer layer of cells increase under the bark, another layer of cells dies off in the sapwood and changes to heartwood. As previously mentioned, sapwood in practically all trees is low in decay resistance, and unless given preservative treatment, is not as durable as heartwood.

Heartwood is neither weaker nor stronger than sapwood fundamentally, but some changes in physical characteristics do occur with heartwood formation. For example, the heartwood absorbs and loses moisture more slowly than sapwood making it more dimensionally stable. However, most heartwood is more difficult to treat with preservative although many varieties are more resistant to decay in the heartwood. While the heartwood of many trees is readily distinguishable from the sapwood by virtue of a darker color, some woods show little color differential. Good all-heartwood lumber may be difficult to obtain, and it is common to find boards with both heartwood and sapwood combined, depending on the species.

SOFTWOODS & HARDWOODS

Woods are grouped into two general classes; hardwoods and softwoods. However, the terms do not necessarily mean that a hardwood is harder than a softwood. The difference between the two classes is purely genetic or botanical in nature. Hardwoods come from trees with broad leaves (called angiosperms), many of which tend to drop their leaves with the seasons. Softwoods, however, come from trees that have needle or scale-like leaves (called gymnosperms), are mostly evergreens, and are often called conifers since they are cone bearing trees. Within each classification there are considerable variations in structure and qualities. The main thing for the novice to remember is that when someone, such as a lumber dealer, refers to a wood as a "hardwood" or as a "softwood", he will be referring to woods with a botanical difference; not to a wood that may be harder than another.

LUMBER SPECIES FOR BOATBUILDING

While there are probably thousands of different wood species throughout the world, most of them are not suitable for boatbuilding. Many woods are unsuitable for at least one of a variety of reasons. They may be too weak, too brittle, too soft, subject to decay, will not hold fastenings well, or the trees may be too short to yield lengths of material suitable for boatbuilding. In the following descriptions, those woods which have been proven in use in boatbuilding over a period of literally generations in the United States are noted, as well as some which may be of only limited value or which are unsuitable, but are often confused with similar suitable types. Even though many types are imported, they are often readily available. The nomenclature of the various woods given is the commercial name. Where the wood may be known under other names, these have been listed in parentheses. Weights of each wood are given per cubic foot and per board foot at 15% moisture content on an average basis. Variations in weights, however, will occur in a given species due to varia-

tions in moisture content, heartwood to sapwood ratio, and other factors. For practical purposes a wood that weighs under 2.5 lbs. per board foot is considered light in weight. A wood that exceeds about 3.3 lbs. per board foot is considered heavy. Woods that weigh between these figures are considered medium weight woods. The descriptions are broken down into the two categories; hardwoods and softwoods. Because of their special qualities and limited uses, not all the woods listed are applicable to boatbuilding with plywood; but they are noted since they are often sold in lumberyards specializing in boatbuilding woods.

HARDWOODS

APITONG
44 lbs. per cubic foot,
3.67 lbs. per board foot.

Abundant in the Philippines, Indonesia, Malaysia, and New Guinea, There are many different species, however, they look very much alike. Sapwood is creamy yellow, gray, or reddish white, while heartwood is reddish purple or brown. The grain is usually straight. The wood is slow to dry, does not take preservatives too well, is moderately low in decay resistance, and somewhat difficult to work. Apitong is very hard, strong, holds fastenings very well, and is often substituted for white oak but it is not nearly as durable.

ASH, WHITE
42 lbs. per cubic foot,
3.5 lbs. per board foot.

A domestic wood grown mainly in the Eastern states. The heartwood is brown, while the sapwood is light colored or nearly white. The wood is hard, fairly strong, straight grained, and suitable for steam bending. It can be substituted for white oak in areas that will not be continually moist. Decay resistance is low. Often used for small boat framing, oars, tillers, and joinerywork.

ELM, ROCK
44 lbs. per cubic foot,
3.67 lbs. per board foot

A domestic wood that grows in the North Central and Northern states. It has only limited use in boatbuilding, mainly because it is suitable for steam bending. The wood is hard, strong, and shock resistant, which makes it suited well for small boats utilizing steam bent frames and laminated members. Decay resistance is fair at best and the wood tends to warp.

GREENHEART
61 lbs. per cubic foot,
5.08 lbs. per board foot

The wood is native to South America and the West Indies, however, it is imported mostly from Guiana. The heartwood is extremely decay resistant and has a reputation for being highly resistant to marine borers that may not be completely deserved when used in tropical waters. The wood was once a favorite with European builders since it is stiff and very strong. It's color varies from pale greenish-yellow to deep brownish purple, with little difference between sapwood and heartwood. The high weight can be a considerable disadvantage in some designs. Being a very hard, dense wood, it can be more difficult to work than other hardwoods.

IROKO
40 lbs. per cubic foot,
3.33 lbs. per board foot

The tree comes from tropical Africa and is much like teak, but not as strong. The heartwood is decay resistant and somewhat resistant to marine borers. The wood is hard, but moderately easy to work. Heartwood is light to greenish yellow, but darkens to brown upon exposure to light and air. Iroko is very popular for boatbuilding in Europe.

IRONBARK (EUCALYPTUS)
62 lbs. per cubic foot,
5.17 lbs. per board foot

Several species of Eucalyptus called red and gray ironbark are native to Australia where they are most used. Heartwood is red to dark brown, and sapwood is light colored. The heartwood has good decay resistance, and is resistant to some forms of marine borers. The wood is very hard, heavy, strong, and shrinks moderately. Because of its high weight, the wood can be a major disadvantage in many types of boats.

LIGNUMVITAE (IRONWOOD)
76 lbs. per cubic foot,
6.33 lbs. per board foot

One of the hardest and heaviest woods known, it is found in Central America and the West Indies. The wood is naturally impregnated with oils which makes it suitable for propeller and rudder shaft bearings (its major function) as long as shaft RPM is not too high. Heartwood varies from olive brown or blue to dark brown or nearly black, while sapwood is cream colored. The heartwood is very resistant to decay and abrasion. The wood is often used for keel and worm shoes, rubbing strakes, etc. Extremely strong with regard to crushing and hardness.

MAHOGANY, AFRICAN (KHAYA, UTILE)
32 lbs. per cubic foot,
2.67 lbs. per board foot

Very similar to genuine mahogany, it comes from Africa. Color ranges from light pink to bright red or reddish brown, but is not as variable as mahogany. The wood is hard, strong, decay resistant, of low shrinkage, and seasons well. There are several species of so-called "African" mahoganies, but those listed above are the most suitable for boatbuilding.

MAHOGANY
34 lbs. per cubic foot,
2.83 lbs. per board foot

True mahogany grows in the West Indies, Central America, the northern part of South America, and some in the southern part of Florida. The types frequently used in boating are called Honduras and Mexican mahoganies. Color varies from deep red to reddish brown in the heartwood, with sapwood a pale yellow. The heartwood is decay resistant, fairly strong, and seasons well, with low and uniform shrinkage. Hardness, weight, and strength can vary depending on where the lumber is from, with the Central American variety being more variable.

MAHOGANY, PHILIPPINE (TANGILE, RED LUAN, WHITE LUAN, TIAONG)
39 lbs. per cubic foot,
3.25 lbs. per board foot

The many varieties of so-called "Philippine mahogany" are really types of tropical cedar common to the Philippines even though they resemble true mahogany. The dark red varieties are harder, heavier, more decay resistant, and stronger than the light red varieties which are usually limited to non-structural joinerywork. The trees yield large, clear boards, although interlocked grain can make seasoning some times difficult.

OAK, WHITE
47 lbs. per cubic foot,
3.83 lbs. per board foot

White oak is a domestic Eastern wood often used in boatbuilding. The problem with white oak, however, is distinguishing it from red oak which is not nearly as suitable for boatbuilding since it is weaker and rots easily unless pressure treated with preservatives. The following characteristics should help in separating white oak from red oak. The heartwood pores will be plugged with abundant hair-like ingrowths known as tyloses, whereas red oak will contain few. The heartwood of white oak is tan or light brown, while that of red oak is reddish or pink. The pores in summerwood are very small and numerous in white oak, but with red oak they are few, large, and open. A chemical test using benzidine-sodium nitrate turns white oak heartwood dark brown or greenish brown, but that of red oak turns light orange. White oak is excellent for steam bending but should ideally be "green" for this purpose and not seasoned. It is durable, stiff, strong, hard, holds fastenings very well, is rot resistant, but is somewhat difficult to work and requires sharp tools. Because of the gallic acid in white oak, it reacts with plastic resin glue when submerged in salt water, and therefore this glue should not be used with white oak under these conditions.

OKOUME (GABOON)
27 lbs. per cubic foot,
2.08 lbs. per board foot.

This West African wood produces large, clear logs of uniform straight grain. The heartwood is salmon pink or pale pinkish brown resembling some types of Philippine mahogany. The sapwood is grayish. It is only fairly strong considering other woods, but strong for its weight, although low in resistance to decay. The wood splinters easily and is best sawn with carbide-tipped blades. It has little use in plywood boatbuilding except in smaller boats where lightweight is more important than durability. Some imported plywood is made from this wood.

TEAK
43 lbs. per cubic foot,
3.58 lbs. per board foot

Probably the most decay resistant wood in the world, but it is not totally immune to marine borer attack. The wood grows in Burma, India, Thailand, and the East Indies. Sapwood is white to pale yellowish brown, while heartwood is a dark golden yellow that darkens with age. The wood has a rough oily feel, is straight grained and coarse, strong, hard, of low shrinkage, and easily worked but brittle, and tends to dull tools. Very commonly used for decking, joinerywork, and frequently left unfinished, it is a very durable wood. Glues used with this wood must be selected with care.

SOFTWOODS

CEDAR, ALASKA
32 lbs. per cubic foot,
2.67 lbs. per board foot

Grows along the Pacific coast from Alaska to Oregon. The heartwood is bright clear yellow, while the thin layer of sapwood which is barely visible is a shade lighter. The wood has a fine uniform texture with low shrinkage, and is moderately strong. Heartwood is high in decay resistance, and works and finishes well.

CEDAR, ATLANTIC WHITE (SOUTHERN WHITE CEDAR, SWAMP CEDAR, JUNIPER)
23 lbs. per cubic foot,
1.92 lbs. per board foot

The wood is soft, brittle, weak, and splits readily. However, it is low in shrinkage even though it soaks up considerable water. Because of this and its decay resistance, the wood is frequently used for conventional planking, especially in areas where the material is grown (notably along the Atlantic seaboard and Gulf states mainly in swamps), and on boats which will be in and out of the water frequently. It has little use in plywood boatbuilding.

CEDAR, NORTHERN WHITE
21 lbs. per cubic foot,
1.75 lbs. per board foot

Very similar to Atlantic white cedar, but because of small trees, its use is limited to small boat construction only, especially conventional planking. It is grown mostly in the Northeastern United States, and has little use in plywood boatbuilding.

CEDAR, PORT ORFORD
30 lbs. per cubic foot,
2.5 lbs. per board foot

Grown in limited areas of Northern California and Southern Oregon, it is the preferred species of boatbuilding cedars. Although only moderately strong, it is the strongest cedar and the heaviest before seasoning. The heartwood is light yellow to pale brown with a distinctive spicy odor. The wood is fine and uniform in texture, moderately hard, shrinks moderately, seasons well, and is very resistant to rot.

CEDAR, WESTERN RED
23 lbs. per cubic foot,
1.92 lbs. per board foot

Grown in the Pacific Northwest, the wood has narrow white sapwood and reddish-brown heartwood. It is rather soft and weak, shrinks very little, and the heartwood has good resistance to decay. The grain is uniform and straight although somewhat coarse and brittle. While often used for conventional planking, it is not highly recommended for this use. However, for veneers for use in cold molded hull planking, the material is excellent.

CYPRESS, BALD (RED CYPRESS, YELLOW CYPRESS, WHITE CYPRESS)
32 lbs. per cubic foot,
2.76 lbs. per board foot

Grown along the Southeastern coastal states of the United States, often in swamps. Heartwood near salt water varies from reddish to almost black, while the heartwood from farther inland is only slightly reddish or yellowish brown. Moderately strong, it is highly decay resistant, but soaks up a lot of moisture. Its primary use is in conventional planking, and therefore has little use in plywood boatbuilding.

DOUGLAS FIR (YELLOW FIR, OREGON PINE)
34 lbs. per cubic foot,
2.83 lbs. per board foot

The best fir for boatbuilding comes from the coastal areas of the Pacific Northwest. Unseasoned green lumber is common and should be avoided. The heartwood tends to be pinkish to yellow in color, with more mature growths being of straight, uniform, and dense grained. Younger trees tend to have more knots. The wood is strong, moderately hard, moderately decay resistant in the heartwood, splits relatively easily, does not bend or steam bend readily, and is fairly easy to work. Douglas fir is sometimes used for making spars in place of Sitka spruce, and in these applications, the wood should be free of defects, well seasoned, and of vertical grain for strength.

LARCH, EASTERN (HACKMATACK, TAMARACK)
30 lbs. per cubic foot,
2.5 lbs. per board foot

The species grows mainly in the Northern and Northeastern coastal states, but is related to western larch. The heartwood is yellowish brown, while the sapwood is nearly white. In boatbuilding, the crooks of the trees (usually in the roots) are used to form natural knees and stems. The wood is moderately decay resistant, tough, moderately strong, and durable.

LARCH, WESTERN
39 lbs. per cubic foot,
3.25 lbs. per board foot

Grown in the Pacific Northwest and

frequently harvested and shipped with Douglas fir. While not a common boatbuilding lumber, there is no reason that it cannot be used if suitable stock is selected. It resembles Douglas fir except the heartwood is russet brown instead of pinkish or reddish. It is strong (actually stronger than Douglas fir), stiff, has moderate decay resistance, splits easily, and has moderately large shrinkage. Knots are frequent but usually tight and small.

PINE, WHITE (EASTERN WHITE, WESTERN WHITE, PONDEROSA, & SUGAR PINE)
25 to 28 lbs. per cubic foot,
2.08 to 2.33 lbs. per board foot

The several types of white pine are available in most of the United States, and grow in many sections of the country. While some types were once popular in boatbuilding, their scarcity and the fact that only second growth stock is sometimes available makes most pine too weak and undurable for boat use. Decay resistance is moderate at best, and its use is best relegated to nonstructural interior joinerywork. These varieties are described to avoid confusion with the longleaf yellow pine type.

PINE, LONGLEAF YELLOW (SOUTHERN PINE)
41 lbs. per cubic foot,
3.42 lbs. per board foot

Grown in the Southern, Atlantic, and Gulf states, there are several varieties of Southern pine. However, the "longleaf" type is best for boat use. The wood is an orange to reddish brown in color, but all species are similar and difficult to differentiate. The dense heartwood is considered almost as decay resistant as white oak. The wood is

strong, straight grained, and hard, however this can vary. The sapwood can be easily treated to improve its decay resistance. Often substituted for white oak.

REDWOOD
28 lbs. per cubic foot,
2.33 lbs. per board foot

Grown along the Northern California coast, the heartwood is light cherry to dark mahogany in color, while sapwood is nearly white or pale yellow. The heartwood is extremely decay resistant, but sapwood is not. The wood is fairly straight grained and free of defects, especially if heartwood. It shrinks and swells little, is easy to work, but tends to be brittle and does not hold fastenings well. The strength is moderate, it does not bend well, and has little use in plywood boatbuilding.

SPRUCE, EASTERN (RED SPRUCE, BLACK SPRUCE, WHITE SPRUCE)
28 lbs. per cubic foot,
2.33 lbs. per board foot

The three species, which are grown in the North and Northeastern states, have similar properties. The wood is light in color with little difference between sapwood and heartwood. It is easily worked, moderate in strength, stiffness, hardness, and toughness. It is not resistant to decay, and is used only where weight is important, and durability is not, or for non-structural work. It has little use in plywood boatbuilding.

SPRUCE, ENGELMANN (WHITE SPRUCE, ARIZONA SPRUCE, SILVER SPRUCE, BALSAM, MOUNTAIN SPRUCE)
23 lbs. per cubic foot,
1.92 lbs. per board foot

These varieties are described only to avoid confusion with the Sitka type of spruce. Grown mainly in the Rocky Mountain states, they are not suited to boat use due to softness, low strength, low resistance to decay, and lack of shock resistance. The sapwood and heartwood are hard to differentiate, and the wood is nearly white in color. It can be used in non-structural joinerywork, however, if not subjected to moisture.

SPRUCE, SITKA
28 lbs. per cubic foot,
2.33 lbs. per board foot

Grows along the Pacific Coast from Alaska to California. Because the trees grow tall, and the material is exceptionally strong for its weight, it is the ideal spar building lumber, even though rot resistance is low. The wood shrinks little and is moderately strong in bending. The heartwood is light pinkish brown and the sapwood creamy white. Where light weight and strength are important, it is ideal.

WOOD USE AND CHARACTERISTICS CHART
The Wood Characteristics chart (see Plate 5-D) is presented as a general guide only, and the qualities listed should be taken with a grain of salt. The reason for this is that there are many variables which must be considered in the application and usage of various wood types. For example, the fact that white oak may be excellent for frame members does not mean that each and every piece of white oak lumber will be suitable for such service. Then too, in some parts of the country, a wood that may be suitable in one area may not be suitable in another for various reasons, such as the quality or quantity available, local practices of seasoning, or any number of other variables. In other words, the recommendations are all relative not only to the locale, but to the services to which the lumber will be applied. Again, the emphasis is made that this listing is general in nature, and the guide to follow is to use those woods which are proven in boatbuilding use in the locale. Also, when selecting a wood from the chart, be sure to look over the adjoining text for that particular species.

WOOD USE & CHARACTERISTICS CHART

HARDWOODS	WEIGHT CATEGORY	STRENGTH CATEGORY	DECAY & ROT RESISTANCE	FASTENING ABILITY	PLATE 5-D COMMENTS
Apitong	Heavy	Strong	Poor	Good	Can be difficult to work
Ash, White	Heavy	Fairly Strong	Poor	Fair	High shock resistance
Elm, Rock	Heavy	Strong	Fair	Good	Good for steam bending
Greenhart	Very Heavy	Very Strong	Very Good	Very Good	For heavy, durable construction
Iroko	Heavy	Strong	Good	Good	Can be used in place of teak in many parts
Ironbark	Very Heavy	Very Strong	Good	Good	For heavy, durable construction
Mahogany, African	Med.	Fairly Strong	Good	Good	Can be used in place of mahoganies
Mahogany	Med.	Fairly Strong	Good	Good	Best of mahoganies
Mahogany, Philippine	Med.	Fairly Strong	Fairly Good	Good	Use dark red variety in boats
Oak, White	Heavy	Strong	Good	Very Good	Don't confuse with red oak
Okoume	Light	Not Strong	Poor	Fair	Suitable for light, small boats
Teak	Heavy	Strong	Very Good	Good	Hard on tools, can remain unfinished
SOFTWOOD					
Cedar, Alaska	Med.	Fairly Strong	Good	Good	Heartwood & sapwood look similar
Cedar, Port Orford	Light	Strong	Very Good	Good	Preferred boatbuilding cedar
Cedar, Western Red	Light	Not Strong	Very Good	Fair	Suitable for veneers in cold mold planking
Douglas Fir	Med.	Strong	Fairly Good	Good	Use only clear, vertical grain
Larch, Eastern	Light	Fairly Strong	Fairly Good	Good	Used mostly for natural knees & stems
Larch, Western	Med.	Strong	Fairly Good	Good	Similar to Douglas Fir
Pine, Longleaf Yellow	Heavy	Strong	Good	Very Good	Can be used in place of white oak
Spruce, Sitka	Light	Fairly Strong	Poor	Fair	High strength to weight ratio

CHAPTER 6 — FASTENINGS

The fastenings usually required for building a plywood boat consist of screws, nails, and bolts. Screws are most often of the flat head wood type, while nails are commonly the annular ring shank or threaded type boat nail. Bolts most frequently are carriage bolts, however, other types are sometimes used such as lag bolts or lag screws, drifts, hanger bolts, machine bolts, flat head machine screws, and threaded rod. All these types will be covered in this chapter (see Plate 6-A).

FASTENING MATERIALS

Basically, metal fastenings can be broken down into ferrous (containing iron) and non-ferrous types, which do not contain iron. As most people realize, ferrous metals such as iron and steel will rust when exposed to the elements, and especially so in a salt water environment. Consequently ordinary steel fastenings have no place in boatbuilding. However, a certain amount of rust and corrosion protection can be given to ordinary steel fastenings by various plating techniques.

One plating technique consists of an electro-plating method which deposits a thin layer of cadmium or zinc onto the metal's surface, and this tends to inhibit the formation of rust to some extent. However, driving such a fastening al-most immediately destroys the very thin layer and rust occurs almost as quickly as if the coating didn't exist. These electro-plated type screws therefore offer poor rust resistance under salt water or even exposed conditions. Their main advantage is that they won't rust on the hardware dealer's shelf.

A better coating process for steel fastenings is a hot dipped galvanized coating of zinc where the fastenings are immersed in molten zinc thereby depositing a heavy zinc-rich coating onto the fastening. Hot dipped galvanized fastenings do not rust when exposed to the weather, however, they may be subject to galvanic corrosion below the water line in salt water conditions when located adjacent to dissimilar metals.

For a boat that will remain for long periods in salt or brackish waters then, hot dipped galvanized fastenings should not be located side by side with bronze or non-ferrous fastenings or fittings since the less noble metal (in this case, the steel fastenings) will begin to deteriorate. It is possible, however, to use the bronze fastening below the water and the hot dipped galvanized fastening above the waterline. For a trailerable boat or for one that will not remain in salt or brackish waters for long periods, the hot dipped galvanized fastening is entirely suitable, especially for boats covered with fiberglass.

Non-ferrous fastenings for boats usually include brass, bronze, and Monel metals, all of which are copper-based. The brass fastening is often considered corrosion resistant, however, this is not actually the case in a marine salt water environment. Such a fastening will de-zincify, which means that the zinc content will leech out of the fastening causing it to rapidly disintegrate. Besides this, brass fastenings are inherently weak, with the heads of fastenings being easily wrenched off when driven hard or otherwise popping off under stress. Because of these problems, brass fastenings are not recommended, with the possible exception of non-structural joinerywork where strength or corrosion resistance is not important.

Bronze and Monel fastenings are superior fastenings, especially for use below the waterline in boats that will remain in salt or brackish waters. There are many different grades of bronze, however the silicon-type is probably best suited for fastenings. Of course, bronze and Monel fastenings are expensive, but as a total percentage of the cost of the boat, the price is only a small fraction. One must consider also that the extra cost of bronze fastenings will probably be more than repaid by the higher resale value of a bronze fastened boat when it is sold.

Aluminum fastenings are also considered as non-ferrous fastenings, however, since they are weak and not corrosion resistant, they also have no place in

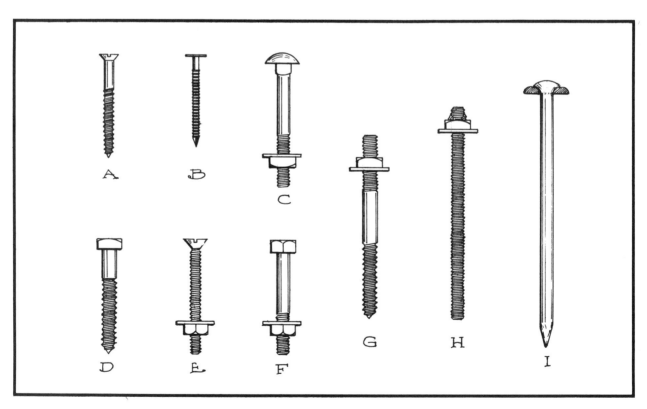

PLATE 6-A—Common fastenings used in plywood boatbuilding include: (A) Flat head wood screw, (B) Ring shank boat nail, and (C) Carriage bolt. Other incidental fastenings may include: (D) Lag bolt, (E) Flat head machine screw, (F) Machine bolt, (G) Hanger bolt, (H) Threaded rod with nut jammed on to form a through-bolt, and (I) Drift with clenched head and ring or washer.

plywood boatbuilding for structural use.

Many people are under the impression that stainless steel is an ideal fastening material. While it is true that stainless steel is ordinarily highly rust resistant, it is not totally free from corrosion. When stainless steel is placed under poorly aerated water conditions or otherwise shielded from air, even by having just a thin oil coating, galvanic action can occur, especially when adjacent to dissimilar metals in salt water. This corrosion usually begins as a very small surface pit trapping salt water which gradually corrodes away to the inner portions of the fastening. Such corrosion is called crevice corrosion and can dissipate a fastening or fitting in the most devious way; from the inside out where it may not be detected until it is too late. The tendency for crevice corrosion to occur will vary depending on the grade of stainless steel. Some grades are more susceptible than others. However, because of the wide array of stainless steel types, and the fact that it is often difficult for the novice to know which type he may be getting, it is usually prudent to avoid stainless steel fastenings for the most part. They are also expensive as well.

SCREWS

Screws come in three main types; round head, oval head, and flat head. The flat head wood screw is the most commonly used in plywood boatbuilding. All head types are available as a slot head or with a cross head type such as the patented Phillips or Read-Prince varieties. These latter types are usually easier for machine driving, however, with the hot dipped galvanized variety, these do not work out so well since the cross head tends to load up with the molten zinc thereby making them harder to drive than the ordinary slot head.

Screw lengths of the standard flat head type range from ¼" to 4" long, however, screws less than ¾" and over 3½" are seldom used in plywood boatbuilding. A number is used to designate the size (diameter) of the screw shank, ranging most commonly from a #2 to a #18. The bigger the number, the larger the screw shank diameter. Relative sizes of the various screws are indicated on the chart shown by Plate 6-B. Screws are sold either by the hundred (1C), or by the gross (144); so when comparing prices make sure you are comparing like amounts.

In driving any screw, it is imperative that the shank and pilot holes be of the proper diameter for the wood being used. Over-drilling or under-drilling will provide poor holding power for the screw or possibly cause the wood to split. Although tables are given recommending the proper sizes, these may have to be varied to suit the work. Obviously, the threads will not cut into oak as well as into a soft wood such as spruce. There are many types of tools available that will drill, countersink, and/or counterbore for screws in one operation, and are well worth the small amount that they cost.

In driving screws through plywood, it is essential that compression wood be left underneath the head (see Plate 6-C). By this term, it is meant that the screw should not be countersunk so far that it will eliminate the top layer of plywood. The top layer of the plywood should be compressed under the screw

43

WOOD SCREWS

When joining wood with screws it is necessary to bore pilot holes, especially in hardwoods. With pilot holes, screws are easier to drive and there is less chance of damaging screws or wood. Bore holes large enough to freely accommodate screw shank in first piece of wood. Bore holes slightly smaller than thread diameters to a depth of half the length of threaded portion in second piece of wood. Screw length should be at least ⅛" less than combined measurement of material being joined.

PILOT HOLE

- COUNTER SINK (C)
- SHANK HOLE (B)
- PILOT HOLE (A)

No. of Screw	PILOT HOLES (A)				SHANK CLEARANCE HOLES (B)		COUNTER-SINK (C)
	HARD WOODS		SOFT WOODS				
	TWIST BIT (Nearest size in fractions of an inch)	DRILL Gauge No. To be used for maximum holding power	TWIST BIT (Nearest size in fractions of an inch)	DRILL Gauge No. To be used for maximum holding power	TWIST BIT (Nearest size in fractions of an inch)	DRILL Gauge No. or Letter To be used for maximum holding power	NO. OF AUGER BIT To Counterbore for sinking head (by 16ths)
0	½₂	66	¹⁄₆₄	75	¹⁄₁₆	52	—
1	—	57	½₂	71	⁵⁄₆₄	47	—
2	—	54	½₂	65	³⁄₃₂	42	3
3	¹⁄₁₆	53	³⁄₆₄	58	⁷⁄₆₄	37	4
4	¹⁄₁₆	51	³⁄₆₄	55	⁷⁄₆₄	32	4
5	⁵⁄₆₄	47	¹⁄₁₆	53	⅛	30	4
6	—	44	¹⁄₁₆	52	⁹⁄₆₄	27	5
7	—	39	¹⁄₁₆	51	⁵⁄₃₂	22	5
8	⁷⁄₆₄	35	⁵⁄₆₄	48	¹¹⁄₆₄	18	6
9	⁷⁄₆₄	33	⁵⁄₆₄	45	³⁄₁₆	14	6
10	⅛	31	³⁄₃₂	43	³⁄₁₆	10	6
11	—	29	³⁄₃₂	40	¹³⁄₆₄	4	7
12	—	25	⁷⁄₆₄	38	⁷⁄₃₂	2	7
14	³⁄₁₆	14	⁷⁄₆₄	32	¼	D	8
16	—	10	⁹⁄₆₄	29	¹⁷⁄₆₄	I	9
18	¹³⁄₆₄	6	⁹⁄₆₄	26	¹⁹⁄₆₄	N	10
20	⁷⁄₃₂	3	¹¹⁄₆₄	19	²¹⁄₆₄	P	11
24	¼	D	³⁄₁₆	15	⅜	V	12

*Sizes of holes recommended for average application. Slightly larger or smaller holes may be required.

#0 #1 #2 #3 #4 #5 #6 #7 #8 #9

ACTUAL SHANK SIZES

#10 #11 #12 #14 #16 #18 #20 #24 #30

To determine Sizes of Screws, lay screws flat within parallel lines shown in border.

Courtesy Southern Screw Co.

PLATE 6-B—Wood Screw Chart

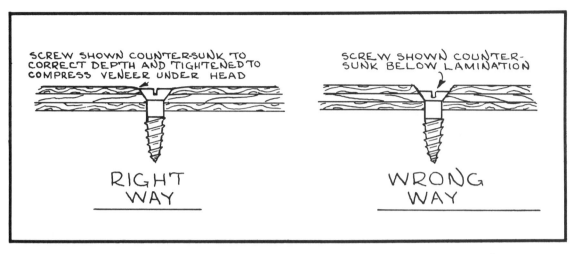

SCREW SHOWN COUNTERSUNK TO CORRECT DEPTH AND TIGHTENED TO COMPRESS VENEER UNDER HEAD

SCREW SHOWN COUNTER-SUNK BELOW LAMINATION

RIGHT WAY

WRONG WAY

PLATE 6-C—The "right" way (at left) to drive a screw in plywood, and the "wrong" way (to right). The screw should compress all the veneers in a plywood panel.

head. This gives much better holding power. Screws in plywood that is under tension, such as in the application of curved planking panels, should never be counterbored. They should be driven just below the surface of the wood. Putty is used to cover the head of the screw. If the hull will be covered later with fiberglass or equal sheathing, such putty should be an oil-free type compatible with resin for a proper bond.

Often in driving screws in hardwoods such as oak, the screws have a tendency to bind and are very difficult to drive. When this is the case, the screws can be lubricated by rubbing them on a bar of soap or paraffin. This will facilitate driving considerably. Avoid driving screws along the very edge of the cross grain on a plywood panel as it can cause the grain to split at the edges. It is better to leave a panel oversize when possible, drive the screws, and then trim to size, such as can be done on the side or bottom planking of a boat at the transom. In extremely fast powerboats or racing boats, it is considered excellent practice to dip each screw in a hard setting glue

before driving it home. When fastening along a length of wood, the screws should be well staggered not only for good holding power, but to avoid splitting the wood. When driving a screw, especially by machine, keep pressure on the screw until it is driven home. If the screw hits bottom but continues to turn freely, it means that the screw has stripped out the hole and has no holding power. When this occurs and the screw is necessary at this point, remove the screw and replace with one of a larger shank size or longer length, or both.

The chart in this chapter (see Plate 6-D) indicates the recommended sizes of screws for various planking and decking thicknesses. However, this may vary considerably depending on the particular boat and the backing member sizes. Quite often screws may require closer spacing or the use of longer screws, or may require larger spacing and smaller screws. This chart should serve as a general guide, but minor variations will not be detrimental.

45

SCREW SIZES AND SPACING RECOMMENDATIONS FOR PLYWOOD PLANKING AND DECKING

Plywood Thickness	Plywood at outer extremities (e.g. at chine logs, keels, and sheer clamps)	Plywood at inner areas (e.g. longitudinal battens)	Plywood to transom and stem
¼″	¾″ #8 OR 1″ #8, 3″ apart	¾″ #8 OR 1″ #8, 6″ apart	1″ #8 OR 1¼″ #8, 2″ apart
⅜″	1″ #8 OR 1¼″ #8, 3″ apart	1″ #8 OR 1¼″ #8, 6″ apart	1¼″ #8, 2″ apart
½″	1½″ #8, 3″ apart	1½″ #8, 6″ apart	1½″ #8 OR 2″ #10, 2″ apart
⅝″	1½″ #8, 3″ apart	1½″ #8, 6″ apart	2″ #10, 2″ apart
¾″	2″ #10, 3″ apart	2″ #10, 6″ apart	2″ #10 min. or larger, 2″ apart

PLATE 6-D—Screw size and spacing recommendation for fastening plywood planking and decking of various thicknesses.

NAILS

Ordinary nails such as the steel common or finish type may sometimes be used for incidental purposes in plywood boatbuilding, but the main nail fastener is the annular rink shank or threaded type boat nail. This nail is usually made from bronze or Monel. There are also machine driven non-ferrous nails or staples that can be used in lieu of this type, but the average amateur may not have access to these, nor to the pneumatic or electric powered gun required to drive them. Regardless of the type of nail or staple used, if it is to remain in the completed boat, it should be made from a suitable marine-type metal.

The ring shank boat nail has a series of serrated circles around the body of the nail. When these nails are driven into the wood, the rings tend to lock with the wood fibers, giving a positive grip that is hard to pull free, once driven, without destroying the surrounding wood fibers. As a general rule, the ring shank boat nail can be used for fastening virtually all flat member junctions in lieu of screws. However, it must be emphasized that these nails do not have the ability to pull the parts together as screws do, and consequently may not provide the proper clamping pressure required for certain types of glued joints. This makes the use of nails for holding planking in

46

place a questionable practice, especially where bending stresses are severe.

If planking is to be fastened with nails, then a clamp should be moved along the backing member and the plywood to hold the panel down, or another worker may be able to physically hold the panel in place, because it will surely pull free if the tension is too great. In most instances, it will be necessary to have someone underneath the backing member bucking it while the nails are driven from the opposite side to prevent springing of the member.

As noted, the annular ring nail comes into its own on flat members such as gussets-to-frames, decking panels, laminations, cabin sides, and cabin tops. The length of the nail is sometimes governed by the thickness of the member to which the plywood will be fastened, but as a general rule, the nail should have a minimum length of three times the thickness of the plywood or member being fastened, and preferably longer. Always stagger the nails in the grain, and drive the head flush with the surface, preferably driving home with a nail set to prevent damaging the surface if appearance is important.

Usually the wire gage of the nail is smaller than the shank size of a similar length screw, but then a greater number of nails (or closer spacing) is used than for screws. Unlike screws, the larger the wire gage number, the smaller the nail shank. With nail shanks larger than about .100", pilot holes are recommended even though most builders will want to pound them in just like the ordinary type. While this rule can sometimes be violated without incidence, such pre-drilling will prevent splitting and increase holding power.

Naturally the pre-drilled hole must be smaller than the nail diameter, and this will vary between 50% and 70% of the nail depending on the hardness of the wood. Softer woods should be pre-drilled with smaller holes, while harder woods should have larger holes. The depth of the hole measured from the top surface where the nail will set should be about 80% of the length of the nail.

Information on the sizes of the ring shank nails for plywood boatbuilding is given on Plate 6-E. These recommendations may need to be varied depending on the type of wood and the pressure required to hold the members in position.

BOLTS & SIMILAR FASTENINGS

The common bolt used in plywood boatbuilding is the conventional carriage bolt. The large rounded head of the carriage bolt has a squared portion just below the head which prevents the bolt from turning in the wood. This means that the nut can be tightened down without the need for wrenching on the head at the same time. This is important in boatbuilding because the heads must frequently be concealed, and yet one must be able to tighten down the bolt both during the construction and perhaps at some time later. No washer is used under the head of a carriage bolt, however, a flat washer of generous size should be used under the nut. Joints where carriage bolts are used include keels to stems, transom knees to transoms and keels, longitudinals like keels and chine logs to frames (especially in larger boats), or other areas where a strong mechanical con-

ANNULAR THREAD NAILS			

NAILS FOR PLYWOOD PLANKING AND DECKING

Plywood Thickness	Nail Size	NAIL SPACING Along Edges	In Hull Battens and Deck Beams
¼"	⅞" x .109"	1½" - 2"	4" - 5"
⅜"	1¼" x .109"	3" - 3½"	5" - 6"
½"	1½" x .134"	3½" - 4"	5" - 6"
⅝"	2" x .165"	4"	6"
¾"	2¼" x .165"	4"	6"

EQUIVALENT GAUGES OF NAILS AND SCREWS

NAILS Wire Diameter	SCREWS Body Diameter	Screw Gauge
.083"	.086"	No. 2
.095"		
.109"		
.120"	.125"	5
.134"	.138"	6
.165"	.164"	8
.180"		
	.190"	10
.203"		
.220"	.216"	12
.238"	.242"	14
.265"		
	.268"	16
.284"		
.300"	.294"	18

TYPICAL QUANTITIES OF NAILS PER POUND
(Counts may vary with different metals.)

Length	Wire Diameter	Approximate Number Per Pound
1"	.109"	350
1¼"	.109"	280
1½"	.083"	425
1½"	.109"	210
1½"	.134"	135
1½"	.165"	89
1¾"	.134"	123
1¾"	.165"	76
2"	.134"	110
2"	.165"	68
2¼"	.134"	94
2¼"	.165"	62
2½"	.134"	84
2½"	.165"	56
2¾"	.165"	50
3"	.165"	45

Courtesy Independent Nail & Packing Co.

PLATE 6-E—Annular thread nail recommendation and reference chart for various plywood thicknesses.

48

nection that will not pull free is required.

In some cases, long lengths of carriage bolts are difficult to obtain. If this is the case, it may be possible to cut the joining members down in size somewhat at the heads or nuts to suit a shorter size without weakening the junction appreciably. Or it is possible to substitute lengths of threaded rod, using a punch to jam the nut at one end to serve as a head, and then securing with another nut at the opposite end. Then again, another type of fastening may be substituted in some cases.

Machine bolts with either hex, square, or flat heads (called "machine screws" in this form) are sometimes called for, but access to both ends of the fastenings must be possible for tightening. Flat head types are used where the head will be flush with the surface.

Drifts or drift bolts are not commonly used in plywood boatbuilding, but are sometimes called for in larger boats, especially for assembling large deadwood members. A drift is actually just a great big nail, and driven with hard blows of a large hammer. A point is shaped on an anvil which does not have to be sharp. The hole for the drift is a little smaller than the drift and a clench ring is placed over the hole. The drift is driven into the hole and through the clench ring. When nearly home, the head is shaped and then driven home.

Lag bolts or lag screws are basically oversized screws but have hex or square heads for tightening with a wrench. They are used, along with drifts, when it is not possible to use through bolts. The holding power of lag screws is dependent on the proper size hole being provided to suit the size of the lag screw as well as the type of wood being drilled. It must not be too large or too small.

Hanger bolts are like a lag screw without a head, and with one end being threaded for a standard nut. The purpose of a hanger bolt is to allow replacement of the adjoining member by simply removing the nut. The stud of the hanger bolt remains in position for repositioning and refastening the member in place. These fastenings are often used as inboard motor or motor stringer hold-downs since it is impractical to continually remove a lag bolt.

CHAPTER 7 — GLUES, ADHESIVES, AND ENCAPSULATION

Glues used for boatbuilding should be so strong, that when used properly, the surrounding wood should fail before the glue joint. Theoretically, if a suitable glue is properly used for a plywood boatbuilding operation, all the fastenings could be withdrawn and the glue joint would not fail. Of course, such a procedure is not advised for most joints, especially for the amateur, since ideal controlled gluing conditions seldom exist or are difficult to maintain. Hence the use of fastenings not only is an aid to construction, but double insurance that a joint will not fail when stressed.

Glue joints in plywood boatbuilding should not fail due to moisture or exposure to marine conditons. Marine use requires special glues and adhesives, but the qualifications for a suitable marine glue for plywood boatbuilding are not as severe as for some other conditions, such as aerospace applications. For example, since boats seldom encounter boiling water conditions, glues that are intended for these conditions are not absolutely necessary.

The most important element when using any marine glue product is to follow the recommendations of the glue manufacturer to the letter. This is especially critical with most types concerning temperatures, proper mixing of the products, clamping methods, and curing requirements. Taking shortcuts in working with glue could lead to disastrous results . . . . . so follow directions!

PLASTIC RESIN GLUE

The plastic resin glue comes in a powder form that is mixed with water. It is technically classed as a urea-formaldehyde type. This type of glue is stain-free, insect, and mold proof. It is virtually waterproof under normal marine conditions as has been proven by years of experience, although most manufacturers rate the glue only as highly "water resistant". The makers of this type of glue are probably reluctant to state that the glue is completely waterproof because the glue joint may fail under stress in boiling or freezing water conditions seldom encountered with boats.

The plastic resin glue is very popular since it is both easy to use and economical. Time available in working with the glue as well as the pot life will vary with the ambient temperature, so only the amount that can be used within a given time should be mixed up. However, since the glue is quick and easy to mix up, if one runs out it is easy to make up more. Using a plastic bleach bottle cut off at the top is ideal for a glue pot since when the glue dries, it will shrink somewhat and readily pull free from the container so it can be re-used.

Joints must be clean, smooth, well-fitted, free of oil or grease, and clamping pressure must be maintained until the joint cures. While working temperatures should be 70° or higher, localized heat can be applied (such as with a bare light bulb or two) to maintain this temperature at the gluing surface. Surfaces should be wiped of excess glue using a damp rag before the glue sets. The product leaves a thin, fine, brown glue line which can be a disadvantage on some kinds of wood if appearance is important.

Plastic resin glue is not recommended for oily hardwoods such as teak, nor for oak when used in salt water due to the possible reaction with the gallic acid of the wood that will destroy the bond.

RESORCINOL GLUE

The resorcinol glue is probably the most respected and time-proven of the marine waterproof glues. The glue comes in a two-part mix with one part being a powder (paraformaldehyde), and the other a liquid hardener (resorcinol resin). Temperatures at which the glue is mixed and used should be 70° or more. As with the plastic resin type, working time and pot life decreases with increasing temperatures, along with curing time. When properly made,

FIG. 7-1—Proper application of glue is important in boatbuilding to avoid a weak "glue starved" joint. While a stick or piece of wood can be used to spread the glue, better practice is to spread an even coat over the mating surface with a brush or a paint roller such as is being used here. Inexpensive brushes and rollers are available in a wide variety of sizes to suit the application.

the resorcinol glue joint is extremely strong and suitable results can be obtained on just about any kind of wood.

Joints should be clean, dry, free of oil, grease, or paint, and slightly roughened. Clamping pressure must be applied until the joint cures. Excess glue must be wiped clean with a damp rag before the glue sets as it will stain. The glue leaves a fine dark glue line that may be objectionable in some applications with certain woods. The glue joint is not affected by mild acids, alkalis, fungus, mold, or rot. It can also be used on many other porous and nonporous materials such as concrete, plastics, and leather.

EPOXIES

Epoxies are one of the newest additions to the family of marine adhesives. There are literally hundreds of different types of epoxies available, formulated for many different applications. It is important to select one that is intended for gluing wood in a marine environment.

Marine epoxy adhesives are two part products usually identified as "A" the resin and "B" the hardener. Proportions of resin to hardener may vary, with ratios in a range from 1:1 to 1:5 most common. Epoxies are used as adhesives, coating, fiberglassing, and making reinforcing fillets. Specially formulated epoxies are made to use as an adhesive. These products are simpler to use, usually 1:1 mix, but are not suitable for coating or fiberglassing. General purpose or encapsulating resins are also used as adhesives often with filler additives. These offer more control over the workability of the epoxy and are multipurpose products.

Epoxies have tremendous strength in themselves and are capable of filling gaps and irregularities. These features don't exist with many other types of glue. Thus, they are excellent for the amateur builder who may not always have close fitting structural joints. Little clamping pressure is required. In fact, excessive clamping is undesirable. Firm pressure is needed but a film of epoxy should bridge between the joining wood members. Properly made junctions are stronger than the wood itself.

Epoxies, in general, will cure at lower temperatures than most other marine adhesives. Many are available with hardeners that will set fast or slow to compensate for ambient temperatures. NEVER vary the proportions of hardener to resin. Always measure accurately, don't guess at the proportions. Mix the hardener and resin thoroughly in clean containers, small quantities at a time. Pour measured amounts of resin and hardener in separate containers. Have several containers ready (and preferably an assistant) to pour the two parts together and mix them on demand. The pot life of mixed materials is limited. If large batches are mixed much of the epoxy may be wasted before it can be used. Curing starts as soon as epoxy components are combined. This curing process generates heat, which in turn accelerates the curing process. It is possible to slow this process by transferring the mixture to a container which gives more surface area thus allowing the heat to dissipate. Placing the resin container in a pan of ice water will also slow curing. Conversely, curing can be accelerated by using a small neck mixing container or placing the container in a pan of warm water.

Epoxy resin, as opposed to epoxy glue, is usually not thick enough to make a good gap filling adhesive. Additives such as micro ballons or spheres, silica, wood flour, fiber fillers, or similar products can be added to the epoxy resin-hardener mixture to thicken it.

Epoxies must be handled with care. The primary hazard with epoxy is skin irritation leading to skin sensitization from prolonged and repeated contact. Safety in using epoxies is covered in more detail under the section on ENCAPSULATION, however a brief overview follows. Keep epoxies off your skin. Use gloves and barrier skin creams. Use a good waterless hand soap to remove any epoxy on the skin. Do not use acetone or lacquer thinner. Such solvents drive hazardous ingredients into your body.

OTHER EPOXIES

One of the epoxy related types suitable for marine use consists of a urea-formaldehyde powder in one part, and a second part of water-like liquid hardener. It has rather unique qualities making it suitable for boatbuilding. This type of glue (one is known as "Aerolite") does not require heavy pressure or clamping and has some gap filling capabilities so that joints do not have to be precise.

The part containing the powder is mixed with water and this is applied to one gluing surface. Then the water-like liquid hardener is applied to the other gluing surface. When the two members are brought together, the two glue components catalyze and cure the joint. Gluing can take place in temperatures as low as 60° with the standard hardeners, and once cured, it will be waterproof, insect, and mold proof. Since nothing happens until the two components come together, the worker has considerable leeway in working time. However, in warm temperatures, the resin portion will tend to solidify if not covered, and the water-like hardener may have to be reapplied if it dries on the gluing surface prior to assembly. The glue dries clear and excess glue is easily removed with a damp rag. As with most epoxy types, the glue can be used on virtually any wood to form an extremely strong joint.

OTHER GLUES & ADHESIVES

The common white vinyl glue for household use is not waterproof and therefore is not recommended for boatbuilding. This type of glue is not suitable for certain hardwoods in any case, especially with oily woods such as teak. Another improved glue that is similar (called aliphatic resin glue) provides better gluing properties and offers better results with difficult woods, however, it also is not waterproof. Either of these glues may be suitable for incidental use in non-structural joinerywork.

In some instances, a so-called marine mastic may be required. A marine mastic is an adhesive that when cured will retain some degree of flexibility. Many types are available including the silicone sealants and polysulphide polymer compounds. These types of mastics are used at water-exposed junctions which are not fiberglass covered, or where a permanent bond may be undesirable. Because the mastics theoretically do not set hard, they will maintain a certain amount of flexibility which will contract and expand with the adjoining members thereby assuring a watertight junction. When using these products, be sure to stick to the recommendations provided with the product.

ENCAPSULATION

Encapsulation means "enclosing in an envelope." Essentially, that is exactly what a coating of marine epoxy resin does to (and for) the wood in a boat. When the process was first introduced, it was called "saturation." In truth, epoxy does not impregnate wood to any great depth. It is actually a coating and does not form a complete moisture barrier. However, as little as two coats, when properly applied, can impede the passage of moisture sufficiently to make the encapsulated material — in this case, wood — quite resistant to water. To put it another way, a marine epoxy will stabilize wood more than any other product readily available and keep absorption of moisture to a minimum.

The term "epoxy" covers many types of products. Be sure the one you decide to use is intended for marine encapsulation. The system described here is used to assemble and encapsulate wooden boats to eliminate rot, worm and insect damage and the effects of moisture (such as warping, checking, delaminating, shrinkage and swelling). Epoxy encapsulation, properly done,

will withstand the effects of water, air, temperature changes, and most chemicals. Epoxy virtually keeps these elements out, both stabilizing the wood and sealing it for maximum durability.

What are the pros and cons of epoxy encapsulation? Well, we've already had a look at some of the "pros" in the foregoing section. Obviously, elimination of many of the traditional problems that can accompany wood construction is a large factor in its favor.

On the other hand, encapsulation is only as strong as its weakest link. It is imperative that all exposed wood be completely covered — edges, sides, everywhere — to eliminate any uncoated area. If the wood is not completely sealed, moisture can enter and problems can arise. At least two (or preferably three) coats of epoxy should be applied to all wood surfaces to assure complete encapsulation.

Epoxy coverings are strong but not invulnerable. As a surface coating, it can be scratched or scraped, again allowing moisture to readily enter. Therefore, it is often advisable to coat all exterior surfaces with a protective layer of fiberglass or its equivalent. Natural elements may take a toll, as well. Over a period of time, epoxy is affected by the ultra-violet (UV) rays in sunlight. This can cause deterioration. Application of paint or a clear coating with UV-protectors can eliminate this problem.

Marine epoxies are two-part products, consisting of resin and hardener. Ratios for mixing these two elements vary, but the most common proportions are usually from 1:1 to 1:5 parts hardener to resin. It is important that you do NOT alter the proportions from those recommended by the manufacturer. If changes in the mixture are necessary, they should be made ONLY in the type of hardener.

Epoxies are somewhat more tolerant to lower temperatures than polyesters, but most work best in the 70 degree F. range. Pot life — that is, the time that the mixed ingredients remain useful and workable — is a variable that must be carefully watched. Since pot life tends to vary with temperature, most marine epoxies are available with either "fast" or "slow" hardeners. Under normal conditions, slow hardener is used for encapsulation. However with some epoxies fast and slow hardeners can be blended to alter pot life to suit the working temperatures.

Please note that epoxy is quite toxic and should NEVER be sprayed. Exposure to epoxy systems without exercising proper safety precautions can cause dermatitis, skin and respiratory problems.

Encapsulation epoxy is not a paint and doesn't act like one. On vertical surfaces, in particular, it tends to run or sag, and can seldom be brushed out to a paint-like finish. Sanding is required to smooth the surface to accept the finish covering, paint or clear finish. For flat surfaces, a special short-nap foam roller works best, allowing the builder to apply thin coats one after another until the desired build-up is obtained.

Horizontal surfaces are easier and quicker to fully coat with epoxy. Some builders advocate pre-coating all parts prior to assembly, then following up with one or more additional coats after assembly. One great advantage of the epoxy encapsulation system is that the glues (which may be the same as encapsulation resin) are specifically intended to be used over previously-applied epoxy.

A coloring agent can be added to epoxy resin, but the final surface will not provide the yacht-like finish that many builders seek. If a first-class finish is desired, plan on painting over a finished epoxy surface. Since epoxy is clear, or virtually colorless, it can be used as a base for marine varnish or clear finish. The initial epoxy surface will need to be sanded smooth, taking great care not to cut through to the wood. Remember that, to be effective, the epoxy must seal the surface entirely. Clear finish over properly sanded epoxy surfaces will build up quickly, thus elmininating many of the successive coats required for most transparent finishes.

Epoxy encapsulation is expensive, and not without hazards or difficulties. For most boat builders, though, the advantages of a properly coated surface, especially in terms of a longer and more care-free boat life, make the process worth serious consideration.

CHAPTER 8 — LOFTING

Lofting, as referred to in boat construction, is redrawing or expanding the lines of the boat to full size. The lines drawing is that drawing which shows the shape or "describes" the configuration of the hull. The main reason for the lofting process is so the builder can pick up the hull contours, transfer these to the members that will be used to build the boat, and thereby duplicate the boat as the designer intended. Of course, if full size patterns are provided with the plans of the boat, the lofting process is not necessary. The use of full size patterns will be described in Chapter 9.

Let us digress for a moment and understand what the designer actually does in his lines drawing. A naval architect or yacht designer does not simply draw a boat; he designs a boat. From the lines drawing he makes all his calculations, determines his various coefficients and balance points, and actually "proves" the boat. Before the lines drawing is finished, he will have determined the designed waterline of the boat in most cases. This will mean that he must calculate for all the weights in the entire boat, not only for the basic hull, but for passengers, motors, fuel, water, etc.

Since an object floating in water will displace or "push aside" an amount of water exactly equal in weight to that of the weight of the floating object, the designer must carefully calculate the volume of the underwater shapes and determine the actual waterline for the proper weight. To do this accurately, the designer must work to the outside contours or extremities of the hull. This is the reason why the dimensions on the lines drawing and as listed in what is called the table of offsets are generally taken to the outside of the hull planking. If this were not done, the architect's figures would not be accurate for his various calculations.

Many individuals interpret lofting as taking dimensions from the table of offsets and drawing out just the section or frame drawings. Nothing could be further from the truth! The designer uses a scale rule to determine all the dimensions given on the lines drawing, including the offsets, or dimensions used to describe the hull configuration. Since a boat is designed to a certain scale, such as $1'' = 1'-0''$, this will mean that in taking the dimensions from the scale drawing, the designer will have to read his rule very closely. On a scale drawing, the thickness of a pencil line could be as much as $\frac{1}{8}''$ in full size. Since this could be a plus or minus dimension, the measurements given are not necessarily accurate. In fact, if they were completely accurate, it would be unusual. In most cases, the lines drawing could have variations by as much as $\frac{1}{4}''$ plus or minus even if the designer did read his scale accurately. For this reason, most designers advise that the drawings never be scaled for accurate dimensions.

While some designers may be more accurate, careful, blessed with better eyesight, or just plain luckier than others, the lofting process should still be performed to correct and prove the scaled dimensions, and to compensate for the fact that the frames must be made to the inside of the planking, since the dimensions are taken to the outside. In lofting, the term "fairing" means compensating for deviations in the dimensions provided on the table of offsets to provide smooth flowing, even, and fair lines that are free from humps and dips or other unfair qualities. Not only are fair lines important to make the construction simpler, but unfair lines can impair the performance of the hull besides upsetting all the calculations the designer may have made.

The nomenclature used for the various items shown on the lines drawing is unique to boatbuilding. Many of these terms are not defined in a standard dictionary. Before attempting to do any lofting, the prospective loftsman should study the various points and terms, and become familiar with them. By reviewing the following definitions and checking to the drawing in Plate 8-A, these terms should be clarified. The three views normally shown on the lines drawing can be located in various manners depending on the preferences of the designer. Also, the station points, which are defined below, may be numbered from the left to right, or vice versa. Regardless of the method or style used by the designer, the nomenclature will be similar.

The various definitions for lofting are as follows:

1. PLAN: The plan of the boat is usually in half-breadth. It is half of the lines of the boat as seen from the top or the bottom. All widths on the plain view are actual or true distances.

2. PROFILE: The profile is the lines of the boat as seen from the side. All heights are true dimensions in this view.

3. BODY: The body is divided into two sections; that showing forward sections or stations, and that showing aft sections or stations. The sections show what the hull will look like when viewed from either the bow or the stern of the boat at those points or stations. The sections are taken at station lines as designated in both the plan and profile view. In these sections, the heights and widths are all true dimensions.

4. STATIONS: The stations are perpendiculars from the base or centerline and are at the same location in both the plan and profile view. The frames of the boat are often situated on station lines, although some of the frames are sometimes omitted.

5. BASELINE: The baseline is a horizontal reference plane given on the profile and body drawings. Dimensions of heights are taken vertically from the baseline. The position of the baseline may vary. The architect may give his height dimensions from the load waterline, a "set up level," or any other horizontal line. In the example shown on Plate 8-A, the keel line and the baseline correspond in the aft portion of the boat. This is not typical of all boats.

6. CENTERLINE: The centerline is just that, the centerline of the boat, and is given on the plan and body view. All dimensions for width are taken from this centerline.

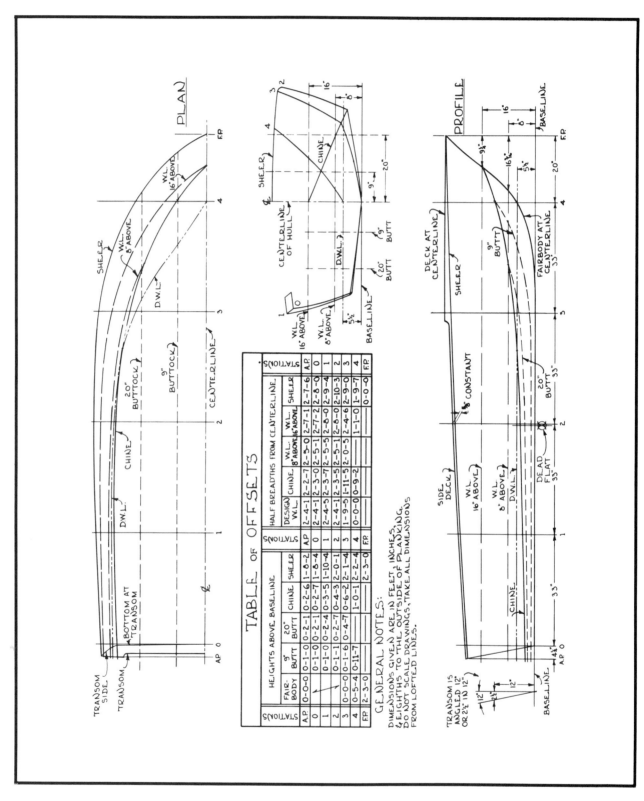

PLAN

PROFILE

TABLE OF OFFSETS

GENERAL NOTES:

DIMENSIONS GIVEN ARE IN FEET, INCHES, & EIGHTHS TO THE OUTSIDE OF PLANKING. DO NOT SCALE DRAWINGS; TAKE ALL DIMENSIONS FROM LOFTED LINES.

PLATE 8-A

7. CHINE: The chine is the junction point of the side and the bottom of the boat. It is seen in all the views of the lines; on the plan, profile, and body. On round bottom boats there is no chine line.

8. SHEER: The sheer is the junction of the side of the boat with the top or the deck. The sheer line is also seen in all views in the lines.

9. FAIRBODY: The fairbody is the junction of the bottom planking with the keel. Actually, it is the rabbet-point if such is given. In plywood boats, the fairbody may coincide with the centerline, as does the example in Plate 8-A.

10. TRANSOM: The transom is the back or the stern of the boat. It may be vertical, raked, or curved. A boat without a transom is called a "double ender".

11. STEM: The stem is the bow of the boat. To put it another way, it is that curved portion at the bow extending upward from the keel to the deck. A few boats do not have stems and don't end in a "point". These boats are said to be "blunt bowed".

12. F.P.: The abbreviation is for forward perpendicular. This is the forward ending of the bow of the boat, or that portion of the boat's lines forward of the ending of the D.W.L.

13. A.P.: This is extreme aft end of the boat, commonly called aft perpendicular. It is that portion of the lines of the boat aft of the aft end of the D.W.L.

14. BUTTOCKS: The buttocks are lines that designate the deviation from a straight line between the chine and the keel, as seen in the body lines. In the profile, these are curved lines, while in the plan they are straight horizontal lines.

15. WATERLINES: Waterlines will indicate the deviation in the side of the boat from a straight line between the chine and the sheer, as seen in the body lines. In the plan view, waterlines will be curved, while, when seen in the profile, they will be straight horizontal lines.

16. DEAD FLAT: Dead flat is sometimes indicated by the symbol ⬠. This is the longitudinal center of the boat measured on its designed waterline length. It has nothing to do with fairing the lines and can therefore be disregarded.

17. D.W.L.: D.W.L. is the abbreviation for the "designed waterline." This is the point the designer has calculated that the boat will settle to when normally loaded. The abbreviation L.W.L., "load waterline," is sometimes used.

18. CENTER OF BUOYANCY: The center of buoyancy is labeled C.B., and is the balance point of the underwater volume. It would be the same as the fulcrum on a child's teeter-totter. The designer must distribute his weights so that the boat is in balance about the C.B., or it will settle or "trim" down at the bow or stern when at rest.

19. TABLE OF OFFSETS: Offsets are merely a method of giving dimensions to a point. The Table of Offsets is the designer's measurements that will be used to plot points to obtain the lofted lines. The dimensions given in a Table of Offsets are usually to the outside of the planking. The table is usually divided into two parts. One is given as a

height above a baseline or some other reference plane, while all widths are taken horizontally from the centerline. The conventional method of giving these dimensions is slightly different from simply writing out inches or feet. These figures are usually written in feet, inches and eighths of an inch. As an example, the figure 3-2-1 would read 3′2⅛″. Some architects prefer to note offsets in inches and eights. For example, the previous dimensions would appear on the table as 38-1 by this method. A "+" is often seen on the Table of Offsets which means to add ¹⁄₁₆″ to the noted dimension.

With the terms used by the architect defined, the "how-to" or lofting can now be described. Lofting may be done on any smooth, flat surface. The area set aside should be enough to allow several feet of clearance on the ends and should also allow this amount of clearance on both sides over the half width of the boat or the overall height, whichever is greater. The drawings, or lofting, can be made on a smooth concrete area or on a wood floor, or a long sheet of plywood or two joined together. It is difficult to spring curves on a concrete floor, as it is impossible to drive nails into it for holding the fairing battens, which are thin wood strips.

The loftings can be drawn on plywood or paper. It is granted that paper will have a tendency to expand and contract with variances in humidity. Such changes are for the most part uniform, and are so inconsequential that they may be disregarded. The larger the boat, of course, the more deviation, but the less in total consequence due to the size of the boat.

For the lofting project a series of pencils will be required. Since many of the lines will be superimposed, colored pencils are preferred. Crayons or the like are not desirable as they will not draw a crisp, fine line. A series of dotted lines and solid lines can be used with standard pencil; however, the colored lines are easier to follow. A good ruler and a six or eight-foot steel tape will be required. A large builder's square will generally suffice for drawing the perpendiculars. For obtaining long straight lines, a chalk line is a valuable asset. If the work is done on a hard surface such as concrete, a series of weights will be needed to hold the fairing battens to shape. Bars of lead such as printers and plumbers use are ideal, although any heavy weight can be used.

If work is done on a wood floor, a hammer and a few nails will replace all weights. As a word of caution, don't jinx the whole job by pounding nails into the wife's hardwood floor or wood-backed linoleum floor. The prospective loftsman is assured that this is not considered good practice unless his wife is a broad-minded boating enthusiast.

Battens are used to fair in the various lines. The size of these will vary with the type of boat. It is good practice to use as heavy a batten as the lines of the boat will stand. The heavier the batten, the smoother the curve. Consider the batten as being the wood member that will later be sent around the hull framing. These fairing battens should be of soft white pine free and clear of knots and imperfections. The one used in the longer sweeps should be several feet longer than the boat, or the longest line, which is generally the sheer. Usually a ¾″ square batten on the larger craft and a ½″ square batten on smaller boats will work out. A shorter length of ¼″ square batten material approximately 8′, is used for the stem. Quite often the bends are difficult and require thinner material.

After selecting the area and having the tools at hand, the builder may start the task of lofting. As previously noted, the lofting surface used must be several feet longer than the boat to be lofted. It must also be wide enough to handle half the width of the boat or the maximum height from the baseline to the highest sheer point as noted on the Table of Offsets. A chalk line is used at the bottom edge of the paper approximately 2″ to 3″ from the bottom to snap a long line at least the length of the boat with a foot or so clearance. This line will designate not only the centerline of the boat, but the baseline in our loftings for reference purposes.

The example used to illustrate a typical lofting problem for a plywood boat will be taken from the lines drawing and offset tables on Plate 8-A. This particular lines drawing has a minimum number of sections, less than would be customary. Since we are illustrating a problem and not actually lofting this boat for practical purposes, the one shown will suffice and simplify the illustrations that follow.

The designer's lines drawing as shown by the example, Plate 8-A, should be referred to for the station spacing. These station points should be laid out along the center and baseline that has just been snapped in, Plate 8-B. At each of these points, a perpendicular line is drawn. Label each of the station lines as the designer has done on his lines drawing. The profile will be the first portion of the lofting to be accomplished. Check the designer's Offset Table and determine the heights above the baseline at each of the stations. Having one individual call out these heights and another measure them and mark them on the loftings will simplify the task. Illustrated on Plate 8-C is a typical example of these points laid out. The heaviest of battens is bent through the various points. Undoubtedly, some discrepancy will be noted. Some of the points may be above or below the batten when bent in a fair curve. By splitting the difference, the batten will hit the points closely and thereby form a fair curve.

Note the importance of the statement "fair curve." The designer's lines are not meant to have bumps, dips, and hollows. The curve must be a fair, clean-looking line. It will be necessary to compensate for deviations in measurements by sweeping the curve fair, hitting as many of the points as possible. When you have sighted the line or curve, it may be held in position by the weights or by tacking nails to the inner or outer surface of the batten. Do not use nails driven through the batten. At the ends allow the batten to extend as much as possible, and place the weight or nail at the tip of the batten rather than at the lines ending points. When all is fair and true sighted, checked, and rechecked, draw the curve in with a sharp pencil. The method just described will be similar for all of the line fairing to be done on the boat.

The portion for the stem will require a little thought. The architect has designed a series of points by giving a certain height and a width on the profile. Duplicate these points on the profile, lofting to obtain the points for the stem. Here again, in springing the batten about the shape, it may be found that

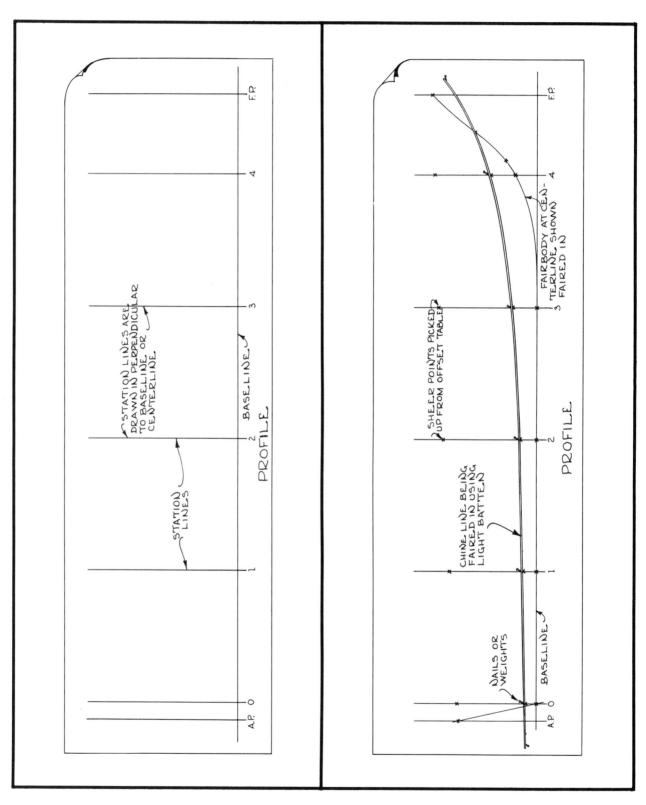

PLATE 8-B

PLATE 8-C

certain compensations will be needed for deviations. The fairing batten for the stem should overlap some distance along the keel, to obtain a fair line from the stem area to the keel. Do not allow a bump or hump to appear. Again, the designer's lines are fair and smooth. Reproduce them faithfully so that your lines are also fair and smooth. It will save a lot of work later.

At this time the lofting for the plan view is started. In practice the lines of the plan and profile would be superimposed. In Plate 8-D, the drawings are entirely separate. This was done for clarification of the lines. If you have drawn the lines of the profile in pencil, use another color pencil for the plan lines and lay them right over the top of the existing profile drawing. The sheer is laid out first, taking the dimensions from the Table of Offsets under the "widths from centerline." Again, use the batten to sweep in the lines fairly. The chine in the plan is laid out by a similar method. The exception will be in locating the point at which the chine intersects the centerline at the bow of the boat. This point is determined from the profile lines that already have been lofted. The distances from the F.P. to the point where the chine hits the stem is projected to the plan view. Check this on Plate 8-D. Upon determining this point, sweep the chine in with the batten, again being careful to fair the curve, compensating for deviations in the architect's scaled offsets.

The basic lines of the boat in plan and profile have now been lofted. If the sections have straight lines from the keel to the chine, and the chine to sheer, the task would be completed except for the drawing out of the sections or frames. In this particular instance, and in most

cases, the lines on the side and bottom in the section will be curved. As defined, buttocks determine these curves in the profile, and waterlines in the plan. It is unimportant which is done first.

Now take the waterlines and plot them (Plate 8-E). Before drawing the curved lines in the plan view, it must be determined where the various waterlines will intersect the chine. To determine these intersection points, the waterlines are laid out in profile. These are lines parallel to the baseline at the heights noted in the architect's drawings, Plate 8-A. Draw in these horizontal lines which, incidentally, need not be continuous in length, for they are used only to determine the intersection point with the chine, the stem, or the sheer line. The intersection of these points is projected to the plan view. The remaining half breadths from the centerline for the waterlines are taken from the Table of Offsets. These are then faired in with a batten as previously described. Be sure that the lines so developed are clean, fair sweeps.

The buttocks are plotted similarly, (see Plate 8-F). It is necessary to draw the horizontal buttocks in the plan view to determine the intersection point of the chine with the particular buttock. In many cases, the architect will also extend the buttock lines in both plan and profile to the stem. This will depend on the particular design and would furnish other fairing points. After plotting the intersection of the buttocks in the plan view, the lines are projected at the intersection of the chine and the buttocks to the profile. The balance of the points for the buttocks are taken from the Table of Offsets under heights for the particular buttock. Again, care must be taken in the sweeping in of these lines

Boatbuilding With Plywood

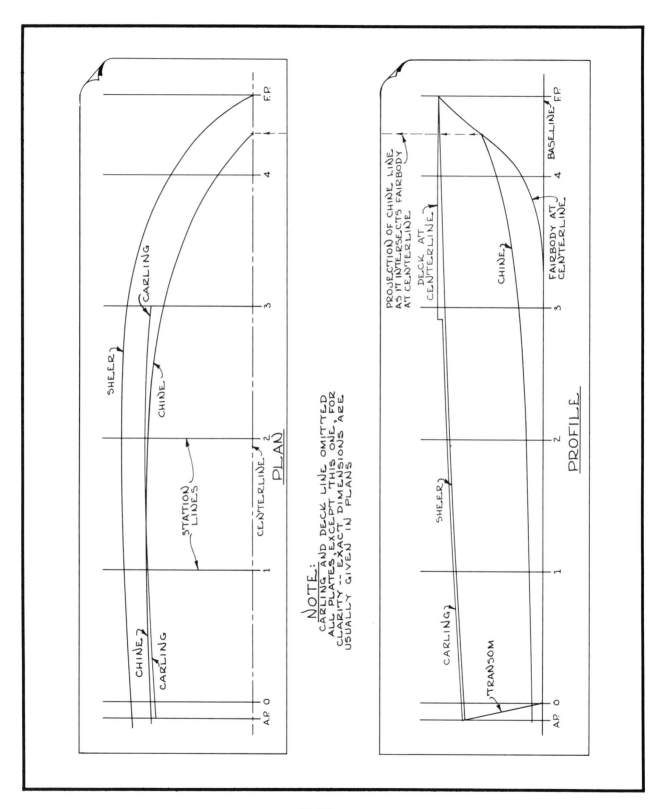

PLATE 8-D

64

with the batten to be sure that they are fair and smooth curves.

In developing the body lines it is best to lay these out on a sheet of paper. The body lines are actually the outer surface of the frame contours, in most cases. By having these on paper, the contour can readily be pin pricked through onto the lumber as described in Chapter 9, being careful to deduct for the planking thickness. Body lines can be superimposed over the existing lines. For those experienced in lofting, this is a simple matter. For those inexperienced, the confusion of the lines will become a maze. A sheet of plywood placed on sawhorses with paper spread over the top will make the task more comfortable. A horizontal line to represent the baseline is drawn several inches from the bottom of the sheet. Again, this sheet of paper must be adequate in height to fit the highest point from the baseline to the sheer in profile view. It must also be more than twice as wide as the half breadth point of greatest beam.

After striking the baseline, a perpendicular is erected from the baseline, and this is the centerline. Horizontally up from the baseline, the various waterline points are struck off which are parallel to the baseline. Spacing of these waterlines must be identical to the spacing used in laying out the profile. The buttocks are put in on both sides of the centerline. These are parallel to the centerline and spaced the same as those noted on the plan view of the drawings. Any station may be plotted first since they are all similar, except possibly the transom, if it is angled or curved.

The various heights and widths that will be required to lay out the sections are taken from the full-scale loftings. Rather than using a rule to determine these measurements, it is preferable to use what is called a "picking stick." A picking stick is a straight, smooth piece of wood about ¾" square long enough to extend from the baseline to the maximum height of the hull, or from the centerline to the maximum half-breadth of the hull, whichever is greatest. The picking stick is used to transfer distances in one view of the lofting to that of another view. The actual distances or dimensions do not matter.

The picking stick is laid on the station lines and the heights above the baseline for the fairbody, the chine, and the sheer, as well as the buttocks, are marked on it. The picking stick is then taken to the body sections and these various heights plotted. In the case of the fairbody, the mark may be put on the centerline. The buttock points may be readily marked as to the height. The chine is located at its approximate width from the centerline. The sheer is handled in the same way. A horizontal line several inches long is drawn at the sheer and chine point so that it will catch the respective width. The picking stick is then taken to the plan view along the same station line. The centerline, chine, waterlines, and sheer are all marked as to widths. These widths marked on the picking stick are taken to the body or section drawing. The distance from the centerline to the chine is plotted. In so plotting the chine and the sheer points, be sure to hold the picking stick parallel to the baseline and at right angles to the centerline. The waterlines are plotted on their respective points as to widths. The deck crown, if required, is then developed from the height above the sheer line by one of several methods. Typical methods are

Boatbuilding With Plywood

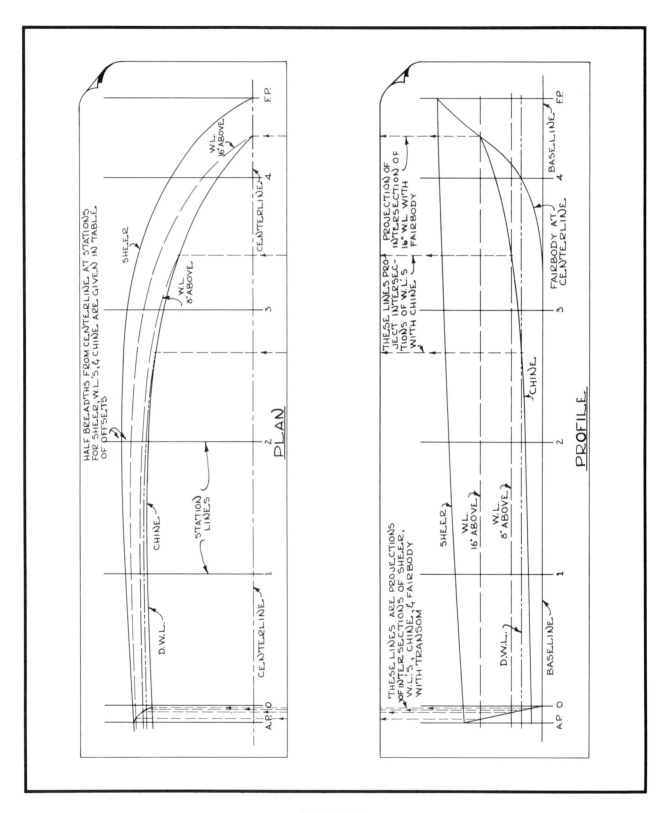

PLATE 8-E

illustrated in Plates 8-I and 8-J. A series of points has been plotted on the section lines.

One other important point arises. Before sweeping in these various curves, it must be remembered that the architect has plotted his lines to the outside of the planking and all of the loftings were made to the outside of the planking. This planking thickness must be deducted. This could have been done in the lofting by using a batten the thickness of the planking in bending about the chine and sheer lines. If the batten is then sprung around the points so that the outer surface of the batten touches the points the inner surface of the batten will then be the actual required point designating the inside of the planking surfaces. Probably the easiest method is to accomplish the planking thickness deduction on the body lines. Admittedly the deduction of planking thickness on sections is not the same as the deduction of the planking thickness on curved lines flowing about the chine or sheer in plan. For practical purposes, however, the difference in the methods for the average plywood boat will be so minor as to be inconsequential. Either method can be used, however the deduction from the body lines or the actual drawings of the frame patterns is the simplest. By this method, a fairing batten the thickness of the planking, is placed inside of the plotted points (See Plate 8-K). Of course, in some cases the batten may be too thick to make all of the curves required, so a thinner batten may be required in addition.

By marking on the inside, the actual frame contour will be noted. If the fairing of the line drawings has been accurately done, the various points should sweep in with a fair, smooth curve. If any deviations occur, a careful check of the offending area must be made. While accuracy is important, a certain amount of deviation is tolerable, but if any line misses a point by more than $\frac{1}{16}''$, it should be checked. Again, the architect does not make humps or bumps in the side or the bottom of the boat. His lines will be clean and fair. In a boat for sheet plywood construction, sides and bottoms will either be straight lines or convex in section. Concavity cannot be obtained with the possible exception of the side in the very forward frame just a few inches from the bow, without severely compounding the plywood panel. Provided all the points are in line, the outer surface of each frame is then drawn. Again, depending upon the whims of the loftsman, all the inner surfaces of the frames or simply the outer contour can be laid out. This, again, is covered in the balance of the text and may be decided on by the individual.

Many feel that obtaining the bevels for the frames is highly important. However, in all but the very largest of plywood boats, determining the bevels and then cutting them in the framing lumber is usually a waste of time. Consider for a moment the bevel that would be required on the side frame member at station No. 3 in the particular boat (Plate 8-G) being discussed. Observe that the bevel or angle to be cut on the side frame at the sheer, Point A, is very small. At the chine, Point D, the bevel is considerably greater. This indicates that the bevel is ever-changing. True, the bevel at the chine, the various waterlines, Points B and C, and the sheer could be marked out. The next question arises, "How would they be cut?" Obviously, you could sit and whittle with a plane on each frame, checking it very

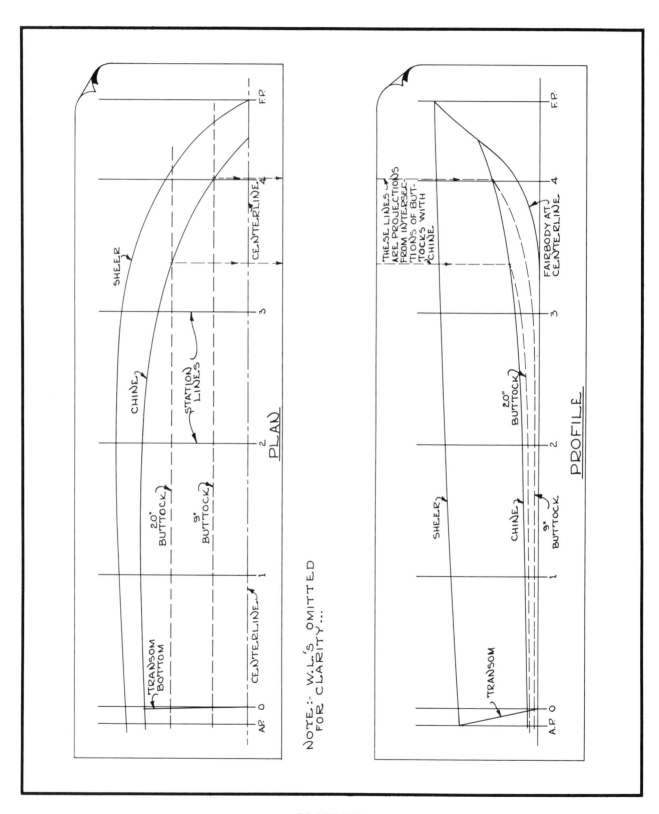

PLATE 8-F

carefully. Other methods would possibly be that of a band saw with one individual cranking the tilting table and another calling out the degrees as he passes through a point. In most cases this is a great waste of time. If the individual feels that he wishes to cut the minimum bevel, in this case the angle given at the sheer, this would be permissible. In most cases, however, the angle cut would be so slight, as to be simply disregarded. Fairing on the completed set up framework will be required and will be described in subsequent chapters. Probably the only point that will be absolutely necessary to consider for the bevel would be a slanted transom as described further along in this chapter. Some individuals do prefer to bevel the side frame member of the frame farthest forward or whenever the bevel exceeds five degrees. Obviously, this will vary with the particular boat.

The stem and knee drawings (if required) may be taken from the profile. The contour of the inner surface or edge of the stem may be laid out, or the assembly joints put directly on the profile, depending upon the type of stem (see Chapter 11). The minimum bevel for the stem may be obtained from either the frame or section closest to the stem, or the sheer, whichever is lesser. Whether it is worthwhile to cut this bevel before the boat is erected on the form is a moot question. Again, in many boats the cutting of such a bevel is a waste of time. If the minimum angle required is considerable, naturally it would be advantageous to cut the minimum bevel on the stem at time of assembly. With a large boat, sections would be taken at various points on the stem and angles thus obtained would give bevels to be

cut.

The expansion, or obtaining the true size, of a slanted transom is probably one of the most confusing problems to the amateur loftsman. The following will describe the lofting of the transom from the lines drawing indicated on Plate 8-G. An enlargement of the lines drawing (Plate 8-H) has been made to represent the plan and profile as it would be lofted. Again, the plan and profile can be superimposed if colored pencils are used to designate the profile frcm the plan lines.

Referring to Plate 8-G, note that in the plan view all widths are true. In the profile view, all heights will need to be taken along the inclined plane of the transom. The true projected transom will show both of these dimensions as actual or true lines. Since a transom has thickness, both the inner and outer lines of the transom surface have been designated. These are noted in the drawing "forward face of transom" and "aft face of transom." To project the transom, extend from the profile to pick up the corresponding point on the plan. For simplification, one particular set of points only will be discussed. Since the method is similar in all cases, the other points may be found.

In the profile, refer to waterline 16″ above. Observe the point "FG," which represents the side of the view of a line. When this ray is projected to the plan view, it will intersect the centerline at a point "F," and it will intersect the waterline 16″ above at the point "G." Referring to this same waterline in profile, note that point "NO," when projected to the plan and intersecting the centerline and waterline 16″ above, will designate the points "N" and "O." Note that this has determined the width of the

Boatbuilding With Plywood

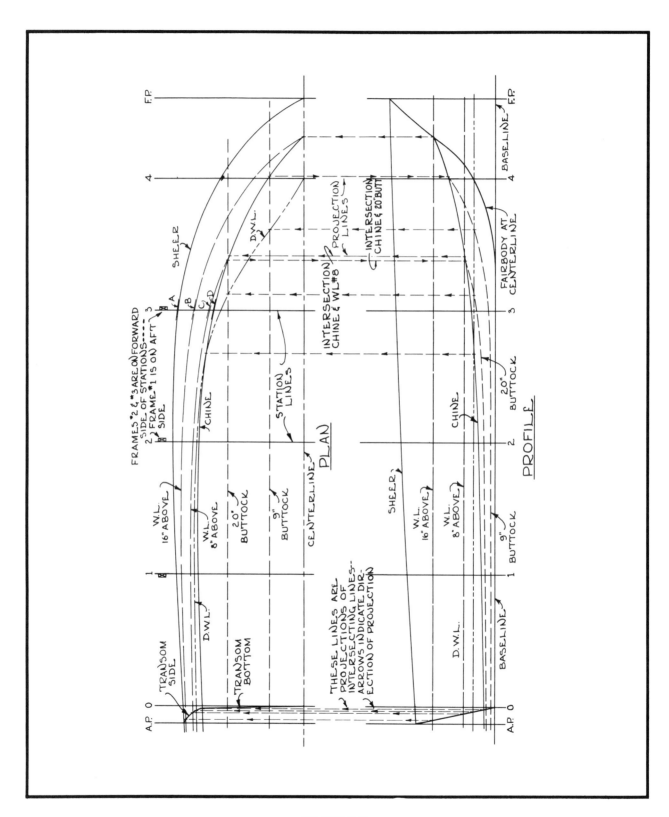

PLATE 8-G

70

transom as seen in the plan. By plotting the other points, the complete plan view of the transom can be drawn. It is simply a matter of using perpendiculars from the baseline or reference plane, carrying each point up from the profile to the plan, and allowing it to intersect its matching point in the plan. This will then give a series of points which may be readily plotted. In sweeping in the contours use the same method as described with the batten sprung between the various points.

After accomplishing the layout of all points in plan and profile, it is possible to obtain the true transom projection. As mentioned previously, the plan view will show all widths as they actually are. The heights, instead of being taken perpendicularly, will be taken on the slanted surface of the transom. From this back surface of the slanted transom in profile, perpendicular lines must be drawn. These are similar to those illustrated at "TT," "AA," etc. Be very careful that the lines or points are extended perpendicularly to the slanted face of the transom. A line parallel to this slanted face of the transom must be drawn to indicate the centerline of the expanded transom; the lines from the slanted face of the transom need only equal the widest point as indicated in the plan view.

After plotting the centerline and the rays, the picking stick is used to pick up from the plan those widths which are true distances. As an example, the sheer point is given in the plan as "HJ." The line "HJ" is taken on its ray in the true transom projection and its width is plotted. The inner surface of the transom is indicated by the symbol "LM." This distance "LM" is picked from the plan and plotted to the corresponding ray "LM"

in the true transom projection.

Referring to the waterline 16″ above that had been previously plotted, note that the point "FG" is plotted from the width taken from the plan and then plotted to the true transom projection view. The point "NO" is done similarly, as are the other points. Observe that the inner and the outer surface, or the forward and the aft face of the transom, are indicated. Unlike the frames, it is a necessity to plot the angle and pre-cut it in the lumber. It would be possible to use the outer line as the size to cut the transom and then bevel this member on the work. It is generally preferable to take the maximum angle and cut it with the saw before assembling the transom and frame. To accomplish this, refer again to Plate 8-H, and note in the upper left-hand corner the various bevels. Plot the thickness of the transom, which was designated in both the plan and profile view as a forward face and an aft face of the transom. These inner and outer faces are designated as No. 1 and No. 2. The point of maximum bevel on the side of the true transom projection is at approximately the point indicated by the figures No. 3 and No. 4. The true width or distance between the lines of the forward and aft face of the transom at No. 3 and No. 4 are measured to the thickness of the transom as noted in the upper left-hand corner. This then will give the amount of bevel. The bevel must be taken at the greatest point, so that during fairing, sufficient material will be available to allow the planking to mate firmly. As with all bevels, a series of points could be picked up and the transom completely prefaired to the ever-changing angle before assembly to the building form. This is considerable work, and generally not

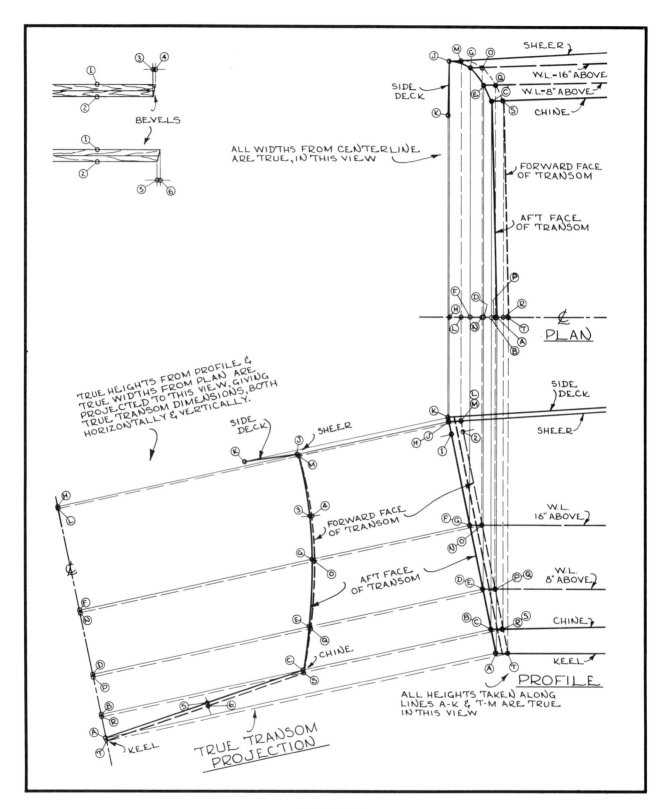

PLATE 8-H

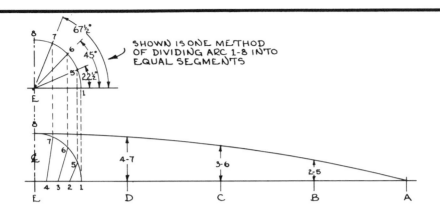

SHOWN IS ONE METHOD OF DIVIDING ARC 1-8 INTO EQUAL SEGMENTS

- A-E = DISTANCE FROM SHEER TO CENTERLINE.
- 8-E = HEIGHT OF DECK CROWN.
- A-E IS DIVIDED INTO 4 EQUAL PARTS SO THAT
     AB = BC = CD = DE.
- ERECT PERPENDICULARS FROM LINE A-E AT POINTS E, D, C, AND B.
- DRAW ARC 1-8 WITH 8-E AS RADIUS.
- DIVIDE ARC 1-8 INTO 4 EQUAL SEGMENTS SO THAT
     1-5 = 5-6 = 6-7 = 7-8 .
- DIVIDE 1-E INTO 4 EQUAL PARTS SO THAT 1-2 = 2-3 = 3-4 = 4-E
- LAYOUT DISTANCE 4-7 ON PERPENDICULAR AT D; 3-6 AT C; & 2-5 AT B.
- USE BATTEN TO FAIR IN ARC 8-A.
- USING SAME DISTANCES BETWEEN E, D, C, B, & A , LAYOUT OTHER SIDE OF BEAM.

PLATE 8-I

DEVELOPING A DECK BEAM

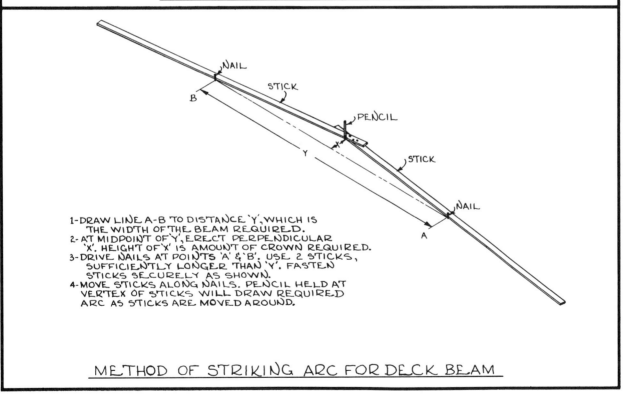

1- DRAW LINE A-B TO DISTANCE 'Y', WHICH IS THE WIDTH OF THE BEAM REQUIRED.
2- AT MIDPOINT OF 'Y', ERECT PERPENDICULAR 'X'. HEIGHT OF 'X' IS AMOUNT OF CROWN REQUIRED.
3- DRIVE NAILS AT POINTS 'A' & 'B'. USE 2 STICKS, SUFFICIENTLY LONGER THAN 'Y'. FASTEN STICKS SECURELY AS SHOWN.
4- MOVE STICKS ALONG NAILS. PENCIL HELD AT VERTEX OF STICKS WILL DRAW REQUIRED ARC AS STICKS ARE MOVED AROUND.

METHOD OF STRIKING ARC FOR DECK BEAM

PLATE 8-J

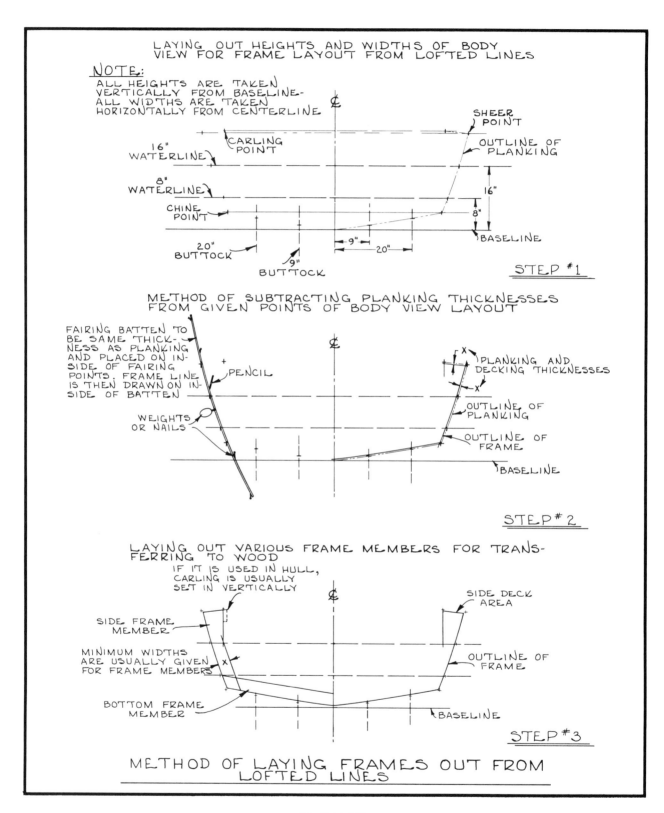

LAYING OUT HEIGHTS AND WIDTHS OF BODY
VIEW FOR FRAME LAYOUT FROM LOFTED LINES

NOTE:
ALL HEIGHTS ARE TAKEN
VERTICALLY FROM BASELINE-
ALL WIDTHS ARE TAKEN
HORIZONTALLY FROM CENTERLINE

SHEER POINT

CARLING POINT

16" WATERLINE

OUTLINE OF PLANKING

8" WATERLINE

16"

CHINE POINT

8"

BASELINE

20" BUTTOCK

9"

9" BUTTOCK

20"

STEP #1

METHOD OF SUBTRACTING PLANKING THICKNESSES
FROM GIVEN POINTS OF BODY VIEW LAYOUT

FAIRING BATTEN TO
BE SAME THICK-
NESS AS PLANKING
AND PLACED ON IN-
SIDE OF FAIRING
POINTS. FRAME LINE
IS THEN DRAWN ON IN-
SIDE OF BATTEN

PENCIL

PLANKING AND
DECKING THICKNESSES

WEIGHTS
OR NAILS

OUTLINE OF
PLANKING

OUTLINE OF
FRAME

BASELINE

STEP #2

LAYING OUT VARIOUS FRAME MEMBERS FOR TRANS-
FERRING TO WOOD

IF IT IS USED IN HULL,
CARLING IS USUALLY
SET IN VERTICALLY

SIDE DECK
AREA

SIDE FRAME
MEMBER

MINIMUM WIDTHS
ARE USUALLY GIVEN
FOR FRAME MEMBERS

X

OUTLINE OF
FRAME

BOTTOM FRAME
MEMBER

BASELINE

STEP #3

METHOD OF LAYING FRAMES OUT FROM
LOFTED LINES

PLATE 8-K

considered necessary.

The transom angle or bevel on the bottom is indicated on the true transom projection at point No. 5 and No. 6. Again, referring to the typical bevels in the upper left-hand corner of Plate 8-H, these points have been plotted as to their distance apart by points No. 5 and No. 6 giving the bevel on the bottom of the transom. Observe carefully that if the individual did not wish to pre-cut the bevel on the bottom of the transom, although it is recommended that he should, it would be possible to cut the transom edge square, picking up the widest point as mentioned, and fairing in the transom on the building form.

Considerable care will need to be taken, and if there are framing or similar additional thicknesses on the inner face of the transom, allowance will need to be made for these thicknesses and for the bevel of these members.

With the fairing operation now completed, the full size loftings can be used to make the framing members which will determine the shape of the hull. As can be seen, the loftings provide virtually a "full size pattern" of the contours for these members. However, with some designs, full size patterns may already be provided as has been noted. The use of these patterns will be covered in the next chapter.

METRIC CONVERSION CHART

$1/32'' = .8$ mm	$1'' = 2.54$ cm	$1' = .305$ m
$1/16'' = 1.6$ mm	$2'' = 5.1$ cm	$2' = .61$ m
$1/8'' = 3.2$ mm	$3'' = 7.6$ cm	$3' = .91$ m
$3/16'' = 4.8$ mm	$4'' = 10.2$ cm	$4' = 1.22$ m
$1/4'' = 6.4$ mm	$5'' = 12.7$ cm	$5' = 1.52$ m
$5/16'' = 7.9$ mm	$6'' = 15.2$ cm	$6' = 1.83$ m
$3/8'' = 9.5$ mm	$7'' = 17.8$ cm	$7' = 2.13$ m
$7/16'' = 11.1$ mm	$8'' = 20.3$ cm	$8' = 2.44$ m
$1/2'' = 12.7$ mm	$9'' = 22.9$ cm	$9' = 2.74$ m
$9/16'' = 14.3$ mm	$10'' = 25.4$ cm	$10' = 3.05$ m
$5/8'' = 15.9$ mm	$11'' = 27.9$ cm	
$11/16'' = 17.4$ mm	$12'' = 30.5$ cm	
$3/4'' = 19.1$ mm		
$13/16'' = 20.6$ mm		
$7/8'' = 22.2$ mm		
$15/16'' = 23.8$ mm		
$1'' = 25.4$ mm		

PLATE 8-L—Metric Conversion Chart listing typical fractions of an inch, inch, and foot increments with their corresponding metric equivalents. To convert inches to millimeters (mm), multiply by 25.4. To convert inches to centimeters (cm), multiply by 2.54. To convert feet to meters (m), multiply by .3048. One pound (lb.) equals .454 kilograms.

CHAPTER 9 — FULL SIZE PATTERNS

Full size patterns, if provided with the design, eliminate the tedious job of lofting and considerably simplify the building of a boat. However, patterns must be reasonably accurate and properly reproduced to be of value. If they are inaccurate, the unfair lines which will not become apparent until during the construction, will have to be corrected when detected. In some cases, such correction could prove to be more work than if the boat required lofting from a table of offsets.

There are several types of patterns available and varying numbers of parts which will be patterned depending on the size and type of boat being built. Generally, the more patterns furnished, the easier the job will be. Usually the designer or plans firm will describe what parts the patterns are provided for in their literature. In some cases, the plans for a given design include the full size patterns automatically in the price, and when this is the case, a table of offsets is not required and therefore may not be provided. If you like the design of such a boat, but also want to loft the lines instead of working from the full size patterns, then you are probably out of luck since the design has already been lofted to provide the full size patterns, and the offsets discarded since they are no longer of any value.

Full size patterns are made by several methods including blueprinted patterns, printed patterns, and cut or drawn patterns usually reproduced on kraft paper. Except for patterns which are already cut, do not cut out any other type of pattern. In some cases only the outer contour of the frame member is provided and the builder sometimes may be required to deduct the thickness of the planking at all points to arrive at the net frame member contour. In other cases, the pattern may include many details such as the widths of frames, size of gussets and floor timbers, etc. Whichever type is provided, there must be sufficient information and dimensions provided on the plans or patterns by which to build the members. Various reference points must also be provided on the patterned members, such as the centerline, set-up level or reference plane, carling points, chine notch and sheer notch points, etc.

It might be argued that, since full size patterns are usually reproduced on paper of some sort, distortion may occur. However, experience over decades proves that even if distortion does occur, it is not only minimal, but evenly distributed so that it does not affect the outcome of the boat to any practical significance if the patterns are made on suitable paper. Sometimes patterns are provided for an entire member, but in most instances, especially on larger boats, only a half-section pattern is provided for the frames or bulkheads since the pattern is symmetrical about the centerline.

FIG. 9-1—Three types of common full size patterns. At upper right is a cut-type paper pattern which designates the outer contour of the member. To middle left is the printed-type pattern which may give inner and outer contours of frame members, as well as other information on how the member is to be built. To lower left is the drawn pattern often used for long members such as stems and harpins. In no case should patterns be "cut out" from the sheet.

FIG. 9-2—The builder is using the cut-type paper pattern. A vertical line representing the frame centerline is drawn on a plywood base. Another line representing the set-up level or reference plane is drawn at right angle to this vertical centerline. The cut paper pattern centerline is carefully aligned to the vertical centerline, and the set-up level or reference plane is aligned to the horizontal set-up line, marked on the plywood. A small straight-edge is used as a guide to mark a series of dashes around the extremeties of the pattern. The pattern is reversed, and the opposite side drawn on the plywood, lining up carefully again with centerline and set-up level.

FIG. 9-3—The use of the printed paper pattern is similar. The centerline is marked on the sheet of plywood, and the centerline of the frame aligned over it. The outline of the frame is transferred to the lumber by pricking through the pattern into the plywood with an awl or icepick at approximate ½" intervals. The pattern is reversed to obtain the other half, just as was done with the cut-type pattern. The builder uses the same paper pattern to mark out the various frame member portions to his lumber. With the cut-type pattern, only the outer edge is marked. However, with the printed type, the inner and outer contours of the various frame members may be indicated in many instances.

FIG. 9-4—The builder uses the outer edge of a cut-type pattern to mark the outer frame contour to the lumber. With the cut-type pattern, only the outer contour is marked. Information for the sizes of members will be provided on the plans. With the printed type pattern, outer and inner contours may be marked to the lumber or information may be included with the plans also.

FIG. 9-5—The marked contour of the frame member is cut to shape on a band saw. In the case of the cut-type pattern where the inner contour may not be marked, the builder can use a marking gage set to the given molded frame width to scribe the inner line from the cut surface. Often it is simpler to take dimensions at the ends of the frame member and draw a straight line for the inner contour of the frame members.

FIG. 9-6—After being sawn to shape, the frame members are tacked into position over the plywood base. The outer contour of the sawn member is carefully lined up with the lines previously marked from the pattern to the plywood surface. Tacking the frame members in position prevents movement or shifting.

FIG. 9-7—The builder assembles the frames on the plywood surface. Each frame is handled in the same manner. Stems, breasthooks, and transoms may be scribed directly onto the material that they are to be cut from, eliminating much of the assembly work.

79

The manner in which a pattern is used depends on the type of pattern. In the case of a one piece member such as a stem, knee, or breasthook, the layout is made directly to the lumber by punching through the pattern at ½″ intervals or with a pattern tracing wheel to indent the lumber beneath. If preferred, carbon paper can be used to transfer an outline to the material. With a cut paper pattern the contour is merely marked around the contour to the stock or plywood base.

With frames or members which may consist of several components, the use of the pattern is more complex. Because the frame or member may be made from many pieces, it can be difficult to hold these pieces in position and assemble them. The methods for handling this situation are shown by the photographs in this chapter. The contours of each of the pieces which make up the completed frame member must be transferred to the material and cut to size. Then the pieces can be assembled using the pattern as a guide.

Experience has proven that assembling this type of member over a wood surface is easier and more accurate than over the paper. A sheet of plywood can be used to which the pieces can be tacked in place once the contour of the member has been marked to the plywood. Since many nails will be driven into the plywood panel, use a panel which, if being used in the construction of the boat, will not be visible. Of course, if the boat is wider than a standard sheet, more than one panel can be used.

To duplicate the outer frame member contour to the plywood panel, first draw a vertical line for the centerline at the center of the panel. Then provide a horiziontal line at exact right angles to this centerline. This line should be drawn at a suitable point, and this is usually noted if it corresponds to the set-up level or reference plane. Align the pattern centerline and set-up level or reference plane to the lines on the plywood using a straight edge. Hold the pattern in place and mark the contours to the plywood using a series of dashes if it is of the cut paper type, or transfer through the pattern as previously noted.

Another method to align the centerline and set-up reference line when using printed-type patterns is to use "sighting holes". These are small holes cut through the pattern at critical points which will enable the reference lines on the patterns to be aligned to those on the plywood assembly board below. Without these it is difficult to see through the paper pattern to the lines underneath. In some cases, the reference lines on the pattern can be extended to the extremities of the pattern and thereby aligned with those on the plywood assembly board. Small brads can also be used at strategic points, and the patterns pushed over the protruding brads to align them over the panel.

If the pattern is of the half-section printed type, mark one half first, and then flip over for the opposite side. When this is done some method of determining the contour of the opposite half of the member must be used. The simplest method is to use two pieces of carbon paper; one face up to the under side of the pattern, and the other face down to the plywood panel. In tracing through, lines will then be put on to the back of the pattern which will then be transferred to the plywood panel when it is flipped over.

Some will question the reason for

TRANSOM BEVELS

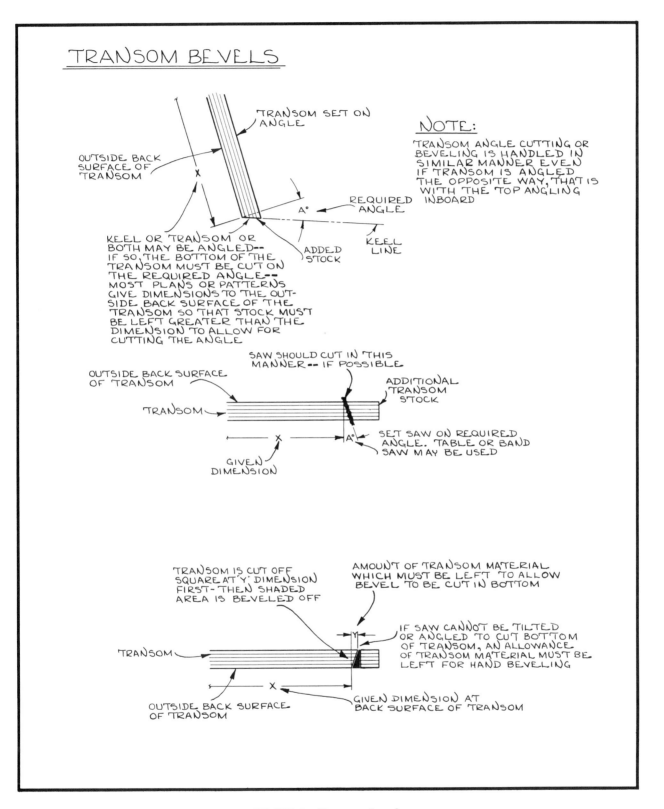

TRANSOM SET ON ANGLE

OUTSIDE BACK SURFACE OF TRANSOM

REQUIRED ANGLE

A°

ADDED STOCK

KEEL LINE

NOTE:
TRANSOM ANGLE CUTTING OR BEVELING IS HANDLED IN SIMILAR MANNER EVEN IF TRANSOM IS ANGLED THE OPPOSITE WAY, THAT IS WITH THE TOP ANGLING INBOARD

KEEL OR TRANSOM OR BOTH MAY BE ANGLED-- IF SO, THE BOTTOM OF THE TRANSOM MUST BE CUT ON THE REQUIRED ANGLE-- MOST PLANS OR PATTERNS GIVE DIMENSIONS TO THE OUTSIDE BACK SURFACE OF THE TRANSOM SO THAT STOCK MUST BE LEFT GREATER THAN THE DIMENSION TO ALLOW FOR CUTTING THE ANGLE

SAW SHOULD CUT IN THIS MANNER -- IF POSSIBLE

OUTSIDE BACK SURFACE OF TRANSOM

TRANSOM

ADDITIONAL TRANSOM STOCK

SET SAW ON REQUIRED ANGLE. TABLE OR BAND SAW MAY BE USED

A°

GIVEN DIMENSION

TRANSOM IS CUT OFF SQUARE AT "Y" DIMENSION FIRST- THEN SHADED AREA IS BEVELED OFF

AMOUNT OF TRANSOM MATERIAL WHICH MUST BE LEFT TO ALLOW BEVEL TO BE CUT IN BOTTOM

TRANSOM

IF SAW CANNOT BE TILTED OR ANGLED TO CUT BOTTOM OF TRANSOM, AN ALLOWANCE OF TRANSOM MATERIAL MUST BE LEFT FOR HAND BEVELING

Y

X

OUTSIDE BACK SURFACE OF TRANSOM

GIVEN DIMENSION AT BACK SURFACE OF TRANSOM

PLATE 9—Transom bevels

drawing out both halves of the frame member. It would seem that one-half would suffice, flipping the frame about its centerline and assembling half at a time. Experience shows, however, that too many errors, or the possibility of them, crop up when assembling one half of a frame at a time.

When cutting out the various members from the patterns, duplicate parts should be cut at one time, one on top of the other. For example, side frame members will be the same on each side of the boat so two should be cut together. The same applies to gussets, as sometimes a frame will require four such gussets. These should also be cut at one time. In assembling the members, align them over the contours marked on the plywood and nail temporarily in place to prevent movement during assembly.

As noted in the chapter on lofting, transoms may require a bevel along the edges unless it is at right angles to the keel. On canted transoms allowances must be made for the bevel during assembly (see Plate 9). If the pattern for the transom is given to the outside back surface, then the transom framing lo-cated on the inside surface must protrude beyond the transom edges by an amount that will provide adequate material for cutting the bevels if the transom angles aft. The angles for the bevels should be noted on the plans or patterns. In some cases, where the transom may be angled forward, the framing members on the inside could be located along the edge of the transom since the bevel would reduce the size of the frame members as it leans forward.

Cutting the bevels on a transom once it is framed can be done on a band saw if the band saw is big enough or the transom is small enough. The table can be tilted to the required angle and the cut made. With some simply shaped or rectangular transoms, a table saw could be used. In most cases, a saber saw will do the job on larger transoms, tilting the saw to suit the angle. Even though the angle of the transom is pre-cut to the noted angle, additional fairing of the transom may be required to suit the planking later, since like a frame, the angle required could be ever-changing, making it impractical to pre-cut at all points accurately.

CHAPTER 10 — FRAMES

In sheet plywood boats considerable strength results from the panel construction of the sides and bottom. Athwartship and longitudinal stiffening members are still required to make a structure of sufficient strength. Longitudinal frames which run fore and aft are excellent in plywood construction, but difficult to use in practice. They are hard to fit and fair in place without having related structural members, such as athwartship frames and longitudinal battens in position first. Hence, the use of longitudinal frames is limited.

Athwartship frames combined with longitudinal stiffeners or battens is the most common and practical framing method used in plywood boat construction, and is the most suitable method for the amateur who may be building just one boat. Athwartship frames may be of many types, including partial frames that may extend only from chine to chine, or fully sawn frames built up from a number of parts, or bulkhead/frames which consist of plywood sheets forming a bulkhead with framing on one or both sides of this. The following will explain the parts of a typical athwartship sawn frame, the nomenclature of the various members, and how they are fabricated While the partial frame and the bulkhead/frame are somewhat different the nomenclature will be similar where similar members are used to build these frames. Not all frames will necessarily contain all the members listed.

Side Frame Members: These are the upright members on the side of the frames, generally running between the chine and the sheer on boats which have a chine. On many small boats, the side members are dimensioned as "molded" or constant size in width. For example, "molded 3 inch" would mean a uniform width of 3". In many instances, the inner edge or contour of the frame is left as a straight line connecting the minimum dimension from the chine and the sheer in a straight line. In other cases, the inside edge of the frame may be used for side paneling, interior framing members, or some other purpose, and may be especially contoured to fit. Side frame members often accommodate or support the side deck area with a widened portion at the top. This is practical provided that the width does not become excessive. When an excessive amount of cross-grain is used, side frames will have a tendency to split. To eliminate this tendency, the side frame should be built up from separate pieces to form a separate sidedeck beam, or laminated with plywood to reinforce the widened side frame portion.

Bottom Frame Members: The bottom frame member is at the bottom of the frame and runs across the boat or athwartships. The bottom frame member may be full width from chine to chine in a single piece, or in two halves joined over the centerline. Whenever

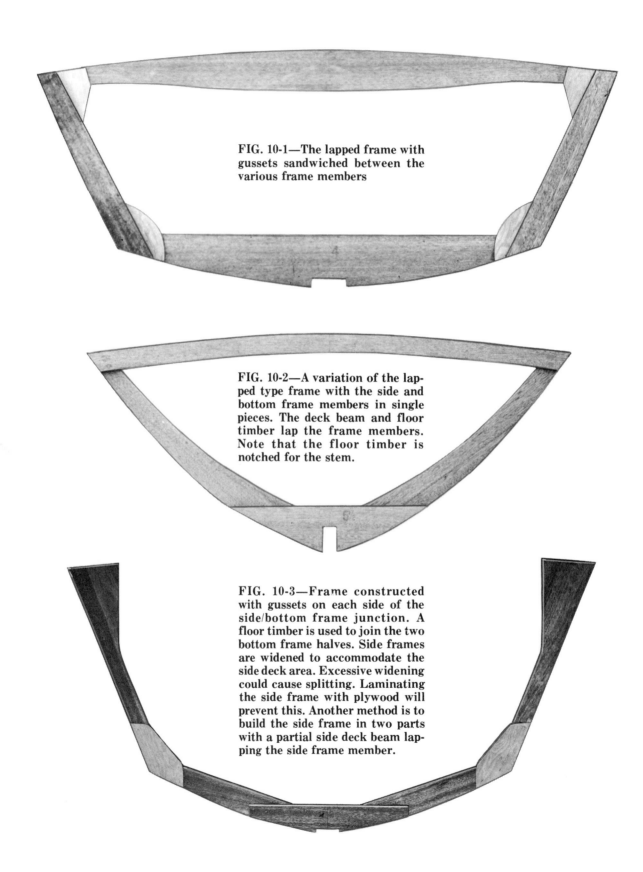

FIG. 10-1—The lapped frame with gussets sandwiched between the various frame members

FIG. 10-2—A variation of the lapped type frame with the side and bottom frame members in single pieces. The deck beam and floor timber lap the frame members. Note that the floor timber is notched for the stem.

FIG. 10-3—Frame constructed with gussets on each side of the side/bottom frame junction. A floor timber is used to join the two bottom frame halves. Side frames are widened to accommodate the side deck area. Excessive widening could cause splitting. Laminating the side frame with plywood will prevent this. Another method is to build the side frame in two parts with a partial side deck beam lapping the side frame member.

possible, a single piece member is preferable. However, when a difference of 6″ or more in the height from chine to keel exists, the frame should be made in two pieces joined across the centerline. Under no circumstances should the bottom frame members be cut as shown in Plate 10-A. The excessive cross-grain as shown will readily split under stress with resultant frame failure.

Floor Timbers: A floor on a boat is not the same as a floor in your house. The surfaces one walks on in a boat are correctly called the "sole", or in some cases "walking flats" or "floorboards". The floors, as referred to on a boat, are the floor timbers which join two bottom frame member halves together over the centerline. The floor timbers extend either side to tie the bottom frame members together with as much strength as if the bottom frame members were in one piece. Even when a bottom frame member may be in one piece, a floor timber may sometimes be used to minimize splitting of such a bottom frame member. Floor timbers may be made from the same material as the bottom frame members, lapping one side of the frame. Or they may be made from plywood which is excellent since this material will not split. In some cases, plywood floor timbers may be used on both sides of the frame and a solid wood filler block inserted between them on top of the frame. Such construction is excellent, since bolts can be used through the bottom frame members and the solid filler blocking to the keel thereby adding strength to the hull structure.

Gussets: Gussets are the scabs or

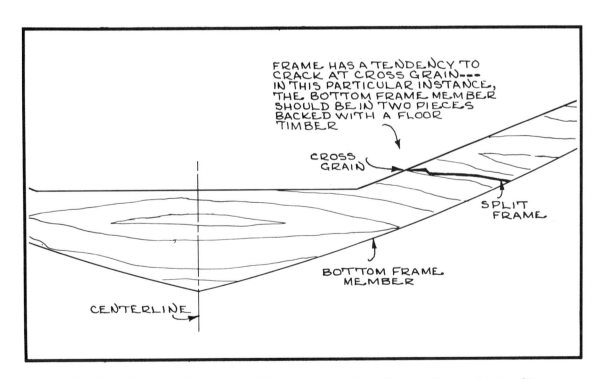

FRAME HAS A TENDENCY TO CRACK AT CROSS GRAIN--- IN THIS PARTICULAR INSTANCE, THE BOTTOM FRAME MEMBER SHOULD BE IN TWO PIECES BACKED WITH A FLOOR TIMBER

CROSS GRAIN

SPLIT FRAME

BOTTOM FRAME MEMBER

CENTERLINE

PLATE 10-A—Excessive cross grain in a frame member will cause the member to split under stress and therefore must be avoided.

FIG. 10-4—Instead of lapping the deck beam, this frame uses a double gusset to join the deck beam to the side frame members. Plywood is used for the floor timber since solid stock in the required width is often not available.

FIG. 10-5—A bulkhead frame does not require gussets or floor timbers to join the frame members since the bulkhead performs the service of these members. In some cases, the side frame members would be on the opposite side, lapping beyond the bottom frame members with the plywood bulkhead in between. Only a portion of such a bulkhead should be cut away at the centerline for the passageway, if required.

FIG. 10-6—This frame uses several frame construction techniques. The deck beam is a lapped gusset type, while the gussets are the same as used on the gusseted frame. However, instead of being double lapped, a partial bulkhead is located on one side to form the gussets as well as the floor timber.

doublers used at the junction of the side and bottom frame members or the side members and the deck beam. Gussets are used on one or both sides of the frames. Solid lumber can be used, although plywood is the most readily adaptable and preferable material, as it has less tendency to split. Gussets on the typical small boat will extend 6″ minimum either side of the joint.

Deck Beams: The deck beam is the athwartship member at the top of a frame, extending from sheer to sheer to support the deck. The deck beam is often molded to a uniform width and crowned to suit the particular boat. The methods of developing a deck crown are illustrated in Plate 8-I and 8-J. Varying methods may be used to fasten the deck beam to the side frame members using carriage bolts and/or screws. These will

be fully covered in the following.

In plywood boat construction the frames are most often "sawn frames" as opposed to "bent frames" found in other traditional methods of wood boat construction. There are basically six types of sawn frame construction methods and each type has certain advantages and disadvantages. Often a combination of frame types will be used on one boat, and some builders may prefer one type over another. The six types that will be described include, (1) plywood, (2) Lap Joined, (3) Lap Joined With Gusset, (4) Double Gusseted, (5) Double Gusseted With Filler, and (6) Bulkhead Frame.

(1) Plywood Frames: Many amateurs are tempted to utilize plywood for frame members both for simplicity and to cut costs. However, except in the very

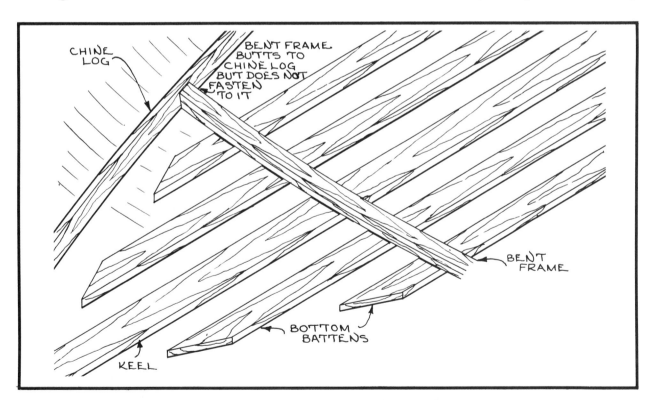

PLATE 10-B—Bent frames are sometimes used in plywood boats for intermediate support to sides and bottoms. They are often placed in the hull after the planking, and span across the longitudinal battens.

smallest of boats, such frames are impractical as well as structurally unsound. Such frames are flimsy compared with those of solid wood, and may contain voids if lower quality plywood is used. A plywood boat will have many longitudinal members which must be fastened to the frames, and since the plywood edge grain holds these fastenings very poorly, such frames are not recommended.

(2) **Lap Joined Frame:** This type of frame is simple and commonly used. As shown by Plate 10-D, the side and bottom frame members, or the side frame members and deck beam member, are joined by a simple lap joint. Usually, at least two carriage bolts are used at each junction to fasten the members after coating the mating surfaces with glue. In very small boats, screws can be used

in place of the carriage bolts. One of the disadvantages of this type of frame is the offset between the side and bottom member. Such an offset will need to be allowed for in lofting to provide adequate stock for beveling during fairing. Frame construction of this type does offer excellent bearing for the longitudinal members adjoining at the sheer and chine. The half-lap junction at the chine and sheer is recommended by some builders. The disadvantage of this type of construction is the limited thickness of solid material available for fastening the chine and sheer members. Unless the frame members were very thick, it would be likely that the screws driven into the edge of this frame at the half-lap joint would hit in-between making for weak holding power. Even if the frame is lapped with a gusset, this

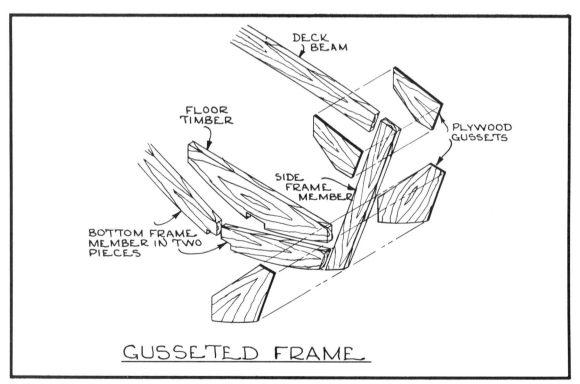

GUSSETED FRAME

PLATE 10-C—Double gusseted frames use plywood gussets lapping each side of the frame member junctions for excellent strength. A solid wood floor timber is shown on one side, however, double gusseted floor timbers as shown in plate 10-F could be used alternately.

inherent problem would exist.

(3) **Lap Joined With Gusset:** This is a variation of the lap joined frame, and utilizes a single gusset between the members as shown by Plate 10-E. A single carriage bolt plus nails or screws holding the gussets will impart considerable strength. This frame method has the disadvantage of an even larger offset between the joining members than the lap joined frame with the resultant problems previously described. This method is often used on smaller craft since it is rugged and simple.

(4) **Double Gusseted Frame:** This method is shown on Plate 10-C and is an excellent way to build a frame. A gusset is used on each side of the frame members at the side/bottom frame junction as well as sometimes at the deck beam/ side frame junction. On boats using 1"

framing, the gussets are usually ¼" or ⅜" plywood. With thicker frame material, thicker plywood could be used. The gussets should extend a minimum of 6" along either side of the joining frame member. The disadvantage of the double gusseted frame is that it takes up room, for example, in the cockpit area or in the cabin on many boats. If the cockpit or cabin sole is higher than the gussets, this will not be a disadvantage In small runabouts it may be that a portion of these gussets may need to be cut away. This may be done to a limited extent in some cases, however, weakening them excessively is not good practice. Ring-type nails or screws can be used to fasten the gussets in place after coating with glue. A minimum of five fasteners per frame member junction should be used. Plywood for the gussets

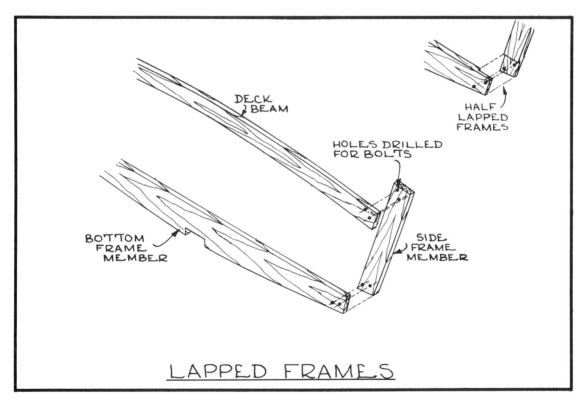

LAPPED FRAMES

PLATE 10-D—A simple lapped-type frame is often used on smaller boats. Sometimes a half-lap (upper right) is used at the junctions, but this has disadvantages as explained in the text.

need not be first grade; any exterior type is usually suitable. Note that with this method the side frame members extend to, and are notched for, the chine and sheer members. This allows suitable solid stock (as opposed to end grain) for the fastenings of these longitudinal members which would not be the case if the bottom frame and deck beam lapped beyond the ends of the side frame members.

(5) Double Gusseted With Filler: This type of frame construction is a variation on the above and is shown by Plate 10-F. The primary difference is that solid blocking is used to fill the area between the gussets. If floor timbers are used and are of plywood on each side, similar filler blocking could be used here, although the frames could possibly be sawn to shape to provide the solid mate-

rial between the gussets in lieu of a separate filler block. The solid blocking in any case equals the frame member thickness and is nailed or screwed in place after applying glue. With the blocking in place, bolts can be used through the frame members into and through the filler blocking for attaching such members as the chine logs and keels, and this makes for a very strong structure. This frame construction method is often used on larger boats, and in these instances, the gussets may be bolted in place in lieu of screws or nails.

(6) Bulkhead Frame: A bulkhead frame as shown by Fig. 10-5 consists of a plywood bulkhead (usually full width across the boat) framed on one or both sides with solid stock. If the solid stock is located on just one side, the bulkhead

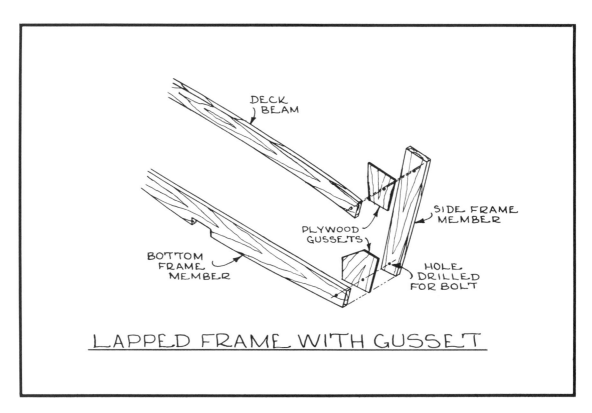

PLATE 10-E—The lapped joined frame with gusset is a variation of the lapped frame.
This method makes a simple but rugged frame usually used on smaller boats.

will not be quite as rigid as if, for example, the side and bottom frame members were on opposite sides, overlapped at the chine area where they would be through-fastened. A similar situation could exist at the floor timber area also. Such a bulkhead frame would be a variation on the Lapped Frame With Gusset method, with the bulkhead forming all the gussets plus the bulkhead as well! With bulkhead frames, the solid wood members are either nailed or screwed to the plywood after coating with glue.

On round bottom boats made especially by the diagonal multiple layer planking methods described in Chapter 19 that do not have a chine junction, such bulkhead frames are common. Since straight members cannot be used to make the curved contours, several pieces of solid wood can be pieced and

joined to frame up the plywood bulkhead. As shown by Plate 10-G, two thicknesses of solid wood are required to provide sufficient overlap on the pieced members for stiffness. The reason bulkhead frames are framed with solid stock in all cases is to not only stiffen the bulkhead, but to provide solid stock for fastening of the various longitudinal stringers and battens.

On high-speed boats such as runabouts, or on boats intended to take quite a pounding at high speeds, it is common to laminate a layer of plywood to solid frame members on the bottom. Such a lamination prevents splitting of the frame. Apply with nails closely spaced and well staggered after coating the lamination with glue.

Frames when they are installed in a boat may or may not actually contact

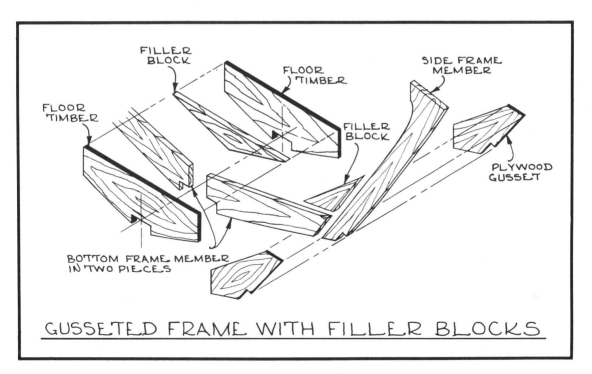

GUSSETED FRAME WITH FILLER BLOCKS

PLATE 10-F—The double gusseted frame with fillers is a variation of the double gusseted type. The main difference is that solid filler blocking is fitted between the gussets and plywood floor timbers, lapping each side of the frame members at junctions. Bolts can be driven through the filler blocking to hold the chine and keel longitudinals in place, making a very strong structure.

the inside of the hull planking. This will vary with the boat. For example, a frame may contact both the side and bottom planking, being notched for all the various longitudinal members such as the bottom battens. Or, the frame may contact just the side planking, but not any portion of the bottom planking. In this case, the frame will rest on top of the bottom battens and voids or spaces will exist between the bottom battens, and the bottom planking and frame edge. In some cases, a frame will not require contact at the side planking either. Frames of these latter two types are called "floating frames". In a boat planked, for example, with the diagonal methods described in Chapter 19, the frame would also make solid contact to the planking at all areas. Only in this case is the planking of both the side and

bottom actually fastened to the frame members. With sheet plywood planking, however, the planking is NEVER fastened to the athwartship frames for reasons which will be covered in the chapter on planking, Chapter 19. Instead, sheet plywood planking is always fastened to the various longitudinal members only.

Two schools of thought exist about notching frames for the bottom battens or allowing the frames to set on the bottom battens as in the "floating" type of frame. A frame is only as strong as its weakest point. For example, a bottom frame member 3″ wide when notched for a 1″ batten would then have the strength of only a 2″ frame member. Therefore, for strength equal to a 3″ bottom frame without the notches would require a 4″ wide frame with notches. A

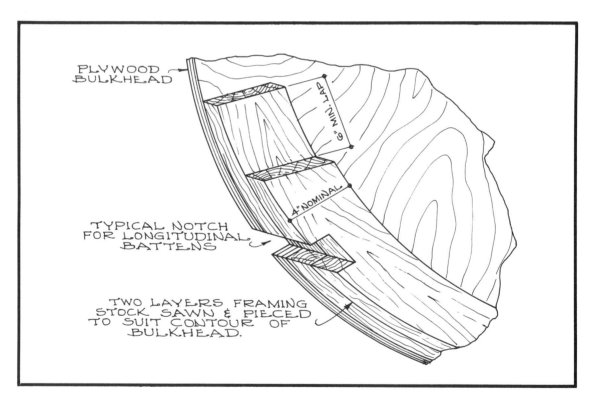

PLATE 10-G—Several pieces of solid wood can be pieced and joined to frame up a plywood bulkhead on round bottomed boats. Two thicknesses are used to provide the necessary overlap on the pieced members for stiffness.

92

problem with the notched frame is that splitting of the bottom frame member may occur between the battens when notches are cut for the bottom battens. Another problem which can occur with frames notched for the bottom battens is swelling of the frames due to moisture which can cause a "washboard" appearance in the bottom that could even affect the performance of a boat. However, an advantage of notching the bottom battens into the frames is in having a positive surface to fair from. The notches can be cut from the faired surface, and the strength of closely fitted notches aids the boat structurally. With frames that do not require notching ("floating frames"), the frames do not require limbers (drain holes) on the outboard sides from the centerline through the frames as do notched frames. The limbers are required in the notched frames so that any water which may come aboard will flow to the lowest portion of the hull so it can be pumped overboard. Either method of designing and installing the frames can be used as long as the boat is suited to the method used.

Bent frames are sometimes used on plywood boats for intermediate support of the bottom or side areas (see Plate 10-B). Bent frames are usually put in after the hull has been planked and righted. They are often sprung over longitudinal battens, for example from chine to chine, and fastened to the keel and bottom battens. There is no practical method of fastening the bent frame to the chines so fastenings are generally not used at this point. Bending oak is often used for these frames, and in other cases laminations of plywood or solid stock can be glued up to the required thickness. Care should be taken to use lumber that is not so stiff that it distorts

the hull. This is especially true if the hull is lightly framed. Bent frames are sometimes utilized for securing bulkheads to the hull when not located at frames in all types of boats.

A type of boat built by professional builders is the so-called "frameless" plywood boat. These are often known as "jig boats" or "stress skin hulls". The name, "frameless" boat, is actually a misnomer. The boats do use frames, but the frame members may be quite different from the types already discussed, and are usually added after the hull has been planked. The construction is approximately as follows: The boat is built over a series of permanent frames on a building form or "jig". The longitudinal members, often only the chines, are sprung around this form, upon which the keel, stem, and transom have been positioned. The plywood bottom and sides are sprung around the members as in any plywood boat. Such a hull is then pulled from the form, leaving the frames on the jig ready for the next boat. The hull at this point consists of four "panels" of plywood (two sides and two bottom halves), with a keel, and chine members in position. In some cases battens or bulkheads are an integral part of the hull.

The athwartship members are then placed in the hull in the form of frames, seat backs, bulkheads, or similar assemblies. In other instances, most of the framing will be longitudinal. Obviously such a hull is not a "frameless" boat, as is often described. It does have frames, but they are different in configuration and the manner in which they are installed. Hulls built this way have a tendency to warp and distort, and for this reason they are most suited to the professional who has the ability and

93

facilities to hold the hull into position while the internal framework is placed into position.

In extremely small boats, such as rowboats, the framing may be little more than seats. In the larger craft, most of the internal member are complete structural items, and are used as frames. For the amateur, such construction is often more complicated than the common sawn frame method. Builders of the so-called "frameless" boat have a period of learning to go through, and hence the practice is only justified when at least several boats will be built from one "jig". Because experience is an important element for anyone building a boat with this method, it is not suited to most amateurs. For the amateur, the sawn frame methods not only are used to determine the shape of the hull, but impart considerable strength to the completed boat, and therefore, they should remain in the hull.

CIRCULAR SAW GUIDE

By using a guide on a table saw as shown by Plate 10-H, several different woodworking procedures can be done, including truing-up an edge of irregular stock to form a straight edge, duplication of parts, making irregularly shaped parts, and making beveled cuts. In all cases, the contours to be cut must be straight lines and not curved.

GENERAL PROCEDURES: The guide is made from any straight stock about 3″ to 4″ wide and about as long as the saw fence. Notches or holes are made into which clamps are used to secure the guide to the fence of the table saw, or the guide could be bolted through the fence.

The guide is located above the table top a distance equal to the thickness of stock which will be cut below, plus about ⅛″ clearance. Set the fence so the guide edge is directly above the outside (the side away from the fence) surface of the saw blade. The saw blade should be set to just come through the stock to be cut, and yet not hit the guide. A straight edge board is nailed temporarily on top of the stock against the guide to control the cut. Always make a trial cut first to check accuracy. By using the proper type of saw blade, a very smooth cut will result.

TO TRUE-UP AN EDGE: A straight edged board at least as long as the lumber being trued-up is nailed to the top of the board as close to the edge as practical. For long members, strike a chalkline to make a straight line on the stock to be cut. Then align the straight edge to this line. The straight edge can be pieced as required if a full length member is not available, aligning the pieces to the chalkline. Then make the cut. This method makes a jointer unnecessary and is actually faster.

TO MAKE AN ORIGINAL PART: Draw, trace, or transfer from a pattern the straight-edged part onto the stock from which the part is to be made. Rough cut the part approximately one inch or so oversize. Then nail the straight edged board on top of the stock directly over the line to be cut. Note that the straight edge must be as long or longer than the rough cut stock. Make the cut, remove the straight edge board, and position onto another line, repeating this procedure until the part is completed.

TO MAKE DUPLICATE PARTS: Straight edged parts serving as a template can be nailed on top of the

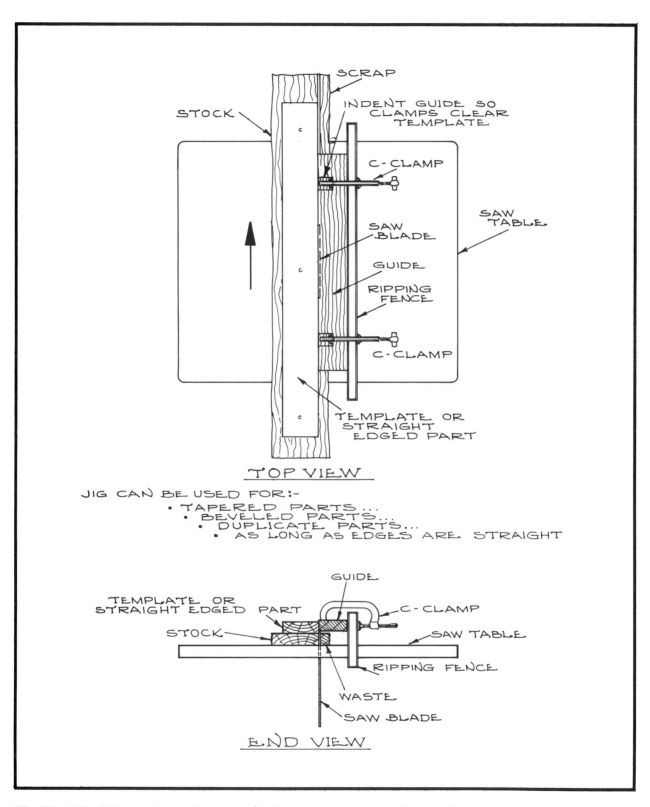

TOP VIEW

JIG CAN BE USED FOR :-
- TAPERED PARTS...
- BEVELED PARTS...
- DUPLICATE PARTS...
- AS LONG AS EDGES ARE STRAIGHT

END VIEW

PLATE 10-H—This simple saw jig can be used to true up irregular stock without using a jointer. It can also be used to make any number of duplicate parts with or without tapers or bevels as long as edges are straight. It is particularly useful for making frame member components.

95

stock to be cut and run through the saw against the guide to make any number of duplicate pieces in the same manner as noted above.

TO MAKE BEVELED PARTS: Follow the above procedures except tilt the saw blade to the desired angle. The height of the saw blade above the stock is critical when making the beveled cut. If it is too high, it will cut into the template. It must be just high enough to clear the stock and not touch the template or the guide. An ideal use for the guide is cutting the bevel along the bottom edges of transoms that have both a frame and the plywood transom attached. The frame and plywood can be assembled oversize then cut to a scribed line with the straight edged board method making the cut to the required angle in a single pass through the saw.

CHAPTER 11 — STEMS & BREASTHOOKS

STEMS

The stem is the portion of the boat's structure that extends from the keel to the deck at the bow and determines the forward profile of the boat. In plywood boat construction the keel is usually notched into the stem and screwed or bolted to it. The shape of the stem has much to do with how it is built and what materials may be used. Plate 11-A illustrates a group of stems fabricated by different methods.

With conventional planking methods used in traditional wood boat construction, the planking joins to the stem in a rabbet or open groove. This rabbet must be cut and shaped into the stem carefully by hand for a good fit which is, needless to say, tedious and difficult. With plywood boatbuilding, such a procedure is not required. With a large panel of plywood on the sides of a boat in a single width from chine to sheer, the builder would be fitting an area perhaps as long as 4'. Attempting to fit this accurately into a rabbet would be extremely difficult. There are easier methods for joining the planking to the stem and they are just as satisfactory.

In plywood boatbuilding, the stem is beveled on each side, and the plywood planking mates to this bevel without the need of a rabbet. The edges of the plywood planking can later be capped to suit. While it would be possible to fit the plywood planking into a rabbet, especially on a straight stemmed boat where it would be relatively easy, there simply is little reason to do so. However, if a rabbet is desired for some reason, note that the stem should be of solid wood as opposed to plywood or laminations. Several stem junctions showing plywood planking are given on Plate 11-B.

The conventional method of building stems from solid lumber usually requires wood 2" or more thick. Such a stem may be in two, three, or perhaps even more pieces, depending upon the shape. It is necessary to eliminate as much cross-grain as possible. Even if the wood were wide enough to cut the stem in one continuous piece, so much cross-grain would be prevalent that it would make the stem weak. For this reason, the joint similiar to that shown in the three piece type (Plate 11-A) is used. In this construction observe that the knee holding the other two parts together is notched in such a manner as to wedge itself in position. This locking method type of construction will prevent working of the members.

The small rowboat-type stem is similar to the three-piece type. In a rowboat, or boats of similar type, the false-nose-type stem (Plate 11-B) is frequently used. That is, the upright part is narrower at the keel and widens out towards the deck. In larger craft, this false nose, or bull nose, may be quite large, glued up of laminations of wood, and

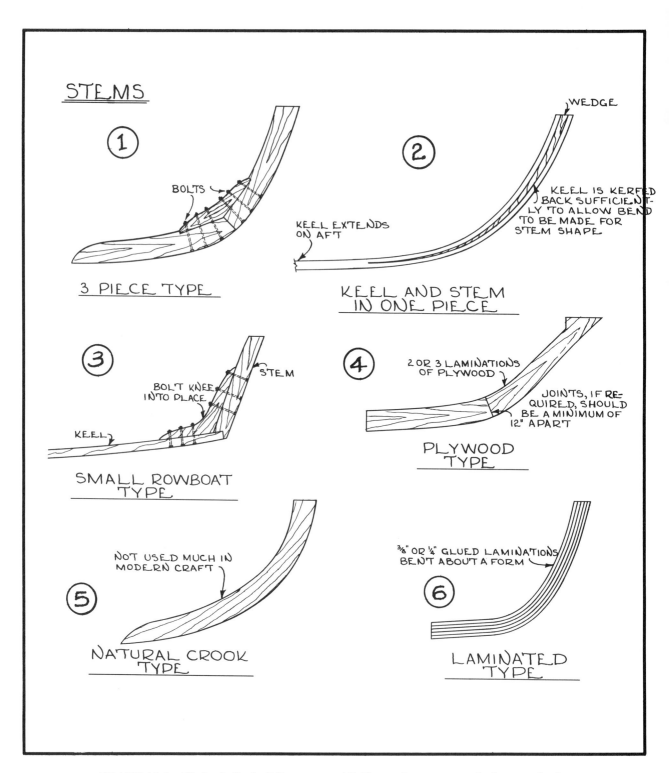

STEMS

① 3 PIECE TYPE

BOLTS

② KEEL AND STEM IN ONE PIECE

WEDGE

KEEL IS KERFED BACK SUFFICIENT-LY TO ALLOW BEND TO BE MADE FOR STEM SHAPE

KEEL EXTENDS ON AFT

③ SMALL ROWBOAT TYPE

BOLT KNEE INTO PLACE

STEM

KEEL

④ PLYWOOD TYPE

2 OR 3 LAMINATIONS OF PLYWOOD

JOINTS, IF RE-QUIRED, SHOULD BE A MINIMUM OF 12" APART

⑤ NATURAL CROOK TYPE

NOT USED MUCH IN MODERN CRAFT

⑥ LAMINATED TYPE

⅜" OR ¼" GLUED LAMINATIONS BENT ABOUT A FORM

PLATE 11-A—Methods for building stems. (1) Three piece type used where a single member is impractical. (2) Stem is made in one piece as a continuation of the keel. (3) Small rowboat stem requires a knee to join it to the keel. (4) Common plywood type may include plywood laminations, or a combination of inner solid wood and outer plywood layers. (5) Natural crook stems are shaped the way a tree grows. (6) Laminated stems can be built up to virtually any contour desired.

contoured to suit. The disadvantage of such practice is the tendency in time for the built-up sections to crack.

The old-time boatbuilder used natural crook-type stems. These were grown in such a manner as to conform to the shape of the stem of the particular boat. Often these were dried by the builder and were structurally quite sound. In modern-day construction, such natural crooks are almost impossible to come by. For practical purposes, they are only of passing interest to the builder of plywood craft rather than something to be seriously considered in current-day construction.

Professional builders of plywood boats often use a combination stem and keel. A combined keel and stem may be built up from a series of laminations

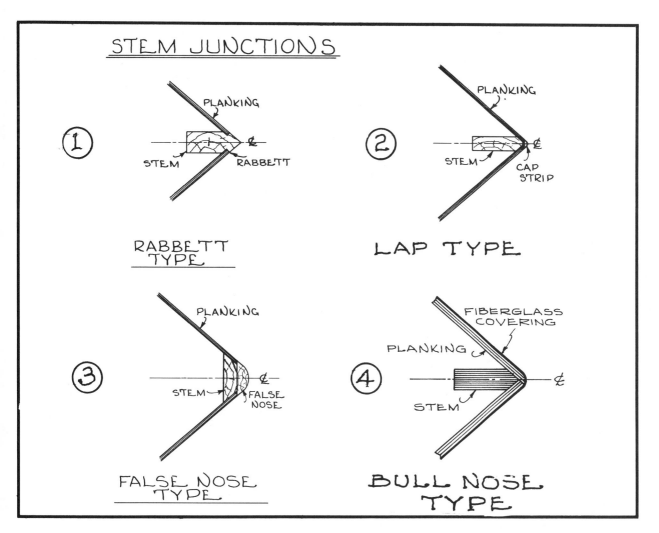

PLATE 11-B—Stem junctions with the planking. (1) The rabbeted type is easy where the stem is a straight contour, but difficult otherwise. (2) Simple lap type uses a cap which, if the hull is fiberglassed, is applied after this material. (3) False nose stem is used where considerable shaping and contouring of the stem is desired for appearance. Fiberglassing over the false nose usually leads to cracking at the joint. (4) Simple bull-nose stem junction with the plywood on one side being overlapped by the opposite side. The junction is radiused and covered with fiberglass.

that are thin enough to bend around the stem curve. The keel-stem member is sometimes steamed from a solid member and bent over a steel jig to form a one-piece keel and stem. In smaller craft, it is possible to slit or kerf the keel to enable the member to be bent about the stem contour. A wedge filler-strip, illustrated in Plate 11-A, is laminated between the slit laminations. Any of these methods are satisfactory, provided that adequate clamps, fixtures, and proper gluing practices are adhered to.

The laminated stem is glued up from ⅜" or ¼" laminations of solid wood or plywood. This method requires the building of a form, plenty of clamps, and closely controlled gluing practices to assure a good bond of the lamination. Properly done, this method of construction provides a very strong stem. This type of stem is more time-consuming to construct than other types. Fastening of the chine members to either the keel and stem, if it is one piece, or the laminated stem is difficult. In the case of the laminated type, a block may be fabricated into the stem to give additional reinforcement to fasten the chines as they meet the stem. This method may also be used with the one-piece keel and stem if adequate material is not available for fastening the chine to the stem.

For plywood construction, the easiest and simplest type of stem is made from plywood. In the smaller craft it is built up from two laminations of ¾" plywood, usually molded a minimum width of about 3" to 4". In larger craft, more laminations and a wider molded width are used. Often combinations of lumber and plywood are used. For example, an inner core of ¾" can be used with laminations of 1" or 1¼" solid lumber on

either side. As long as the laminations are liberally spread with glue, and the joints are staggered a minimum of 12" apart, such a stem is perfectly sound, although considered unconventional by the old-time boat builder. In fastening laminations together, screws or annular-thread nails are used, spaced a maximum of 6" apart. The reader may question the feasibility of fastening the planking skin with screws driven into the end grain of the plywood stem. Closer investigation will show, however, that the screws are not driven into the end grain. They are driven angularly through the plies, thus affording good holding power, although longer screws than usual should be used as a precaution. There are several advantages to the plywood type of stem, in addition to the ease of construction. The stem may be made longer than would be conventional practice. It is good construction to allow the stem to extend to the first frame aft of the bow of the boat. By nesting the stem between the bottom frame members and butting to the floor timber, an integral, strong unit can be developed (See Fig. 11-1). Notches or ledges for forward frames, breasthooks, chine blocks, or partial bulkheads are readily incorporated in stems built from plywood laminations. The expansion and contraction of dissimilar wood is prevented by using plywood for stems.

BREASTHOOKS

The breasthook is the member that secures the sheer clamps to the stem. In conventional wood boatbuilding this member is usually made from solid wood. In some cases solid wood breasthooks are used on plywood boats, however, with most plywood boats the breasthook will be made from laminations of plywood. Usually, ¾" plywood in two or more laminations is sufficient for most boats. A typical plywood breasthook is shown by Fig. 11-2. Note that the breasthook in this case is made up from two layers of plywood, with one layer that rests on and fastens to the top of the stem, and the lower layer notched to lock around the stem at the top. On larger boats, more layers may be used, and in some cases, solid wood laminations alone or alternated with plywood could also be substituted. Regardless of the manner of construction, the principle is the same.

Note that the breasthook must be notched for the sheer clamps which join to the side of the breasthook. If the sheer clamps are sprung around the boat so they are vertical, this notch will be cut vertically also. However, if the sheer clamps are angled to be parallel with the side planking, then the notch must be beveled so the sheer clamps will mate flat to the breasthook. In most cases, this bevel can be approximated while assembling the breasthook and pre-cut for the most part. However, some fairing will be inevitable due to the fact that the angle will be everchanging.

Some may question the fastening strength of the breasthook junction just described. As noted for the stem-

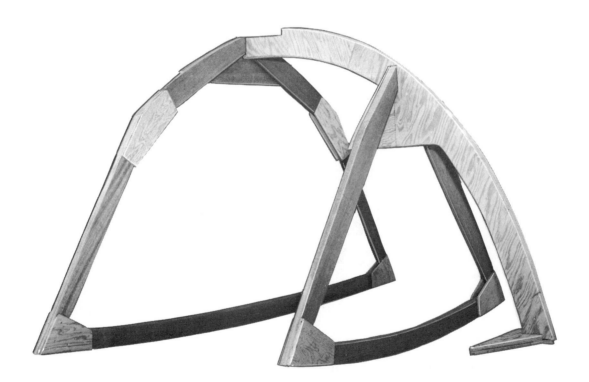

FIG. 11-1—A plywood stem assembly shows how the use of plywood can provide a member that can be contoured where required for an adequate landing to adjoining frame members. The forward frame is notched over the stem and butts to it, thereby providing a positive mating junction. The aft frame has the bottom frame members notched so the stem butts to the floor timber. Such an assembly with the breasthook can be securely anchored to the building form.

planking junction, in many cases the screws for the sheer clamps may approach the breasthook at an angle thereby giving good holding power. Or if the builder prefers, he can use solid wood laminations (or at least one solid wood layer) which will be used to receive the sheer clamp screws. But through experience it has been shown that these precautions, while acceptable, are not really necessary because once the deck has been laid and fastened in place, the resultant structure will be more than ample.

CHINE BLOCKING

The chine blocking is similar to the breasthook, except that it is used to join and brace the chine logs where they meet with the stem. While not usually a required member, it does simplify the junction of the chine logs to the stem in many cases. Fitting chine logs to the stem can be difficult for the amateur, and the chine blocking eliminates much of this problem. Determining the proper angle for the chine blocking and fitting it to the stem is a cut-and-fit project, and for this reason it is sometimes installed after the positions of the chine logs have been determined on the stem.

The chine blocking shown by Fig. 11-3 is made to notch around the stem, bearing on a ledge provided. In other cases, it will be difficult to predict the exact point where the chine logs will mate to the stem, and consequently the installation of the chine blocking is best left until the chine logs have been located. Drive screws angularly through the chine blocking into the stem to provide adequate holding power. Although the angle of the chine blocking which

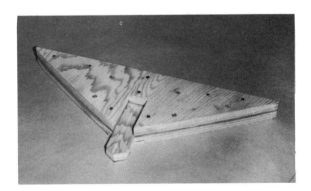

FIG. 11-2—A plywood breasthook made in two laminations. One half fits on top of the stem, while the other half notches around the stem at the top. The sheer clamps fit along each contoured edge which must be notched away to suit the net thickness of the sheer clamp members.

FIG. 11-3—When chine blocking is specified, it is similar to the breasthook. The chine blocking is located between the chine logs and lock-notches around the stem. Beveling is required for solid contact with the chine logs.

will mate to the chine logs is preferably pre-cut, some fairing will be inevitable.

The chine blocking is made the same as the breasthook, and usually two or more layers of ¾″ plywood are required.

In addition to fastening the chine logs to the chine blocking, they are also fastened into the stem angularly for better holding power (see Chapter 15).

FIG. 11-4—A plywood stem assembly with breasthook and chine blocking in position. Note the sheer clamps and chine logs joining with the breasthook and chine blocking respectively. The sheer clamp in this instance is a laminated type set in vertically.

CHAPTER 12 — TRANSOMS

The transom is the athwartship covering or "planking" at the stern or back of the boat. As noted previously, if a boat is pointed at both ends (a "double ender") it will not have a transom. The construction of the transom will vary depending upon whether the particular boat is a sailboat, or inboard powered boat, or will have an inboard engine driving through a transom-mounted outdrive unit or jet drive unit, or if it is an outboard powered boat. The sailboat and conventional inboard powered boat may have a transom that is lighter and less rigidly built than any of the other types listed since there will probably not be as much stress on this part of the boat.

In traditional wood boat construction the transom is built from a framework and then covered with a series of planks glued and fastened to the required width. This method is not only a lot of work, but the planks have a tendency to warp and split with the drying out and soaking up of water that a boat is subjected to. The result can be leaks. Plywood is the most practical and preferable choice for covering this area of the hull. With most boats, it is possible to make the entire transom from a single plywood panel thereby making not only a much stronger structure, but also one that is leak-free.

Depending on the boat, the transom can be simple or quite complex. For example, a transom that is vertical or at right angles to the keel is simple to build since bevels along the edges will not be required, or will be only minimal in nature. With outboard boats, the transom will almost always require a certain angularity to suit the mounting requirements of the outboard motor. This means pre-beveling of the members at least along the bottom will be necessary. It may also require a motor cut-out that must be sized to suit the motor used. The builder should plan carefully when laying out and assembling the transom to include all the elements that are required to suit the particular boat due to the many possible options.

OUTBOARD TRANSOMS

The transom on any but the smallest outboard hull is a minimum of ¾" thick plywood. Usual practice is to frame this plywood transom with framework similar to the other frames used in the boat (Fig. 12-1). In some instances, builders use thicker plywood or two layers of ¾" or 1" plywood glued together. This eliminates the framework as the notches for the longitudinal members are put in one layer of the plywood transom. The latter is not considered good practice, as the planking and longitudinals then must be fastened to the end grain of plywood. As previously

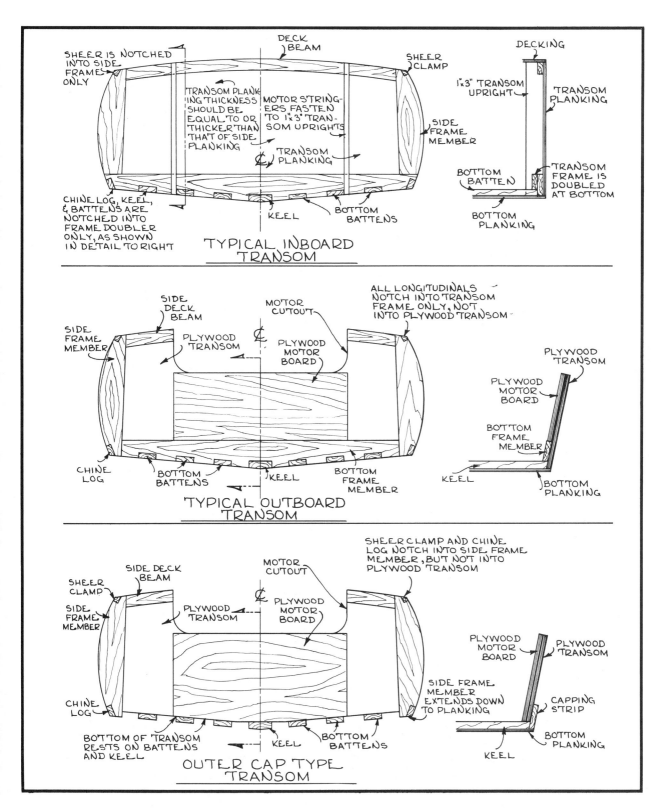

PLATE 12-A—Typical transom construction methods

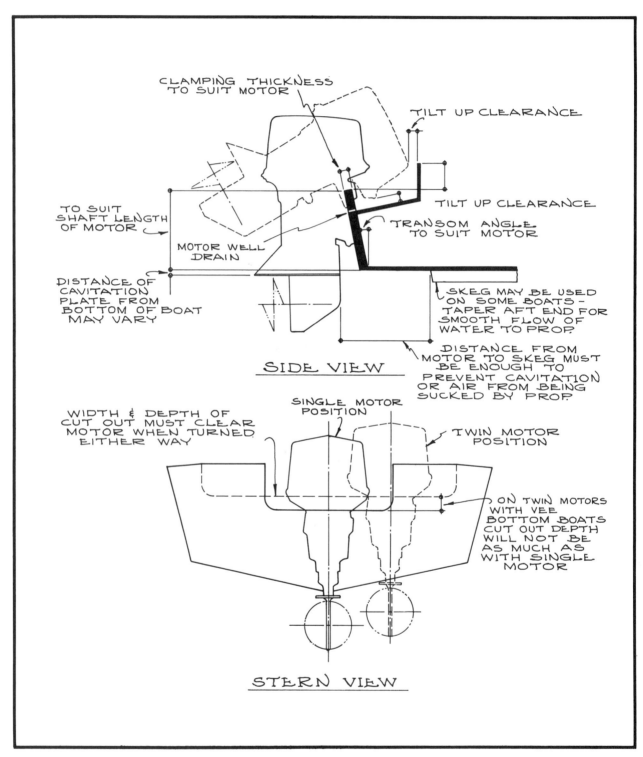

CLAMPING THICKNESS
TO SUIT MOTOR

TILT UP CLEARANCE

TILT UP CLEARANCE

TO SUIT
SHAFT LENGTH
OF MOTOR

TRANSOM ANGLE
TO SUIT MOTOR

MOTOR WELL
DRAIN

DISTANCE OF
CAVITATION
PLATE FROM
BOTTOM OF BOAT
MAY VARY

SKEG MAY BE USED
ON SOME BOATS -
TAPER AFT END FOR
SMOOTH FLOW OF
WATER TO PROP.

SIDE VIEW

DISTANCE FROM
MOTOR TO SKEG MUST
BE ENOUGH TO
PREVENT CAVITATION
OR AIR FROM BEING
SUCKED BY PROP.

WIDTH & DEPTH OF
CUT OUT MUST CLEAR
MOTOR WHEN TURNED
EITHER WAY

SINGLE MOTOR
POSITION

TWIN MOTOR
POSITION

ON TWIN MOTORS
WITH VEE
BOTTOM BOATS
CUT OUT DEPTH
WILL NOT BE
AS MUCH AS
WITH SINGLE
MOTOR

STERN VIEW

PLATE 12-B—These details through a typical outboard motor well and motor cut-out show several considerations unique to outboards. The motor well is sloped so that any water that enters will drain out and not enter the boat. The builder must consider the transom height in relation to the shaft length of the motor, the transom angularity required for the motor, motor clamping thickness, and tilt-up clearances. In addition to these dimensions, the width of the cut-out and turning axis clearance must also be considered. All such dimensions and tolerances are usually provided by the motor manufacturer.

106

mentioned, end grain of plywood does not hold screws very well. The conventional framework fastened to the plywood transom is superior. In some cases, the frame is on the outer portion, but most generally the frame is on the inside of the transom. Such a frame will have all of the notches pre-cut for the longitudinals. Longitudinals should not extend through the plywood transom, as they will have a tendency to leak. The longitudinal members, however, may be extended through the transom frame and plywood if the exposed ends are capped with an outer frame. For extra strength, a combination of inner and outer frames on the transom is frequently used.

To be as thick as possible, the clamping area for the outboard motor should at least be doubled with additional laminations of plywood. The thickness of a transom at the motor area of course must not be greater than the maximum clamp opening for the outboard motor that is to be used. Such added thickness

of a motor board may extend completely athwartship across the boat. In other instances, when the transom is rather wide, the thickness is added at the motor area only.

The height for the motor cutout and the width required for the motor as well as the fore and aft depth to tilt the outboard motor will vary. It is always preferable to check with the motor manufacturer for his recommendations on the motor that you intend to use. Standards are difficult to give, for they are constantly changing as manufacturers improve and alter their models.

The motor-clamping area must be reinforced to take the stesses and strains that will be imparted by the outboard motor. At the center of the transom, a knee brace is often used extending from the keel as high as possible up the transom to meet the motor. The height of this knee will depend upon the clamping area required by the motor to be used. Such knees on the average outboard hull should be a

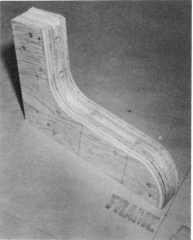

FIG. 12-1 (left)—Typical plywood transom framed with solid stock. Note that the framework is notched for the various longitudinals which do not go through the plywood transom. FIG. 12-2 (right)—A transom knee as used on outboard boats built up from plywood laminations. Plywood used for knees takes advantage of the material's uniform strength in all directions.

minimum of 12″ on the lower leg. Knees may be fabricated from solid lumber, although it may split in use. Plywood can be used to eliminate that possibility. Such plywood knees can be laminated from ¾″ plywood to any desired thickness. On the smaller boats, a minimum of two laminations, and in the larger hulls, perhaps four or even more laminations would be used (see Fig. 12-2). Additional knee braces from the longitudinal battens in the form of plywood webs are desirable. These often form motor-well sides, as indicated in Fig. 12-4. Such plywood knee braces on the plywood runabout would generally be a minimum of ⅜″ thick. They should be securely anchored to the longitudinal battens, and to uprights provided at the transom, as well as tied into any longitudinal deck structure members. Such knees impart considerable rigidity to the transom and take the stresses and thrust of the outboard motor, distributing them through the hull structure. Figures 12-6 and 12-7 indicate the typical bracing of the transom on outboard runabouts and cruisers intended for single-motor operation. Twin motors would be handled similarly.

It is possible to obtain or to make metal knees or use metal reinforcing at stress points at the transom. This is particularly true with the larger outboard motors. Such construction is highly recommended and has less tendency to fail in use. In all cases when metal reinforcing members are used, they should be bolted securely in position. If made of steel, such members should be hot dipped galvanized after fabrication to prevent rusting.

A built-in motor well for the outboard motor is recommended for any outboard craft. Such a well is water-tight, and allows any water that splashes over the transom to drain overboard through drain holes provided in the back of the transom. A motor-well is not only a safety feature to eliminate swamping the boat, but also adds considerable structural strength to the hull (see Fig. 12-5).

INBOARD & SAILBOAT TRANSOMS

The transom for a plywood sailboat or inboard powered boat, whether it be a conventional inboard, inboard with an outdrive, or jet drive, is made similarly to that of an outboard. As noted, the sailboat or conventional inboard powered boat transom may be more lightly built since there will not be an engine or a drive unit hung on or protruding through the transom. This is not to say that such a transom can be weak, however. For example, on some large sailboats, the transom may be fitted with the chainplate that connects the backstay from the transom to the masthead. In this case the transom must be strong and rigid enough to support the loads imposed by the backstay. Fittings, such as chainplates, gudgeons, and pintles, which fasten to the transom, should always be backed with blocks of either solid wood or plywood of sufficient thickness and size to adequately distribute the stresses over the plywood transom. On sailboats with outboard transom hung rudders, the transom must likewise be sufficiently strong to take the rudder forces and fastenings, which are frequently also backed up on the inside with blocking.

On inboard powered boats using a jet

FIG. 12-3—These photographs depict a motor well assembly in a small outboard runabout. The clamping area for the motor is reinforced with additional laminations of plywood. The transom knee is bolted both to the keel and the transom. A heavy athwartship member is screwed to the knee and the transom.

FIG. 12-4—For additional reinforcement, the motor well sides extend completely to the bottom of the boat, fastening to bottom battens. These plywood motor well sides are also fastened to solid lumber uprights on the transom.

FIG. 12-5—The motor well bottom is fastened in position to provide a self-bailing well. Any water splashing over the transom cut-out will immediately drain back out thereby preventing or minimizing the possibility of swamping the cockpit.

109

FIG. 12-6—A motor well area for an outboard cruiser. The motor well sides extend to the bottom battens. The floor battens are also used to support these upright members.

FIG. 12-7—A plywood bulkhead built into the motor well area. The opening below the motor tray is for checking the bilge or for access to a drain plug.

FIG. 12-8—In small runabouts the transom is often braced by an extension of the coamings acting as motor well sides in addition to the transom knee. The self-draining splash well may be quite small in such boats.

FIG. 12-9—Small hydros or race boats do not have a splash well and utilize considerable bracing to longitudinals to spread out the stresses caused by the outboard motor. Often aluminum or other metal braces extend from the transom forward to longitudinal members to provide additional strength.

drive or outdrive unit mounted on the transom, some modifications are usually required from the standard inboard boat transom. For example, if the transom is made from ¾" plywood, quite often additional plywood layers will be required on the inside to suit the mounting requirements of the drive system, both for the mounting bolts and for additional strength. In some cases, the transom may be specified to be a certain angularity as noted by the designer, and this angle may not suit exactly the angle required for mounting a particular drive. If this is the case, the builder must either change the angle of the transom or provide beveled blocking to suit the drive being used.

It is common practice on inboard powered boat transoms to provide uprights on the inside which lap and join to motor stringers that run longitudinally in the hull. The uprights serve much the same purpose as knees on the outboard type of transom, and in fact, sometimes knees may be called for. If the uprights are specified and do tie in with the motor stringers, the spacing of these uprights must be made to suit the motor stringer spacing.

When building sailboat and inboard boat transoms, a standard frame is built from the same material as used for the regular athwartship frames. If the transom plywood is very thin, gussets may be used at the side/bottom corners on the forward sides of such framing. In this type of transom the plywood need be little or no thicker than the side or bottom planking. A better transom, that is almost as easy to make, uses two bottom frame members laminated together and notching only the forward lamination for the various longitudi-

nals. The inner aft or concealed bottom frame lamination is not notched, but instead receives the fastenings for the bottom planking. This practice all but eliminates the possibility of leaks along the bottom transom edge. A variation of this theme would be to laminate one of the bottom members on the outside of the transom to cap the ends of the longitudinals and receive the planking fastenings. The other bottom frame member is fastened on the inside of the transom for receiving the longitudinal members and fastenings. With this variation no notches would be required as the frame member is offset to match the thickness of the longitudinals (see Plate 12-A and Fig. 12-11 which show similar methods). Some may not care for the appearance of this method, and another drawback is that it is more difficult to cover with fiberglass.

A natural finished wood transom such as mahogany is considered traditional on boats and is often desired. This type of transom can be made by using a mahogany faced plywood, though some will prefer to use solid wood planks with plywood backing. When planks are used, they should not exceed 6" in width. The thickness will depend on the size of the boat, with ½" thick being a minimum in most cases. The planks are generally fastened from the inside through the plywood backing and into the solid planks after applying glue. This eliminates any fastenings showing when viewed from the outside. Or the fastenings can be driven from the outside well counterbored. The screw holes can be fitted with matching wood plugs preferably, or filled with matching putty.

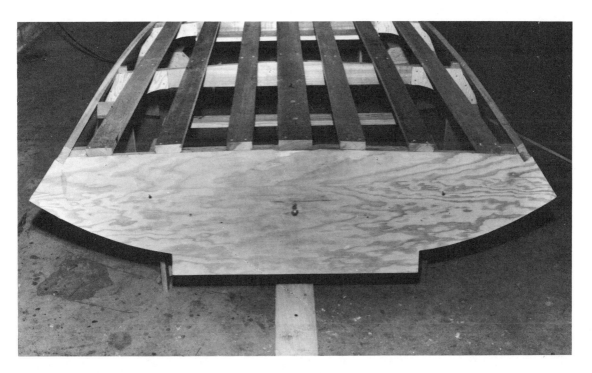

FIG. 12-10—A transom that has no internal framework. The battens rest on top of the plywood transom.

FIG. 12-11—A capping member is used to cover the exposed ends of the battens, and the bottom planking is fastened to it.

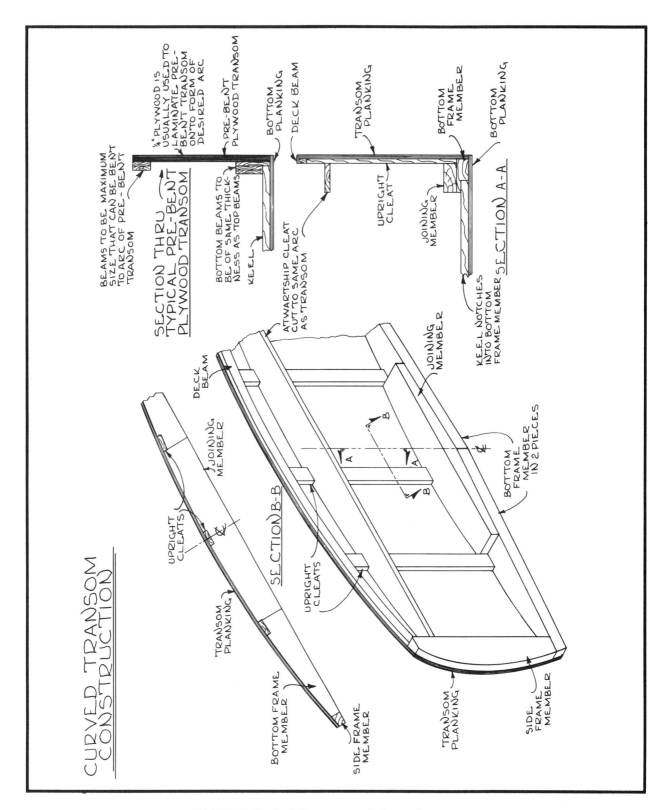

BEAMS TO BE MAXIMUM SIZE THAT CAN BE BENT TO ARC OF PRE-BENT TRANSOM

¼" PLYWOOD IS USUALLY USED TO LAMINATE PRE-BENT TRANSOM ONTO FORM OF DESIRED ARC

PRE-BENT PLYWOOD TRANSOM

BOTTOM PLANKING

DECK BEAM

TRANSOM PLANKING

BOTTOM FRAME MEMBER

BOTTOM PLANKING

BOTTOM BEAMS TO BE OF SAME THICKNESS AS TOP BEAMS

KEEL

UPRIGHT CLEAT

JOINING MEMBER

KEEL NOTCHES INTO BOTTOM FRAME MEMBER

SECTION THRU TYPICAL PRE-BENT PLYWOOD TRANSOM

SECTION A-A

ATWARTSHIP CLEAT CUT TO SAME ARC AS TRANSOM

JOINING MEMBER

DECK BEAM

JOINING MEMBER

BOTTOM FRAME MEMBER IN 2 PIECES

SECTION B-B

UPRIGHT CLEATS

TRANSOM PLANKING

UPRIGHT CLEATS

TRANSOM PLANKING

SIDE FRAME MEMBER

BOTTOM FRAME MEMBER

SIDE FRAME MEMBER

CURVED TRANSOM CONSTRUCTION

PLATE 12-C—Building a curved plywood transom

114

CURVED TRANSOMS

Curved transoms are preferred by many from an appearance standpoint. They are considerably more difficult to build than the flat type. Some methods of curved transom construction are shown on Plate 12-C. Provided the transom is curved in one direction only, building up the transom from a series of plywood laminations is probably the easiest method. This is done by building a jig or fixture to the desired or specified arc. A minimum of three laminations of ¼" plywood should be used. With larger transoms, and provided that it is possible with the required radius, heavier material may be used. Each lamination is sprung around the form and spread liberally with glue. Proper gluing practice as to temperature and clamping should be strictly observed to prevent voids between the laminations. A conventional frame is used around the extremities of the transom. At the bottom transom member, it is usually necessary to saw a member to fit the curved portion of the transom. It is possible to build the curved framework from laminations. This is not considered best practice, as screws driven into the laminations have poor holding qualities. Another method of making a curved transom is to build a framework from solid material and spring the standard plywood transom around the curvature. Here, again, several laminations may be required to obtain the desired thickness. It must be understood that plywood transoms, as described, can be curved in one direction only. The limitations of the material will not enable an arc to be made in two directions. It is always possible to use strips of plywood and build up almost any contour for a transom, but this is very uncommon in use.

TRANSOM CONSTRUCTION

Regardless of whether the transom is for an inboard or outboard, it is seldom that the transom is at right angles to the keel or bottom of the boat. When the transom is canted back, as is typical in both inboard and outboards, an allowance must be made for the bevel. This is covered on Plate 8-H, in the chapter of lofting. Details on allowing for the bevel of the transom when full-sized patterns are used are also given in Chapter 9, Plate 9-A. When the transom is thinner than the framework, as could be the case in an inboard, the plywood is fastened to the frame with annular-threaded nails or screws spaced approximately 3" apart. When the framework and the transom are relatively the same in thickness, it is the usual practice to fasten the framework to the plywood transom. Usually screws are used, spaced a maximum of 6" apart and well staggered. All joints and mating area should be thoroughly coated with a hard-setting glue before assembly. On transoms that are larger than the standard 4' x 8' sheet of plywood, a larger piece of plywood can be used, or smaller panels can be butt joined to form the larger transom. Another method is to use two layers of plywood laminated together, staggering the joints between layers as far as practical. Methods for butt joining are similar to those noted on the chapter covering planking (see Chapter 19).

CHAPTER 13 — SETTING UP

The first procedure in setting up the hull is making the building form, and the first thought that the builder will have is just where should the building form and the subsequent hull construction take place? Virtually any area that is big enough for the hull including access around the sides will suffice. Naturally, there must be room enough to get the boat away from the building site as well (remember the boat built in the basement story?). From a working standpoint, the more room the better, and the builder should be planning also at this time how he intends to right the hull once it is completed, as this can have some bearing on the space required. Consider also electrical power available on the site, weather protection in many climates, and how building your boat will affect your neighbors. Some local officials may scorn your idea of having an "ark" on your front lawn for any period of time, so check local ordinances. In many areas, space can be rented to build a boat, and there are even facilities which encourage this sort of thing. Working around other boatbuilders is often encouraging and enlightening to the amateur, so check around if your backyard or garage is not up to the task.

It is easier to set up or build the average plywood boat bottom side up. This applies to almost any hull of reasonable size, as handling sheets of plywood while the boat is right-side up is impractical, to say the least. Most texts on boat construction will refer to the building taking place on a level wooden floor. While a nice, level, flat floor is an excellent building area, the catch is that most builders are limited for such a space to build their boat. Most will work on a concrete or even a dirt area. There are several methods of setting up that would require a wooden floor to be practical. In these particular cases, one could be built. Actually the surface or contour of the floor is incidental in most set-up methods, as long as a form can be leveled and anchored to it.

When mention is made of setting up, some reference point or plane must be taken into consideration. Obviously, a group of frames, stem, and transom without a reference plane could not be sensibly built into a boat. The reference plane is generally a horizontal line in the profile of the boat. Such a line may be above the sheer, one of the waterlines, or even below the bottom of the boat, if the hull is to be built right-side up. If the builder is lofting the boat himself, any reference plane could be struck, depending on how the individual decides to build his boat. Any of the methods in this chapter can be used. When the designer has lofted and given dimensions for the frames, or furnished full-size templates, the set-up level and the set-up method will usually be noted.

The building form is an important part in the construction of a boat. All of

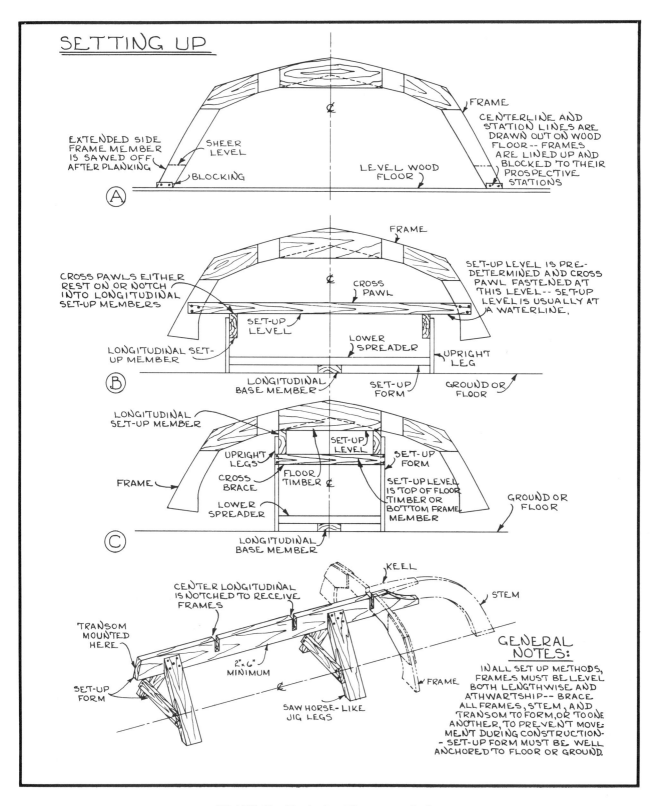

PLATE 13—Typical setting-up methods

the time and effort spent in lofting or accurately building frames will be wasted if the framework is not accurately located and precisely held in position on a form, jig, or fixture. Do not use a haphazard form, or one that will spring out of shape when the longitudinals are sprung around the hull. The builder is going to be leaning, pushing, shoving, and forcing members about a framework. Spend a few dollars, and make the form by whatever method is preferred, but make it strong and accurate. A few examples of typical building forms are illustrated.

Plate 13 shows three common methods for choosing set-up levels and how each would be utilized to set up frames for building. Method "A" would use a set-up level or reference plane drawn above the profile. This is the method simplest for those fortunate people who are working from a level wooden floor, or care to build one. Another common method of setting up is illustrated in "B". This utilizes a cross pawl or athwartship spreader on each of the frames. This method would be used when the set-up level or reference plane is a waterline. In building this type of form, it is essential that the cross pawl be accurately located and level

FIG. 13-1—While a prime consideration in selecting a building site is to have enough room to work on the boat, another consideration is how to get the boat from the building site to the water. This builder had plenty of room in his backyard, but no room to move the boat out of the yard. The solution? Hire a crane for a brief period of time.

FIG. 13-2—A building form for an outboard runabout. Since the builder is working on a concrete floor, a longitudinal central member is used, anchored to the concrete with expansion bolts. The legs and blocking for the stem assembly are all built from this base member.

FIG. 13-3—A sinple building form for construction of an inboard. In this instance the base member has been eliminated, and each of the support legs anchored to the floor individually. The longitudinal motor stringers are mounted on these legs and the frames fitted into notches provided in the stringers.

119

athwartships on the frames. Frames are constructed on a form that consists of two longitudinals extending fore and aft, long enough to hold all or most of the frames. Such longitudinals are heavy members, seldom less than 2" x 4", spaced as far apart as possible, depending upon the widest width available on the cross pawl.

An excellent method of setting up consists of striking a level for the floor timber or the inside level of the frame, whichever the case may be ("C"). This level is carried constant throughout the boat, or it may vary, as long as the offset is taken up by notching or blocking up from the reference plane the amount of the variance. Using this method in inboard hulls, the longitudinal motor stringers are used as the set-up members. Each is notched to lock around and space or locate the frame. This is an especially rigid type of construction. In small runabouts or cruisers, inboard or outboard, it is possible to arrange flat floor boards by this method. The same thing could be done by any of the other set-up methods if taken into consideration at the time of lofting. This method probably takes more thinking from the amateur's standpoint if he does the lofting himself. When working from frame dimensions or full-size patterns, the task is greatly simplified and well worth consideration.

A method used by some designers is to use the sheerline as the set-up level. This can only practically be done when the sheer is a straight line. A flat floor, partial floor or level longitudinals should be used to support the cross pawls on the frames located at the sheer line to position each frame accurately. Such frames will seldom be at right angles to the waterline by this method. If

bulkheads are required, this could well put them out of plumb. Since straight sheers are not common, this type of building form method can be considered for specialized instances only.

Regardless of the method of mounting the frames or setting them on the building form, the general procedures will be the same. The frames should be erected at a convenient working height. Seldom is it practical to have the closest point less than 6" from the floor. If a wood floor is available, nail the form down. If working on a concrete floor, use expansion plugs driven into the concrete. These are small and are hardly noticable, so they will not get you in trouble with your spouse or the landlord. If you aren't able to drill into the concrete, and are working in a garage, it is often possible to send braces over the plates of the building or to brace the structure to the walls and ceiling. Some of these braces may have to be shifted when applying the planking, but be sure you have enough to make the structure strong and rigid at all times. If working on a dirt area, the problem is somewhat rougher. Stakes will have to be driven into the ground, or heavy posts provided to hold the longitudinals. The shape of the ground is not important; it is the leveling and keeping level of the set-up members that will support the frames that is essential. The boat should be built on the form and left in one spot until completion. If at any time it is absolutely necessary to remove the hull in a semi-finished state, it must again be realigned and levelled to be finished.

Any longitudinal set-up members must be level both lengthwise and athwartship. They must not only be carefully leveled, but they must be kept that way during the entire construction.

FIG. 13-4—The following pages of photographs depict the setting up of a typical boat. Although the method of holding the frames to the form may vary, the general principle of building a hull and setting it up will be similar in all cases. When the longitudinal set-up members are notched, both of the forms (in this case the motor stringers for an inboard) will be clamped together and the notches cut at one time. This will insure accurate frame spacing.

FIG. 13-5—The longitudinal members, or motor stringers, are mounted to the building form so they are level both fore and aft, and athwartships. The form for holding these members is bolted securely to the concrete floor to prevent movement.

FIG. 13-6—All the frames are slipped into their respective notches. The frames should not be permanently anchored in place until all preliminary alignment and adjustment is done. If any of the frames have full deck beams, it would be necessary to thread the frame over the longitudinal members before assembly to the building form legs.

FIG. 13-7—Each of the frames is plumbed in vertically. If the longitudinal stringers are level in both directions, it holds that a level or a square can be used to carefully align the frame. A brace can be used from one frame to the next to hold each in vertical alignment.

FIG. 13-8—A chalk line stretched over the centerline of the frames is used to position each one. A forward frame and an aft frame are centered in position. The chalk line stretching over the frame centerline simplifies aligning the remaining frames.

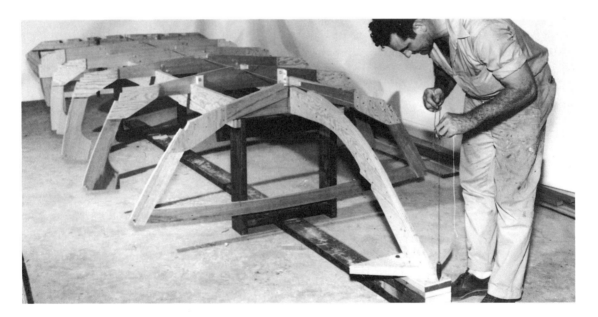

FIG. 13-9—A chalk line sprung over the centerline of the frames with a plumb bob will determine the position for the center of the stem. Care should be taken that the height of the stem or breasthook, as taken from the full size loftings, patterns, or plans, is the correct distance from the building form set-up level or reference plane. When aligned properly, the stem or breasthook assembly is fastened to blocking to prevent movement.

Use adequate legs and braces to keep these members level and true. The frames are mounted on the building form and spaced accurately from the dimensions given on the plans. In most instances the frames aft of amidships will be placed behind the station line. Those frames forward of amidships will be placed on the forward side of the station line. When deck beams are a part of the frames, it is often necessary to thread the frames over the set-up members before anchoring these members in place. A chalk line or steel wire between the set-up members will provide an accurate centerline. Each frame must be accurately centered in position, as well as spaced per the frame spacing given on the plans. After spacing and centering the frames they must be aligned vertically. When the frames are perpendicular to the set-up level, as is the usual case, a plumb-bob, level or builder's square used from the set-up level will assure vertical alignment. Be very careful in vertical alignment of frames. A frame out of alignment, either athwartships or vertically, could cause considerable problems. This is particularly the case if a bulkhead is to be located on a frame.

After all of the frames have been carefully aligned, temporary battens are sprung over the bottom frame portions, and also along the sides of the frames to check the alignment of the frame-work. The battens should sweep in with a clean, fair line without humps, bumps, or hollows between frames, If the framework is not sufficiently accurate so that a sweep of the plane will remove the excess, some checking as to the error should be made. When all is checked and accurate, the frames should be securely fastened in place, and braced to one another, to the floor, or to the form to prevent movement.

Mounting and alignment of the stem must be carefully done. The height of the stem at the deck can be obtained from the full-size loftings, or, if the hull has been lofted, from the dimensions on the plans. The distance to this point from the set-up level must be carefully measured and the stem blocked into position. Use a chalk line with a plumb-bob to accurately line up the stem. The stem should be securely anchored in position by diagonal bracing, or, if a breasthook is part of the assembly, it can be bolted to blocking that is fastened to the floor. The stem will have a tendency to spring out of position when the longitudinals are sprung around the framework. Be extremely careful and brace it adequately to prevent such movement.

Aligning the transom must also be done with care. If the keel is a straight line, as is the case with many small boats, the transom may be brought into position by the use of a straight-edge over the frames. This will give the up-and-down position. If the particular boat is an outboard and has a knee, this knee may be bolted to the keel to determine the proper angularity of the transom. Careful measurements should be made at both chine points, to assure equal spacing from the first frame forward to the transom. Without the knee, and with an arched keel, careful measurements will need to be taken from the set-up level, both for the height of the transom and also for the correct angularity. Often in such cases, the transom angularity and position are incorporated into the building form. After the transom has been carefully aligned, it should be securely fastened, either to the building form or to the frames, to prevent movement.

In securing the various frame members to the building form, remember that these members will have to be removed from the form later. Therefore, use temporary fastenings which can be readily removed. An exception to this is with boats where the set-up members form the motor stringers. These motor stringers will remain in the boat and therefore can be permanently fastened to the adjoining frame members. Types of blocking for such motor stringers are more fully described in Chapter 22.

CHAPTER 14 — KEELS

Webster defines a keel as the principle timber extending from the stem to the stern at the bottom of a boat, and supporting the whole frame network. Many naval architects prefer to call this member "keelson"; others, "keel batten", or "inner keel". For purposes of simplification, this text will refer to the inner member on the bottom of the boat at the centerline as the keel. The outer member will be referred to as the skeg, deadwood, or outer keel batten (see Plate 14).

The inherent stiffness of plywood panels used to plank a boat forces all of the stresses and strains to the junctions of the various panels. All "working", or the tendency to work, is concentrated at the weakest point of the structure. The bottom of a boat takes the beating, and since the two halves of the plywood bottom are usually joined over a single central member, keel failures of early plywood boats were quite common. Since the keel is the point of constant stress on a plywood boat, it should be made as large or larger than is ordinarily used for traditional planked-type wood boats. Another alternative is to build up the keel from laminations, or to laminate the inside of the keel with a layer of plywood. Such practice reduces or eliminates the tendency for splitting the keel. Keels made up from laminations of plywood can also be made, however, considerable care should be taken to assure a proper glue bond. Such a keel

is more difficult to fair than a solid wood keel due to the plywood layers. This type of keel does eliminate the expansion and contraction of a typical wood keel, but the moisture prevalent along the keel should be considered due to the exposed plywood edges. Such exposed edges should preferably be sealed, or at least treated with a wood preservative. Because expansion and contraction are eliminated, the possibility of cracking the outer fiberglass covering along the planking junction at the keel is greatly reduced if such covering is used.

Plate 14, "A", illustrates the bottom planking butt joint used on the keel of most plywood boats. This method is, by far, the simplest, and for most construction, it is not only satisfactory but recommended. One of the disadvantages of this method is that the planking must be flattened at the centerline for the skeg. Provided the skeg is rather wide, this may be difficult, particularly if the boat has a pronounced vee or dihedral. Plate 14, "B", depicts another common method for keel construction. This method utilizes a skeg fitted between the two plywood planking panels. One of the difficulties of this method is the fitting along the skeg to provide a good joint. Fitting the garboard strake on a conventionally planked boat, and fitting the large plywood panel on the plywood craft are quite different. Any long fitting of joints that must be accurately done is difficult with large

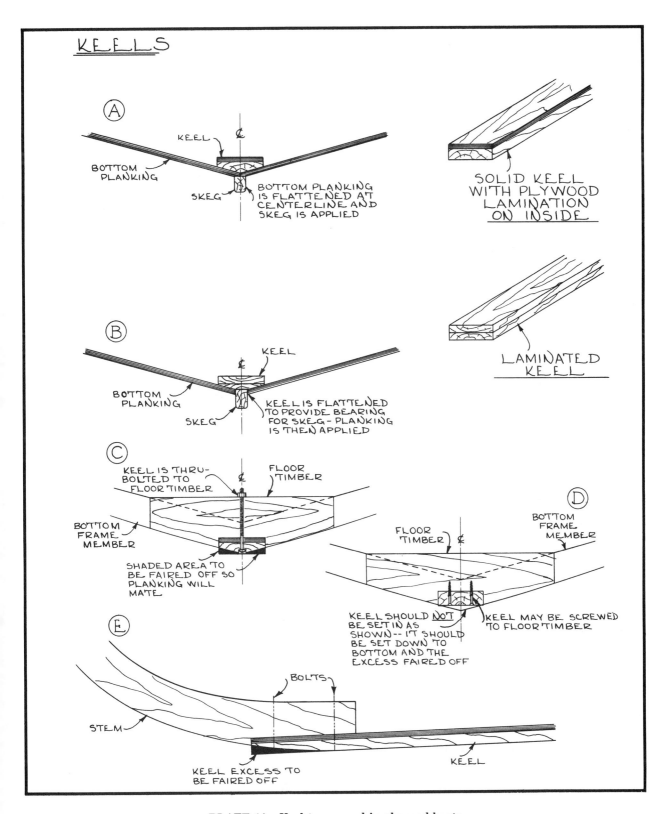

PLATE 14—Keel types used in plywood boats

plywood panels. The method illustrated in "A" eliminates this problem, as any voids are readily filled and capped by the outer skeg. On the other hand, the method shown in "B" is quite common and recommended by many architects, although covering with fiberglass is more difficult.

The keel is notched into the frames and screwed into position on most plywood craft. Plate 14 "C" and "D", illustrate the amount of notch required in the frame. Adequate material must be left on the keel to fair for the planking. If the keel is set in too far, material will not be available for the planking to mate. This type of construction is referring to the standard frame method, where notches are cut for the longitudinals, and they do not simply ride on the frames. Both of these construction methods are described in Chapter 10. In smaller boats, the keel is fastened to the frames by screws, while in the larger craft, bolts are used. The junction of the stem and the keel is preferably through-bolted. Plate 14, "E", represents a typical joint at the stem-keel junction. Note that, although the keel is notched into the stem the builder need not bend the keel to the shape of the stem. Although it is desirable, in many instances it is simply not possible to spring the keel to the contour of the stem, particularly when the keel is a heavy, stiff member. The excessive amount of keel is later removed by fairing.

The skeg, or outer keel when specified, will vary in size, depending upon the type of boat as well as the size of the craft. With the construction method shown in Plate 14, "A", it will be necessary to flatten the area along the keel to provide a flat mating for the skeg member. In small outboards, the skeg should never extend to the transom, but should end a minimum of 15" to 18" forward. With large outboard boats or those using inboards coupled to an outdrive, this distance should be increased to about 4' (see Plate 12-B, Chapter 12). This will eliminate the tendency for the skeg to cause cavitation when the boat is turned sharply. The aft end of the skeg should always be tapered to allow a smooth flow of water to the propeller. This holds true particularly when a large skeg is installed on an inboard craft.

For the installation of the skeg, screws or bolts are usually used. If the hull is not to be fiberglassed, bed the skeg in mastic. If the hull is to be fiberglassed, it is preferable to fiberglass the hull first, and then install the skeg. When the latter is done it is good practice to bed the skeg in a strip of fiberglass cloth or mat lying along the keel, well saturated with resin. Just before the resin has hardened, a razor blade or utility knife is used to trim off the excess along the junction of the skeg with the bottom of the boat. This provides a solid bearing and the fiberglass acts as a gasket to take up any slight irregularities in the bottom of the boat.

In arc-bottom plywood craft, it is quite common to use bilge stringers, bilge keels, or rolling chocks. These members are parallel to the keel and are located somewhere between the centerline of the boat and the chine, usually closer to the chine. Their purpose is to prevent rolling, and designers claim that they act as baffles in some instances to give additional lift to the bottom. Be that as it may, these longitudinal strips that usually extend along the aft two-thirds of the boat do have the

FIG. 14-1—Glue is used at the contact point between the frame and the keel. The keel this builder is installing is laminated with plywood on the inner surface to prevent splitting.

FIG. 14-2—The junction of the keel with the stem. The keel is narrowed or tapered at the end to be the same width as the stem. To prevent excessive bending at the tip of the stem, the keel is set slightly higher at its forward ending, to be faired off later to match the contour of the stem.

advantage of lessening the roll on an arc-bottom plywood hull underway, and they also offer protection on a smaller craft when it is beached or grounded.

Long members are often specified for the keel which may not be available. When this is the case, usually the laminated keel can be substituted, staggering the laps as far apart as practical, with at least 6' being a common recommendation. Or the keel can be made from two shorter members butt joined with a butt block. Such a butt block should be made from the same size stock with the joint occuring between frames and the butt block running the entire frame space length. Such a butt joint is preferably located where the keel will be a straight line. If not, then the butt block must be shaped to suit. Fastenings in the keel must never be located where the shaft hole will be bored on inboard boats, and should be spaced so as not to interfere with fairing later.

CHAPTER 15 — CHINE LOGS

The chine log, more often simply referred to as chine, is the backing member at the junction of the bottom and side planking. In plywood construction, the importance of the chine log cannot be over emphasized. The tendency towards racking and working is most often concentrated at the junction of bottom and side planking. Inferior materials, poor fitting, or undersized members cannot be tolerated at this critical point. Boats which are round bilged do not have a side bottom planking junction, and consequently will not have a chine log member.

The chine log can be bent around the frames to follow the contour of the side planking, or it can be angled to allow equal bearing for both the side and bottom planking. Typical examples of these joints are shown in Plate 15. The type of chine joint illustrated in "A", Plate 15, was initially construed to be the most practical for plywood construction. With the advent of superior plywood and with more plywood boats being subjected to rough usage, this was proven untrue. The fitting of the capping batten, or outer chine, was very difficult, to say the least, and since this member was generally made of some material other than plywood, it had a tendency to expand and contract considerably. The simpler method illustrated in Plate 15, "B", is most common in plywood construction today. With this type of chine, the plywood is either butted together or the bottom lapped over the side, depending upon the contour of the boat. As described in Chapter 19, both conditions are common in the average, vee bottom boat.

The chine log member shown in Plate 15, "A", is built up from laminations of plywood by many professional builders. Their claim is that such a chine is not subject to the expansion and contraction of standard lumber. This is true; however, the inherent difficulties of assuring a proper glue bond, the deterioration of the exposed edges of the laminations, and the difficulty in fairing, all make this type of chine more difficult to install than one of solid lumber. For practical application, as the simplest and the most advantageous to use, the average builder will find the solid-lumber type of chine most suitable and easiest to build.

The frames of the boat are often pre-notched for the chine log. In other instances, the frames are notched while on the building form. Two schools of thought prevail, and the better method is merely a matter of opinion. Probably, most builders will prefer to pre-notch the frames even though the bevel will have to be filed in the frame to allow the chine to mate solidly.

The chine log is a curving member that intersects each frame at a varying or different angle. In lofting, the angles for these junctions could be picked up and incorporated in the frame chine

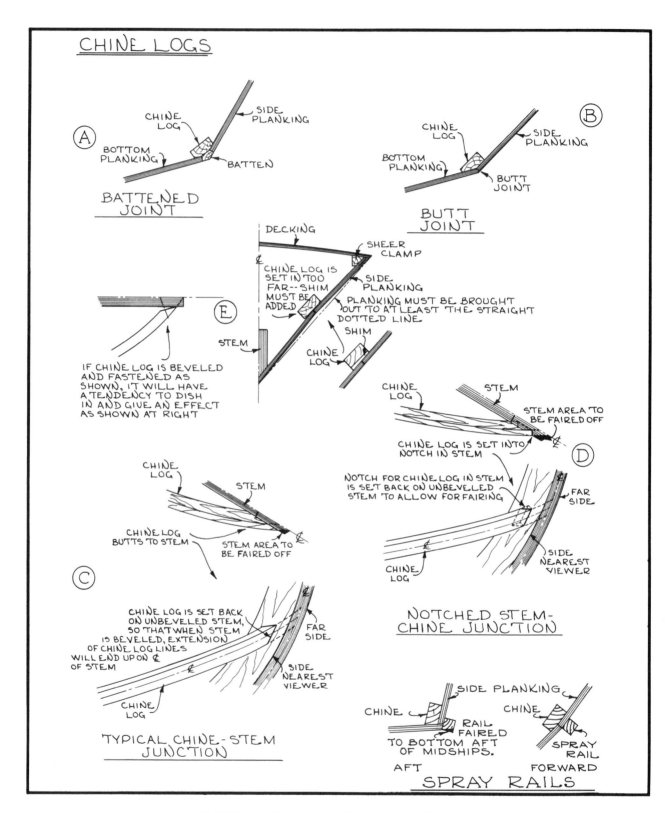

PLATE 15—Chine log configurations and junctions

notch before mounting on the building form. In plywood boats it is usually simplest to hand-cut the bevels on the building form. The chine log member should be carefully selected as to grain, and should be a foot or more longer than required to provide cut-and-fit material that is needed at the stem junction.

If full length chine logs are not available, two shorter members can be used with a butt joint located between frames. Back the joint with a butt block of the same size material, locating the joint preferably in the aft hull areas or where the lines will be fairly straight so that shaping will not be required, or will only be minimal. The butt block should be as long as the frame space, and be fastened with at least four bolts per joining member, or at least eight good size screws per joining member.

Scarf joints are also practical when epoxy adhesives, with their gap filling properties, are used. Such joints have ratios from 1:8 to 1:12; the longer being preferable. Methods of scarf joining plywood, as described in Chapter 19, will work well for solid stock as well. Care must be taken to insure a good fit and the glued junction held at the proper duration and temperature for maximum strength. Other longitudinals, such as sheers, battens, etc. may also be joined by either of the methods described.

The chine log is sprung around the frame work, and the angle required at each frame to allow the chine log to mate properly is marked. This is illustrated in Fig. 15-1. In the aft frame notches, very little will need to be removed in most plywood boats, but considerable bevel will be required up forward. The notch for the chine should be such that the outer surface of the chine

log parallels or follows the contour of the side frame member. On the bottom, sufficient material should project to fair off. Fairing of the chine is described in Chapter 18. Fig. 15-2 shows the builder cutting the notch to the required bevel with a back-saw. This is done at each of the frames. A wood rasp is used where the portion to be removed is minor.

The fitting of the chine log at the stem requires some thought. This applies particularly when the stem is not pre-beveled. Consider this carefully: The extension of the line of the chine must end up at the center of the stem. The fixture shown on Fig. 15-5 may be used to properly locate the set-back of the chine at the stem. Another alternative would be to bevel the stem at the approximate point of junction with the chine. This particular photo shows a chine blocking, which may be helpful if details are furnished in the particular plans. In some cases, the chine is notched into the stem, as shown in Plate 15, "D". This is good practice, particularly with the solid-wood-type stem. The simple joint illustrated in Plate 15, "C", although not considered good practice on planked hulls, has proven quite satisfactory on plywood hulls. With this joint, the chine log sides to the stem in a long taper.

In fitting the chine log to the stem, spring the member about the frames, and be certain that it is an even sweep, ending at the stem. In many cases, the position of the chine logs on the stem can be varied up or down along the stem for a considerable distance. Unless chine blocking has been installed, the ending point on the stem is not critical as long as the chine forms a fair curve. Do not attempt to force the chine logs into a curve that they will not naturally

FIG. 15-1—The chine log is clamped at the transom and roughly sprung around the framework. The chine log is used as a guide to mark the notch or the angle required at the frame. The chine log must mate firmly to each frame, and not bear just on one edge.

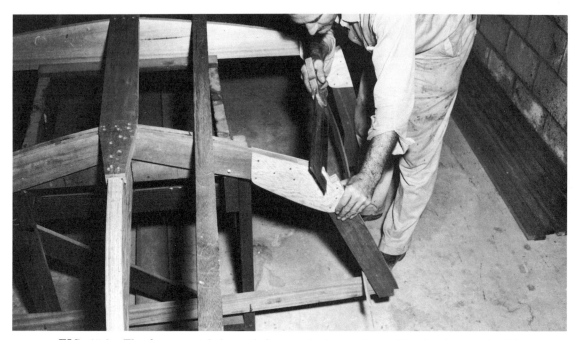

FIG. 15-2—The frame notch is angled properly by sawing with a back saw. In this particular instance, the frames were pre-notched before assembling to the building form. The angle could have been picked up from full size loftings, but it is generally considered easier to take it from the work as shown.

FIG. 15-3—Note the appearance of the chine log at the forward frame. Adequate material has been left on both the side frame member and the bottom frame member to bevel for the planking.

FIG. 15-4—In fitting the angularity of the chine log as it junctions with the stem, the chine log is sprung around the hull framework. It should be allowed to extend past the transom to enable several cuts to be made on the stem angle. Here the builder uses a saw against the side of the stem as a guide to the required angularity of the chine log.

FIG. 15-5—The chine log at the stem must meet at the proper position to assure that, when beveled, the stem vee and chine log will be a smooth, flowing, and continuous surface. The checking block shown in the photo will simplify the determination of this point. It may be necessary to shift the chine log slightly in or out to obtain the point where a continuation of the line of the chine will end on the center of the stem.

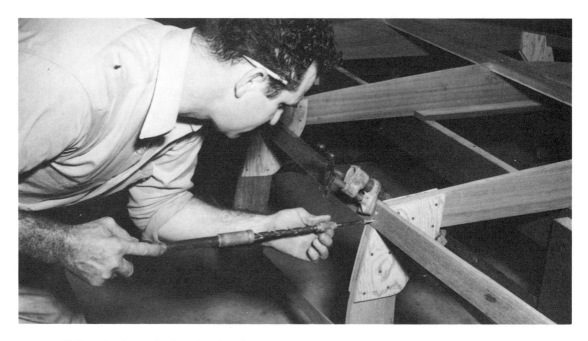

FIG. 15-6—In anchoring the chine log to the frames, it is advisable to use a pipe clamp to pull the chine log firmly into the notch while driving the screws.

assume. The chine may need to be twisted as well as bent around the hull, particularly toward the stem. To do this, you need a large "C-clamp" or, even better, a long pipe bar clamp. Attached firmly to the chine, the clamp can be used as a handle to make the bending and twisting easier, by using leverage instead of muscle.

Allow the chine to extend past the transom. Using the stem as a guide, saw a bevel on the chine log, as shown in Figure 15-4. Re-spring the member into position. You will probably have to do some hand-filing to obtain a good joint. Take care in trying to make the pieces fit. Do not cut the bevel in such a manner as to dish the chine (unless the plans call for such a configuration). See Figure E, Plate 15 for an illustration. On the other hand, try to avoid cutting the bevel too much the opposite way. This can severely bow the chine, although in most instances it will not do any significant harm.

Check to be sure that the chine is twisted and bent in such a manner as to provide adequate material on which to fasten the side planking, preferably without fairing. First, mock up or simulate the sheer clamp position. Then use the method shown on Page 158, Fig. 18-10, to assure that the side planking will mate flat to the chine. If the chine doesn't provide a solid footing for the planking, perhaps more twist in the chine is required.

Twisting the chine will vary the point where it joins the stem. If the boat is being built upside down, twisting the lower section of the chine outward will force the chine toward the hull deckside. Likewise, twisting inward (which is seldom required) will do the opposite. Use the bar clamp, as described above,

for better twisting leverage.

If the space between the stem and first frame is excessive, the chine twist may flatten out the natural arc or curve. Use a wedge spreader between the chines to force either the lower edge (assuming the boat is upside down) or the entire member outward. A temporary partial frame may even be in order. Just be sure the chine will provide a flat surface for the side planking from the stem to the first frame.

Regardless of the foregoing instructions, some builders may position the chine incorrectly. In some rare instances, the boat design itself may make adequate twisting and bending impractical. This condition is readily corrected by gluing a shim on the chine, such as shown on Plate 15, Detail E. Make the shim the same width as the chine, and of the thickness required to eliminate the problem. Also make it long enough to extend from the stem to about the first frame. Then glue it in place using clamps or temporary fasteners until the glue sets.

A shim must be tapered with care to blend smoothly into the chine fore and aft, so that a bump or dip does not occur. It must also be bevelled or faired to receive both the bottom and side planking (as described in Chapter 18 — Fairing). When planking is applied, remember to use longer fasteners than would ordinarily be required. This will ensure that fastener will go through the shim and anchor solidly in the wood of the chine.

Bear in mind that it is possible to avoid having to use a shim. Be sure to check (and correct) the alignment of the chine, as described, BEFORE the chine is finally fastened.

From broken chines, the amateur

FIG. 15-7—Springing in both chine log members at the same time will eliminate excessive strain on one side or another of the hull. Note that the keel is in position to prevent the frames from being sprung out of position. Bracing each frame to the building form is a necessity to prevent distorting the framework.

FIG. 15-8—To eliminate the tendency of the chine log members to spring the stem out of alignment, braces are used to the building form. In this instance the construction is utilizing chine blocking and the braces extend directly from this member to the building form base member.

boat builder usually furnishes a considerable amount of scrap lumber to fireplaces. To prevent this problem, several methods are worth noting. If the bend is particularly severe, the member should be steamed. In other instances, boiling water poured over the point of greatest stress will suffice. Fastening the chine log to the frame at the point of greatest stress most often causes the fracture, which usually takes place in the forward part of the boat where the bend is severe. You cannot drive several large screws into the typical small boat chine log without weakening it. The average amateur builder breaks the chine on this forward area by excessive drilling and counter-sinking for the screws. In practice, it is much simpler to eliminate the screw at the point where the bend is excessive. A clamp can be used to hold the chine into the frame notch until the glue dries. A finishing nail can be driven in as an alternative. After the planking has been applied, drive a long, single screw through the planking and chine to the frame. This eliminates the tendency to create the weak point, and has been proven successful many times when the chine log is rather stiff.

In larger plywood boats, the chine log is often bolted into position. On smaller boats, screws are most often used. At the stem, the same holds true. One or two screws driven angularly into the stem will hold the chine securely in position for all but the largest of boats.

In installing the chine, start by having a helper hold the member obliquely out from the side of the boat, and drive a screw or bolt into the stem. Spring the chine around the framework until its angular position in profile is determined by hitting a frame. When this has been done, drive another screw through the chine into the stem. If the stem has a tendency to distort or be pulled from its alignment when the chine is sprung about the frames, both chines may be sprung in at the same time, as illustrated in Fig. 15-7. This is excellent practice, as it equalizes the stresses on the framework. After springing in the chine log, preferably clamp it to a frame at the approximate center of the boat. Using a clamp adjacent to the fastening area will provide a perfect positive bond of the chine log to the frame, as illustrated in Fig. 15-6. Progressively put in the screws through the frames, taking into consideration the bend and the possible elimination of screws at the frame of greatest stress, usually very near the bow, as previously described. Trim the chine to fit into the transom last to be sure you don't cut the member short. Use a hard setting glue at all chine joints.

FIG. 15-6—Chines on flat bottom boats, with considerable flare at the bow, will require twisting the chine tending to force it down toward the sheer. Decreasing the twist and fairing the chine so the side planking mates solidly will help solve the problem. Note that the keel has been tapered to create a landing area for the chine as it sides to the stem.

139

Outer chines, spray deflectors or spray rails are often advantageous on plywood craft. These longitudinal members parallel the chine log and are installed after planking. One of their functions is to protect and seal the exposed edge of the plywood bottom planking. Their most important function, however, is to knock down spray. Due to the convex curve in the bottom of the plywood boat, water or spray tends to rise vertically, with a swirl that may put it on the deck or in the face of the passengers. A spray rail will help to keep the spray where it belongs, under the boat. Some deflectors run from the stem to the transom. Actually for spray protection, they need run only from the stem to midships. When run completely to the transom, that portion aft of amidships should follow the contour of the bottom. In the forward section the rails should have a crisp lower edge to better deflect spray. Such rails should be screw fastened or bolted securely in place. They are usually considered expendable and are applied after planking and fiberglassing if such covering is to be used. They may be bedded in mastic or fiberglass and resin similar to the skeg previously described. However, bedding in resin would make future replacement more difficult.

FIG. 15-9—The final position of the chine logs against the unbeveled stem is actually somewhat back from the stem edge. Once the stem has been faired, however, the beveled edge of the stem and the chine log surfaces will come into alignment so that the planking will mate flat to both the chine logs and stem.

CHAPTER 16 — SHEER CLAMPS & HARPINS

The sheer clamp, more commonly called sheer, is the backing member at the junction of the side planking and decking. In conventional planking procedure, the clamp is the inner member supporting the deck beam, fastened to the inside of the frames. The sheer backing member was usually the size of or very little larger than one of the battens used on the planking seams. With plywood sheet planking, however, all of the concentrated stresses are at the fastening points, thus requiring this member to be heavier than would be required on a conventionally planked boat.

The harpin is the inner backing member often used in place of the sheer clamp and is also used at the junction of the side planking with the decking. Harpins are sawn to shape and laid flat, whereas the sheer is bent or sprung to shape. In some instances, a combination of both may be used. When this is done, the harpin is commonly used up forward in the more severely arced section of the sheer or deck line where bending a sheer clamp would not be possible or practical.

SHEER CLAMPS

Several types of sheer clamp members are used. Where the bends are gentle, a relatively small sheer clamp that follows the contour of the side planking can be used. If the boat has considerable flare up forward and the sheer is a straight line or hogged (meaning bowed or arced upward slightly as viewed in profile—see Plate 16-A), you are simply not going to bend much of a member around the sheer line. Such a sheer line requires not only a bend around the hull, but also twisting as it is forced into position. If the member is of any size, such a two-way bend will provide more wood for the fireplace. If too lightweight a member is used, the sheer will take on a variety of humps and bumps at the point of the bend. Most architects take the type of sheer into consideration in the design. The one-piece sheer clamp is best, as heavy as possible, as long as it will make the bend. With the conventional-type sheer, it is usually possible to bend a single member with less difficulty, as this is the shape the lumber wants to follow. If it is impossible or impractical to spring the sheer clamp into position, use the method described in the following paragraph.

In an effort to flare and contour the bow in plywood boats, attempting to force the sheer member into position became a headache. To overcome this problem, the laminated sheer was developed. This sheer is built up from two or more laminations of material. The sheer laminations from midships forward are set in vertically. This eliminates the distortion of the sheer clamps,

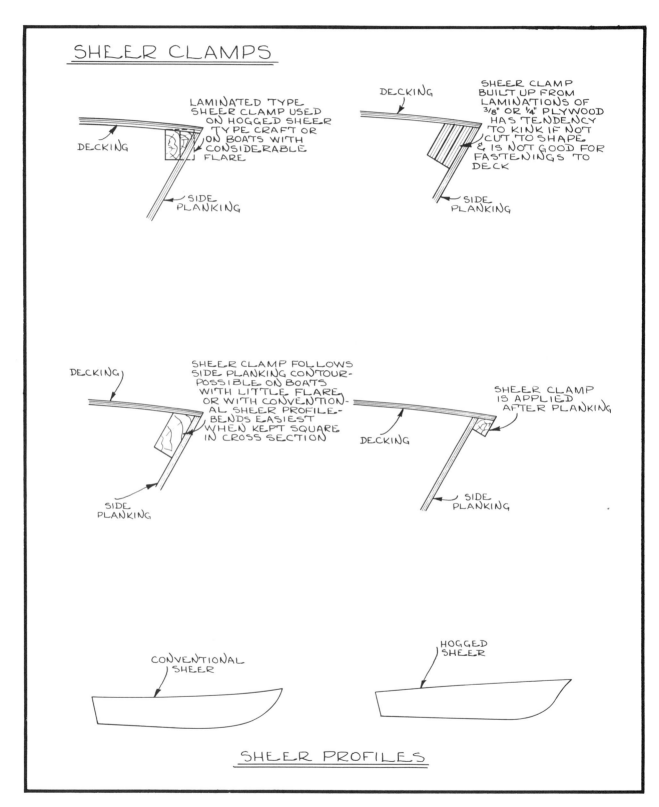

SHEER CLAMPS

LAMINATED TYPE SHEER CLAMP USED ON HOGGED SHEER TYPE CRAFT OR ON BOATS WITH CONSIDERABLE FLARE

DECKING

SIDE PLANKING

DECKING

SHEER CLAMP BUILT UP FROM LAMINATIONS OF 3/8" OR 1/4" PLYWOOD HAS TENDENCY TO KINK IF NOT CUT TO SHAPE & IS NOT GOOD FOR FASTENINGS TO DECK

SIDE PLANKING

DECKING

SHEER CLAMP FOLLOWS SIDE PLANKING CONTOUR- POSSIBLE ON BOATS WITH LITTLE FLARE OR WITH CONVENTION- AL SHEER PROFILE- BENDS EASIEST WHEN KEPT SQUARE IN CROSS SECTION

SIDE PLANKING

DECKING

SHEER CLAMP IS APPLIED AFTER PLANKING

SIDE PLANKING

CONVENTIONAL SHEER

HOGGED SHEER

SHEER PROFILES

**PLATE 16-A—Typical sheer config-
urations and sheer clamp details**

FIG. 16-1—The notches in the frames must be angled similarly to those of the chine. In the example shown, the builder is cutting the bevel for a laminated-type sheer clamp that will be set in vertically.

FIG. 16-2—After beveling all of the frames, the sheer clamp is beveled at the junction as it will meet the stem. The first lamination is fastened to the breasthook after coating all areas thoroughly with glue.

FIG. 16-3—The first lamination is sprung around the hull and fastened into position with annular thread nails or serews.

FIG. 16-4—The second lamination is applied over the first layer of the sheer clamp. Glue is used liberally between laminations. To hold them while the glue is setting, either clamps or annular ring nails driven from the inside of the laminations out should be used. Screws are driven through both laminations into frame junctions.

and makes the bend easier, although it does make for excessive fairing, particularly up forward. Laminated sheers overcome the bending problem, and a steam box is not required. It is felt that the over-all task is much simpler than attempting to spring in difficult members that will often fracture. One disadvantage of this method is that in installation of the decking, the fastenings may be driven down parallel to the laminations. With screws or fastenings well staggered, however, there is little possibility of fracturing or splitting the laminations, and good holding power will result.

In some instances, sheer clamps have been made from plywood laminations. These are cut to shape from scrap planking materials, usually ¼″ or ⅜″ in the smaller boats, and built up into a series of laminations to a thickness of 1″ or more. The disadvantage of this method is found in fastening the deck into the

FIG. 16-5—This photo shows the inner third sheer clamp lamination often added to a laminated sheer clamp to provide extra material after fairing. Note that the lamination runs between the breasthook and the forward frame.

end laminations of the plywood and obtaining a solid glue bond. With such a method it is difficult to obtain smooth, fair lines as the thin laminations tend to distort from shape. Usually, such sheer clamps will need to be sawn to shape, and not just installed in strips to form the desired shape. Because of the difficulties in fairing, fastening, and gluing, the built-up plywood member is not recommended.

In smaller craft, the planking is often applied without a sheer clamp in position. The sheer clamp member is later sprung around the outside of the plywood planking panel. Such a sheer junction is illustrated in Plate 16-A. If the sheer bend is not too tough, this method can be used. If the sheer is hogged and the hull has good flare, it may be very difficult to spring into shape unless such a member is very light or hand-fitted. Another disadvantage will occur in the planking operation; without some method to clamp the plywood side planking at the sheer line, the plywood application may be rather difficult.

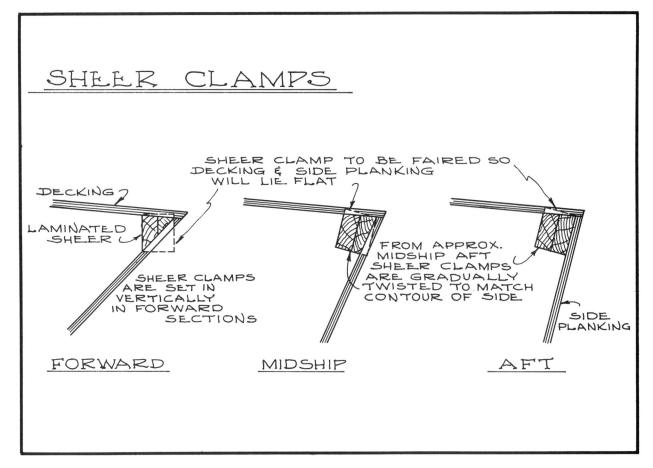

PLATE 16-C—The laminated sheer clamp set in vertically can be "twisted" in the aft areas of the hull to have the member conform to the side frame contours. This "twisting" reduces the amount of fairing required in the aft areas, and will vary the notches somewhat at each frame where the "twisting" begins.

If a solid one piece member is used, installing the sheer clamp is done in much the same way as the chine logs. Each of the frames must be notched, or the notches if pre-cut, must be beveled to enable the sheer clamp to mate flat at all contact points. This procedure is illustrated in Fig. 16-1. As with the chine log, the frame notches in the forward areas will require considerable bevel, while the aft section in most boats will require little beveling. The sheer clamp must not be set into the frame notches too deeply in order to provide adequate material for fairing. Cut the ends of the sheer clamps so they side to the stem in the same way that the chine logs join, leaving the members long at the transom for final fitting. Spring the sheer clamp around the frames, fastening at each junction progressively towards the transom.

As with most longitudinal members, where a single long length piece is not available, two shorter members can be butt joined in the straighter areas of the hull, backing the joint with a butt block of equal size material. Alternately, a laminated sheer clamp can be used, staggering the joints between laminations about 6' apart. Optionally a scarf joined member can be used, however, this is usually more work.

With laminated sheer clamps, the laminations are installed progressively, one at a time. The notches are beveled and the laminations are fitted in the same manner. The first lamination is fastened at each contact point with only enough fastenings as required to hold the member in position. Then the second lamination is installed after this, using as many clamps as possible to hold the members together. If plenty of clamps are not available, nails can be used to bond the laminations, driving them from the inside. Take care to drive the nails near the deck side of the member and to use nails which won't be so long that they will interfere with fairing for the side planking. These nails should be spaced about 6″ apart. Screws can be substituted for nails in most cases, and would be utilized in a similar manner. After laminating, fasten with screws through the laminated member at all junctions with the frames, stem, and transom. Use several screws into the breasthook as well, which are previously described in Chapter 11.

In the case of the laminated sheer clamp installed vertically around the boat, it is common that sufficient material will not remain after fairing for the side planking. With an acute flare to the side planking, so much material may be faired off, especially in the forward areas, that only a triangular shaped portion of the sheer clamp member will remain, thereby not allowing sufficient material to receive the planking and decking fastenings later. When this occurs, a third inner lamination must be added to the sheer clamp on the inside of the member before fairing, and cut to fit between frames. This lamination is installed similarly to the other laminations, but does not have to be installed in the frame or breasthook notches. In short, it is simply a double member between frames to provide adequate material along the sheer clamp after fairing, and should be the same size material as that used for the sheer clamp laminations.

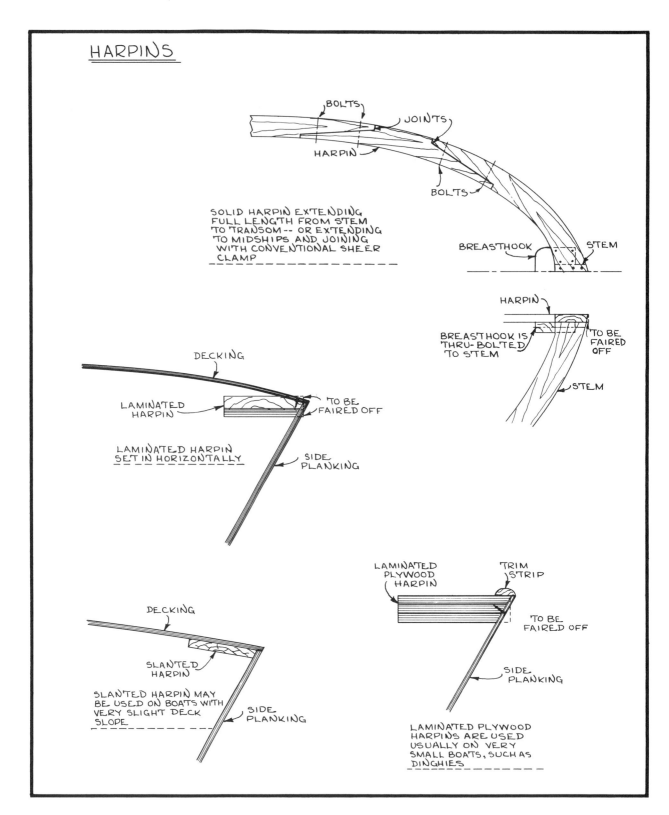

PLATE 16-B—Typical harpin configurations and details

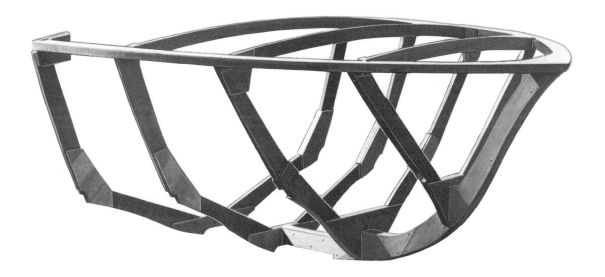

FIG. 16-6—A harpin assembled with the stem and forward frames for an inboard cruiser.

FIG. 16-7—A harpin being installed in a smaller craft. This partial harpin is set in without twisting and is being fitted to butt against a frame. A notch is provided for the sheer clamp that will, in turn, bolt to the harpin and extend aft to the transom.

HARPINS

The conventional construction method for harpins is to cut the member from solid lumber with joints as illustrated in Plate 16-B. Such harpins may be sawn to width to a nominal dimension, providing excessive cross-grain is avoided. The standard method of construction calls for bolting the joining members together using long scarf joints.

Another method of harpin construction takes advantage of plywood. Plywood is used as a bottom layer, and solid lumber is laminated to this to form the harpin. Usually, the plywood is ⅜" to ¾" thick, laminated with 1" nominal stock. The plywood is furnishing the longitudinal strength, and the planking skin is fastened to the solid material. By using this method, sawing the harpin to uniform width without excessive cross-grain is practical since the plywood lamination ties the solid members together. In very small craft, plywood may be used for the entire harpin. Such usage is confined to dinghies or similar boats, as the plywood will not hold fastenings well in the end of side-grain areas (see Fig. 16-8).

When installing the harpin, a breasthook is used at the bow to couple the two halves to the stem. Such a breasthook may be of solid wood bolted to the stem, or a plywood web, depending on the design. At the landings on the frames, either screwed or bolted junctions are used. Care must be taken to allow material to fair for both the deck and side planking. On most small boats, the faired area for the decking should be at least 1", and preferably more as illustrated by Plate 16-B. The harpin is almost always set in flat or horizontally.

Attempting to curve the contour to follow the crown of the deck will generally distort the shape of the harpin, although it is possible to twist the harpin slightly if the crown is very minor.

Fabrication of the harpin is preferably done directly over the loftings of the boat, or from full size patterns if available. The minimum bevel for the side planking can be pre-cut at the time of assembly to eliminate much of the fairing that will later be required. Fig. 16-6 and 16-7 show typical harpins with a plywood lamination. Note in Fig. 16-7 the notch for the sheer clamp that will be used in the aft section of the boat. The forward portion, or the most severe bend, is a harpin, while the aft portion is the conventional sheer clamp member. Bolts or screws fasten the sheer clamp to the harpin, depending on the size of the boat.

FIG. 16-8—The young lady is watching Dad assemble a full plywood harpin on a small dinghy. In this particular instance the boat is only 8' long so the entire harpin is sawn from a sheet of ¾" plywood with built-in corner knees and reinforced bow area.

150

CHAPTER 17 — BATTENS

Battens are longitudinal stiffeners along the bottom or sides of a boat. The battens on the bottom are not installed until after the side planking, however, as it is much easier to wipe up any excess glue if the battens are not in the way, as well as for ease of fitting and installing the side planking. These members are extremely important as they provide the necessary stiffness for the plywood planking as well as longitudinal strength required for the hull. The battens rest on top of the frames (in the "floating frame" type of construction), or notch into the frames depending on the type of construction. Battens should be made from stock that is as robust as can be made to conform to the hull contours. The battens begin at the transom and extend as far forward as possible. However, a batten should never end on a frame, as this will set up a localized stress that will often begin to break or crack the planking skin at this point. Instead, the battens should always end just short of a frame.

The statement to extend battens as far forward as possible is often confusing. If at all possible, the battens should extend completely forward, and join to the stem or the chine. In boats with a generous amount of vee up forward, this is often not possible. The battens must match the curvature of the plywood planking, and often the attempt to conform the batten to the shape, and also to end it on the stem or chine, are simply not compatible. There are several methods to enable the battens to extend farther forward or completely to their ending point, junctioning against the chine or stem. One of these is to slim down the batten in the forward portion, decreasing it in either width or thickness, to more readily conform to the required contour. Kerfing the ends of the battens is often resorted to. This means splitting the batten in its horizontal plane back far enough past the severe bend to make the batten bend easier. Although this does weaken the batten, it can, if properly done, be relatively strong and is surely better than ending the batten too short.

When battens are kerfed, it is best not to fasten them to the forward frames if they do not end on the chine or stem. This statement may also apply to some battens which may not be kerfed. Let them "run wild" instead as far as they will practically conform to the hull shape without unfair lines being formed later. During the planking operation, the ends of the battens can be fitted with screw eyes and wires can be used to pull the battens down to the building form so as not to make contact with the plywood planking. After the planking is installed, the slit area of the kerfed batten, as well as the contact area with the planking, can be coated with glue. Then the wires to the screw eyes are released and the battens are allowed to conform to the inside surface of the planking.

Fastenings can be driven through the planking and into the battens afterwards. Machine screws are recommended to force the plywood planking and the batten contour together. An example of the kerfed batten is shown by Plate 17.

The use of plywood for battens is relatively limited. The strength of longitudinal strips of plywood is not comparable to similar-sized pieces of solid lumber. Plywood battens do have the advantage of overcoming the tendency to split, and such plywood battens are used in very small plywood boats. In some instances, plywood battens are built up from a series of laminations to a thickness that would be too great to spring around the hull form. With good gluing practices, such a method is entirely feasible. Care must be taken with thin laminations of

this type to prevent distortions of the running surfaces of the boat. Plywood laminations are often glued on solid lumber to be used for battens to eliminate splitting, particularly in the higher-speed type of boat.

At the transom, good practice calls for the battens to be tightly notched into the transom frame, especially if a double laminated transom bottom frame is not used. With a doubled bottom frame, in some cases the corners of the notches are rounded rather than tightly notched. This is considered practical to achieve faster and simpler construction when the frames and notches are cut on a shaper or router. When an outer transom bottom frame member is used to receive the planking fastenings and the inner member is used for the batten fastenings, the inner member may not

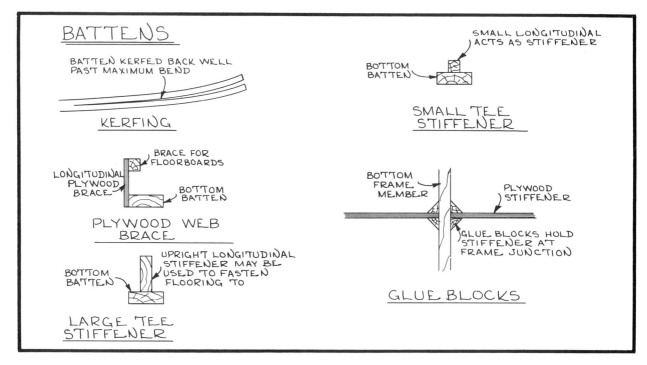

PLATE 17—Various batten and hull stiffening configurations

FIG. 17-1—The battens in the bottom of a hull may be applied before the side planking. It is preferable, however, to install the battens after all fairing has been accomplished, and the side panels have been applied. It is more convenient to clean off the glue on the inside with these battens omitted, and by carefully notching the frames to the exact depth of the batten, little additional fairing should be required. Obviously, the foregoing applies to frames that are notched for battens.

FIG. 17-2—Notches called "limbers" should be cut in the frames alongside all the longitudinals on the outboard side to allow bilge water to drain aft. A notch is made on the battens near the transom to allow all bilge water to drain to the center or lowest portion. With a drain plug at this point, it will be relatively simple to wash out or clean out the bilges of the hull on a trailerable type boat.

require any notches as previously noted in Chapter 12, since it serves more as a blocking member only.

In the trailer-type boat, notching or grooving the battens crosswise near the transom to allow the bilge water to run to the center along the keel aft is excellent practice. These notches or grooves (which are actually limbers or drain holes) are shown in Fig. 17-2. These together with limbers on the outboard side of all bottom longitudinals, or with "floating" frames, makes washing down the boat after use much easier. Mopping up excess water between the battens is eliminated because the water all drains to a common point. A drain plug installed through the transom on each side of the keel eliminates any water standing in the boat during storage. Note, however, that notches or grooves across the battens should not exceed about half the batten thickness, and backing blocks as thick as the notches are high, should be scabbed onto the battens for reinforcement.

The location of the longitudinal battens is usually specified by the designer, although an excess of battens rather than too few is preferable. The bottom rigidity is increased considerably, and stresses are widely distributed by these longitudinal members. Some consideration should always be given to the batten position. It is often possible to use them as cabinet junction points or for attaching plywood seat braces, motor well sides, or similar structural interior members of the boat. Since the points of major stress in the sheet plywood boat are at the chine and keel joint, it is good practice to have the battens adjacent to these members closer than usual. This will tend to distribute the stresses of the screws in the chine and the keel member to the adjacent batten.

Bottom battens are most often bent flat-wise to make the bends previously described. To increase the longitudinal rigidity several methods can be used. Plywood webs may extend between the frames from the side of the batten to the height of the frame. With a continuous floor batten running full-length, the web structure will offer exceptional longitudinal strength. In other instances, thicker solid lumber, usually 1″ thick, is contoured to lay on top the bat-

FIG. 17-3—The battens on this cruiser extend completely to the stem whenever possible. The are either junctioned at the stem by a simple long bevel or fitted into notches in the side of the stem. More battens can be made to end on the stem if the battens are spaced so as to be closer to the keel in the forward area than at the transom. In other words, the battens fan out with the apex of the fan being at the stem.

ten. At the junctions of these webs with the frames, corner blocks are used for additional rigidity, as shown in Plate 17. This method is especially advantageous in racing monoplanes to hold the bottom running surfaces true and straight. A"T" batten section can be used, built up from solid lumber, to strengthen the battens between frames. If these are notched into the frame, they have a tendency to cause the frames to split. If run between frames on top of a batten, the rigidity is not as great as the previously described methods. A typical example of a "T" batten is shown in Plate 17.

Battens on the side of a plywood boat are used when the side planking is thin, or the frame spacing quite great. In most small craft, battens are not re-

quired on the sides. When outer bumper rails are used, these will often suffice, and actually be stronger than battens notched into frames. In cruisers, the interior cabin structure may fasten to the sides of the hull with longitudinal strips called "cleats". These also will serve to impart rigidity to the side of the hulls. It is also possible to construct the frames so that the battens will ride on the outer surface, and not be notched into the frames. Such a method is entirely practical, although not too common in the smaller craft. In the case where the side battens are used, it is well to take into consideration the eventual use of these battens for such purposes as fastening seats, interior cabinets, cabin soles, cockpit soles, etc.

FIG. 17-4—In this outboard runabout, a plywood upright is used alongside the batten connecting to the side of a longitudinal running on the inside of the frames. This not only reinforces the batten, but provides a rigid support for the floorboard junctions.

CHAPTER 18 — FAIRING

Fairing is the "bugaboo" of the amateur boat builder. It is tedious, confusing, misunderstood, and a lot of work. If the more timid readers have been frightened by that prologue, they have good reason to be—fairing is all that has been stated. It is, conversely, very simple when understood. The photographs and the following text should clarify the problem in the builder's mind. In fairing, as in most phases of boat building, the solution is simply a matter of proceeding step-by-step. A careful job in fairing is important. Proper solid contact of the planking to the hull structure is necessary to achieve a strong boat. Fairing also affects the appearance of the boat, giving sweet, smooth lines, or lines with humps and dips which will prove to be an eyesore and possibly affect the value of the boat. Finally, fairing is an aid to the performance of the boat in many cases. So take care in the job, standing back and sighting along the hull lines frequently to assure that the boat will be a credit to your ability.

The term fairing means beveling, shaping and trimming the framework members, such as stem, keels, sheers, chines, and frames, so that the planking skin will lie flat or mate to all members. In the flat-bottom boat or one with very little vee up forward, the fairing problem is minor. The vee-bottom plywood craft involves more work and thought on the part of the builder. On the average vee-bottom power boat, very little if any, fairing will be required on the bottom frames in the aft section. Boats with a great deal of flare and with harpins or laminated sheers will require a great deal of material to be removed from the frames and longitudinals to enable the planking panels to contact properly.

The tools required in fairing vary considerably with the preference of the builder. Each person seems to have a pet tool that he thinks is best. If you have available a variety of tools, try them all and find out what suits you. Usually in the hand tool range, a long smooth plane is the best in fairing long, flat sweeps. A block plane is used on the short sections, as well as heavy wood rasps and files. In the hand/power tool group, the power plane will make short work of fairing the long sweeps. On the frames or battens, particularly in the flatter areas, some builders use a router running on a fixture. A heavy disc sander, properly used, is excellent to remove excess material. This tool, in the hands of an expert operator, can be used for almost all of the fairing. For those inexperienced with this tool, the tendency to dig in and remove too much material is common.

If the frames are to make contact with the bottom and side planking, it is easier and simpler to fair the frames before the battens are installed. First of all, the notching will be done from the faired surface of the frames. A hand-power saw set to the exact depth of the batten material will make short work of the notching. If the battens are installed before fairing the frames, it may be necessary to remove material from the battens instead. Some minor fairing will be required on the battens, mostly up forward. Such fairing will be inconsequential if care has been taken in the frame fairing. If the "floating" frame type of construction is used, however, the above process does not hold true.

In any areas that are to be flat or straight fore and aft along the longitudinal lines of the boat, a straight-edge should be used in checking the battens. This portion of the fairing is very important particularly on high speed power boats. The hull lines when viewed in profile on such a craft should be straight lines free of humps (called "rockers") or dips (called "hooks"). If a hook or rocker is built into the bottom of the boat, espe-

cially in the after ⅓ portion to the transom, the high-speed performance could be disappointing as well as dangerous. Not only should the fairing be done carefully in this area, but the builder should check the building form to make sure it is rigid, and when removing the hull from the building form, he should make sure that the boat will not distort or "rack" and thereby affect these running lines.

Fairing is started at the stern of the boat along the keel or chine. The chine will be used as an example. At each of the frames, a notch should be filed in the chine with a wood rasp following the contour of the bottom. If the chine has been set in properly, very little, if any, fairing will be required along the side area on the chine (this may vary with the type of chine used; see Chapter 15). After filing these notches in the chine,

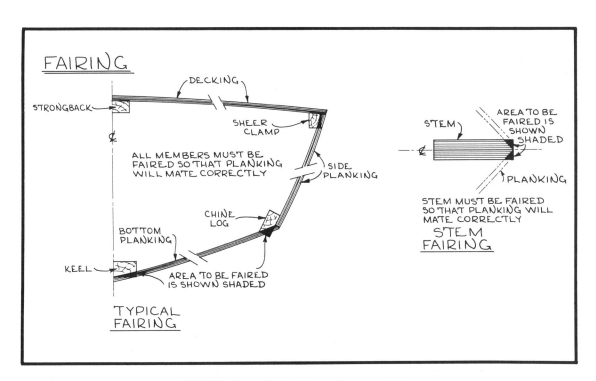

PLATE 18-A—Typical members requiring fairing or beveling on a plywood boat

157

FIG. 18-2—This is the same area as depicted in the photograph at left after fairing. The planking skin will now mate firmly to all points and not rest just on corners.

FIG. 18-4—After fairing, the plywood panel will mate flat to the keel and chine log.

FIG. 18-1—The builder is illustrating the fact that the planking skin will not lie flat to all members. It will be necessary to fair or bevel both the chine log and the keel members to enable the planking skin to mate flat.

FIG. 18-3—In the forward portion of the hull, it is best to use a short length of plywood to check the fairing as shown. The planking skin will not mate securely so it will be necessary to fair both the keel and the chine log.

FIG. 18-6—The longitudinal member, in this case the chine log, is faired between these notches so that a clean, fair sweep will result.

FIG. 18-8—In many small inboard and outboard runabouts, the longitudinal lines in the aft portion of the boat are straight lines. When this is the case, great care must be taken to use a straight edge, checking over a group of frames at one time to insure the accuracy of the lines.

FIG. 18-5—To determine the amount of bevel required on the longitudinals, such as the keel, chine logs, and sheer clamps, a bevel is filed at each frame point. In this instance, the builder is beveling the chine log to the amount required for the bottom planking.

FIG. 18-7—The builder should always stand back and sight along the lines of the hull during fairing. All lines should be fair and smooth, without humps or hollows.

as depicted in Fig. 18-5, a plane is used to fair between the frames. Use the notches as a guide to the amount of material that will have to be removed, being sure that the lines between the frames along the chine are clean, even sweeps. This operation is depicted in Fig. 18-6. Bumps or hollows cannot be tolerated, and the change in bevel as the chine is faired progressively forward must be uniform and consistent. In fairing, stand back and sight along the lines at frequent intervals. If you inadvertently "goof", and remove an excess of material, it is better to laminate another section of material in with glue and to refair, rather than let the defect remain. This is not considered good practice, but it is better than allowing the dip or hollow to remain in the structure.

As the frame closest to the stem is approached along the chine log, careful fairing is required in order to provide adequate fastening surface for both the side and bottom planking (see Plate 18-B). A line is draw along the chine log surface from the beveled notch or faired point at the forward frame to the center of the chine log where it intersects

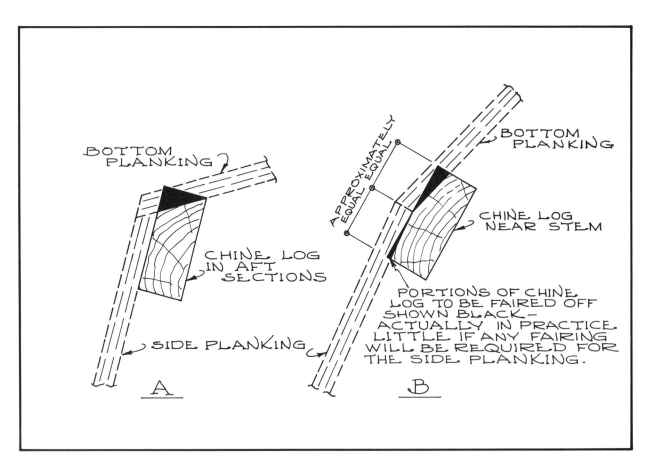

PLATE 18-B—Fairing along the chine log will change progressively from the stern (a) to the forward areas near the stem (b). In the forward areas the side and bottom planking will butt join and lay in more or less the same plane. Fairing to the center of the chine log at the stem will allow adequate fastening material on the chine log for both the side and bottom planking.

160

FIG. 18-9—A line is drawn on the chine log from the faired point at the forward frame to the center of the chine log as it intersects the stem. The portion above this line will be faired to receive the bottom planking, while the part below this line will be used for the side planking.

FIG. 18-10—Since the chine log is set in to meet the contour of the side frame member, no fairing is usually required on this member for the side planking. Here the builder is checking to determine the amount of material to be removed from the sheer.

against the stem. The bottom planking will be fastened to that portion of the chine log above this line, and the side planking to the portion below. This procedure is shown by Fig. 18-9. If there are several frames close to the bow of the boat, use the faired points at each of the frames as guide points in springing a batten in to mark the line.

On the usual vee-bottom boat, the side planking and bottom planking will meet in a butt joint and lay more or less in the same plane with one another over the forward portion of the chine logs. Very little, if any, material will need to be removed for the side planking, provided that the chine log has been set in parallel to the side planking contour.

The keel is handled in the same manner in the after-section. But, as the keel approaches the stem, the problem becomes more difficult. The bottom sections of the usual plywood boat are arced in section. When this is true, the stem cannot be beveled by the use of a straight-edge between the chine and sheer. It will be necessary to approximate the arc by springing a length of plywood from the chine to the stem, as shown in Fig. 18-12.

The sheer clamp is faired in much the same way as the other longitudinal members. The member must be beveled where required so the side planking will mate flat at all points. With the laminated vertical sheer clamp, considerable fairing will be required, especially forward. As noted previously in the chapter on sheer clamps, the sheer clamp member may be faired away so much that only a triangular portion will remain, and this is why a third layer is often added. However, when the sheer member sets into the notches so that the surface is flush with the side frame con-

tours, (as with the single sheer clamp type) little if any fairing is required for mating of the side planking. But with either type of sheer clamp, additional fairing on top of the sheer clamp must be done for the decking. However, this portion of the fairing is not done until the hull is righted.

As shown in Fig. 18-13, each of the frames will need to be beveled. In some instances, very little material, if any, will be removed in the mid-section or aft portions of the boat. In the forward frames, where there is quite a good deal of flare, considerable material may need to be removed. Remember that the frames are ever-changing in bevel between the chine and the sheer. A ¾" square batten, approximately the length of the boat, may be used to determine the angularity of the frame bevel at a series of points. The batten is sprung around the framework much as one of the permanent battens would be. The amount of bevel required will be clearly indicated and may be filed at each frame. A series of points can be used to indicate the varying amount of fairing required on the side and bottom frame members. Fairing between these notches in a smooth even curve is done similarly to that previously described. On sheet plywood boats, the planking is not fastened to the side or bottom frames as will be noted in the chapter on planking. Because of this, especially on the side frames, it is not necessary for the frames to even make contact to the planking. In fact, it is better to have a slight void between the frame member and the planking in many cases, such as when the frame member does not actually determine the planking contour, than to have the frame member protruding unfairly against the planking

FIG. 18-11—A short length of plywood sprung about the sides of the boat is a good check to determine if the fit at the sheer is being made properly.

FIG. 18-12—A short length of plywood will also be of assistance in determining the amount of bevel to be removed along the stem and along the chine log for the bottom planking. The bottom planking contour is usually convex, so care must be taken to simulate this condition.

163

FIG. 18-13 (above)—The frame contours must be faired where required. In the forward section of the hull, the forward part of the frame will need to be beveled or removed. In the aft section, the reverse will hold true except on some boats with straight parallel lines aft. The frames should be a clean sweep from chine to sheer so that the planking will not be deflected by the frames.

FIG. 18-14 (below)—When any of the lines, particularly in the aft section of the boat, are straight lines, constant checking should be done with a straight-edge. Here the builder is fairing the keel.

FIG. 18-15 (right)—In boats with a severe "vee", the fairing must be carefully done at the stem section. Here the builder is checking with his plane to be sure that the stem is properly beveled for the plywood bottom planking.

and thereby forming a "hard spot" or stress concentration.

Fairing of the transom and the stem from chine to sheer is done similarly. The major portion of the fairing is finished with the exception of the battens. If not previously installed, the battens should be notched into each of the frames at the required depth. Minor fairing of the battens may be required especially up forward when the battens are not kerfed or do not end against the stem.

After roughly cutting the planking panels to fit the side and bottom, further touch-up fairing may be necessary. Often, the large plywood panel will bend differently than the approximated curves in the forward vee portion. Be sure that the planking panel contacts all the mating surfaces. Any projecting edges or corners should be removed so that the planking will mate properly to all members.

THE "RABL METHOD" OF FAIRING

A method of determining the bevel required for fairing on the bottom of a plywood boat has been developed by that sage of yacht designers and amateur boat builders, Sam Rabl. The Rabl Method (see Plate 18-C) is a simple, effective way of determining the required bevel at any number of points along the keel and chine or the chine and sheer.

The process is accomplished on the bottom of the boat as follows: Divide the chine and keel line into an equal number of parts starting either where the chine and keel (or stem) meet or at the approximate midpoint of the hull where the vee is convex. In so doing follow the curve of the members; not a direct straight line. The points are identified, starting at the bow, calling the first points from the stem along the keel

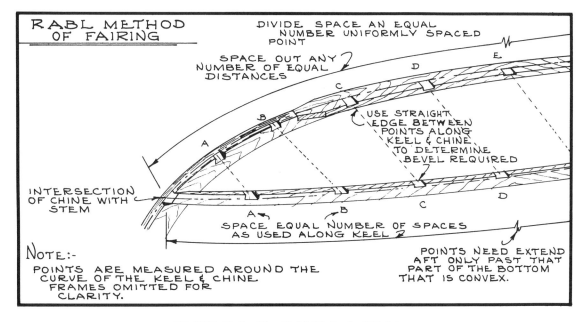

PLATE 18-C—The Rabl Method of Fairing

(or stem) and along the chine A, the next point B, etc. By laying a straight edge across the corresponding points, A on the chine, to A along the keel, the amount of bevel required may be observed. Bevel these points as previously described with a wood rasp. Use a plane sweeping in between the points in a fair line without humps or bumps.

This method is especially adaptable when the boat has considerable roundness or convexity to the forward sections. The builder will not have to guess at the curvature of the plywood sheet while fairing. Rabl's Method will assure the builder of an exact bevel, as basically the lines are the radians of cones used by the architect to develop the surface for plywood planking in sheet form.

CHAPTER 19 — PLYWOOD PLANKING

SHEET PLYWOOD

Most neophytes have the opinion that planking the sheet-plywood boat is difficult. When handled in a step-by-step manner, however, the project is relatively simple and fast. The method of applying plywood planking will vary, depending upon the type of boat, the amount of vee, and the chine construction. The construction depicted in the photographs is the most common. The application of the planking would be similar in any vee-bottom plywood craft.

Full-length plywood panels are desirable for planking. These plywood panels come in lengths to fit almost all plywood boats that are built by the amateur. In some localities, however, the long-length plywood panels are not available, and some builders prefer to use the standard 4' x 8' panels as a cost-saver. The methods used to join such shorter panels will be described in the following.

When building all but the smallest boat, it will be necessary to join the plywood planking. When long lengths of panels are available, they are scarf joined from 8' panels in most cases. Seldom are long length plywood panels made without joints. Some companies specialize in scarf joining plywood to almost any practical length. Since these sources are not wide spread, most build-

ers will need to join standard 8' long plywood to make the required lengths. Two methods are common, scarf joining and butt joining. Strengthwise, both have proven to be as strong, or stronger, than the plywood being joined.

SCARF JOINTS

When you purchase a full-length plywood panel longer than 12', it will undoubtedly be factory-spliced by the scarf-joining method. Such a joint properly done is stronger than the plywood panel. Special machines are used for factory scarf joints, and the gluing and clamping are carefully controlled. The amateur can scarf-join his own plywood panels, but he must be very careful in his workmanship to control the glue conditions and clamping pressure. If the work is carefully done, the scarf joint is completely practical. If improperly done, scarf-joined panels will fail in use.

The scarf joint shown (Plate 19-A) is at a ratio of 1:12 but some use a 1:10 ratio up to ½" and 1:8 for thicker plywood. The scarf joint length is found by multiplying the thickness of the plywood being joined by the ratio. As an example, at a 1:12 ratio, ¼" thick plywood would have a scarf joint length of

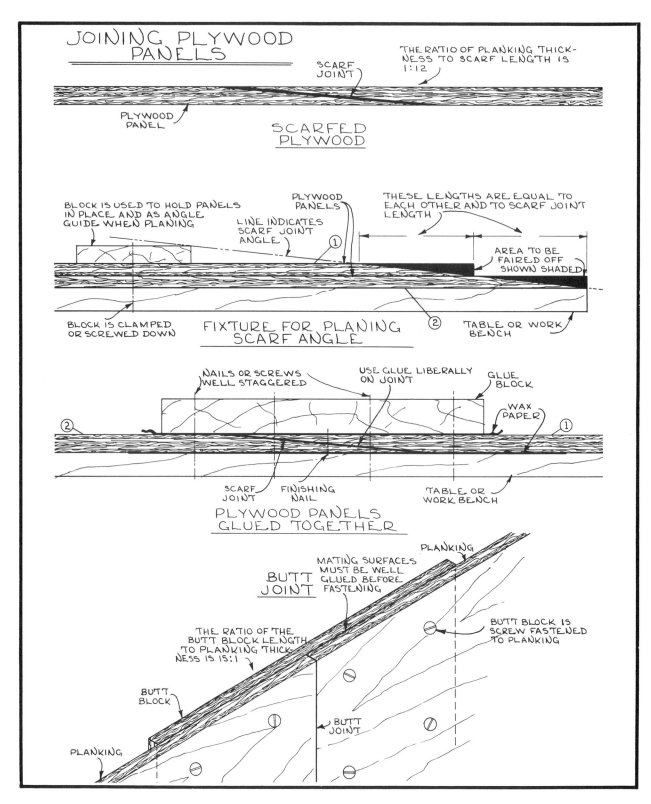

PLATE 19-A—Methods used to join plywood panels to form longer lengths

3″. Always cut the plywood panels to the minimum width, as wide panels are more difficult to join.

As shown in Plate 19-A, the ends of the two plywood panels to be scarf joined are aligned on the edge of a flat table or a sheet of ¾″ plywood. The upper panel is set back from the lower panel the distance of the scarf joint. Align the edges of the two plywood panels to be joined, the edge of the table or work surface, and the clamping block, so they are precisely parallel. Clamp, nail, or screw the block through both panels to the table or work surface. Both plywood panels are tapered simultaneously with a hand or power plane, or a disc sander for preliminary rough cutting. The panels are finished to a smooth surface, with a long base joiner or smooth plane. If the base of the plane is not long enough to extend from the block to the table edge and provide planing movement, use extensions clamped to the side of the plane.

Either resorcinol or epoxy adhesives (or epoxy resin with filler additives) can be used. Epoxies are preferable because of their gap filling properties. Remove the panels from the fixture and give both surfaces a liberal coat of glue. (Pre-coating the mating surfaces when using epoxy products is usually advised). Place plastic film between the work surfaces to prevent them from being glued to the joining plywood panels. Use finishing nails, driven through the scarf joint into the table, to prevent slipping. Screw or nail the blocking clamp over the joint with enough temporary fasteners to provide solid, even pressure until the glue sets. When gluing with epoxy, avoid excessive pressure that may force too much of the glue out. CAUTION: BE SURE

THE JOINT IS LEFT AT THE RECOMMENDED TEMPERATURE, AND TIME REQUIRED FOR COMPLETE CURE. If you are working at lower temperature, use plastic, cardboard, or a blanket to make a hood or "tent" over the joint. Under this "tent" use an electric light as a heater, or an electric heater, to maintain the proper temperature. The holes caused by temporary fasteners can be filled with a hard-setting putty. Always make scarf joints in the flattest area of the boat and place the pointed exterior edge of the scarf toward the stern.

BUTT JOINTS

Another method of joining plywood panels to obtain longer lengths is by the use of a butt joint backed with a butt block as illustrated by Plate 19-A. This

FIG. 19-1—Fitting a butt joint to join two panels of plywood used for bottom planking. Note that the butt blocks are fitted between the battens.

MAKING LONG LENGTH PLYWOOD PANELS THE EASY WAY

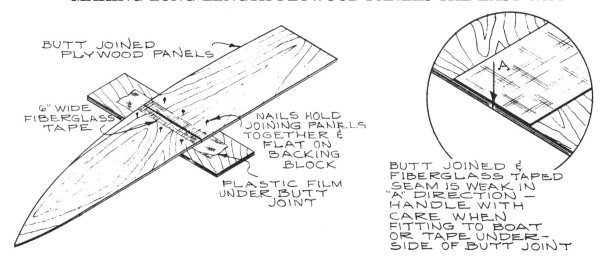

BUTT JOINED
PLYWOOD PANELS

6" WIDE
FIBERGLASS
TAPE

NAILS HOLD
JOINING PANELS
TOGETHER &
FLAT ON
BACKING
BLOCK

PLASTIC FILM
UNDER BUTT
JOINT

A

BUTT JOINED &
FIBERGLASS TAPED
SEAM IS WEAK IN
"A" DIRECTION —
HANDLE WITH
CARE WHEN
FITTING TO BOAT
OR TAPE UNDER-
SIDE OF BUTT JOINT

Obtaining plywood panels longer than 8′ in length is often difficult, costly, or impossible. Scarf joining panels does take time and care and many builders simply don't want to try it. Butt joining methods work fine, but in some instances will flatten or make a bump in the butt joined area. Here's a method of joining panels that is easy, requires little skill, and eliminates bumps.

First rough fit the panels to the boat leaving them oversize for final fitting. Butt the panels as required and make a mark at right angles to the butt joint for aligning purposes. Remove the panels and lay them on a flat surface. It is preferable to work on a wooden surface. A sheet of heavy plywood is fine. Butt the panels together and tape the joint with a strip of masking tape on what will be the INSIDE of the butt joint and then turn the panels over. This can be a chore as the masking tape is easily torn away. Some find it easier to place the masking tape on the underside of one panel then place the butt joining panel on top and press it down on the "sticky" side of the tape. The tape is used to prevent the resin from seeping out, and gluing the panels to the work surface. However, clear plastic should also be used as shown in the sketch.

The butting panels should be aligned and held in place to make a tight joint outside face-up. Use small nails driven through the planking into wooden work surface, or clamps (if they can reach to provide positive clamping) to hold the panels together. Precoat an area with epoxy resin about 4″ either side of the joint and then apply 6″ fiberglass tape, 8–10 ounce weight, centered over the butt joint. Saturate the fiberglass tape with epoxy and allow time for cure.

When handled with care, the resultant joined panel is usually strong enough to place on the boat side or bottom for final fitting, gluing, and fastening. The panel is weak at the joint if the panels are bent AWAY from the tape side (see sketch). Bias cut or bi-axial fiberglass cloth or tape will improve the strength. A strip of the fiberglass tape can also be used on the inside, taking care to OMIT the tape in way of the chine, sheer, battens, keel or other longitudinal as the plywood must mate firmly to these members. After fastening the plywood panel to the boat, back the junction with a plywood butt block. Usually a butt block is the same thickness as the joining plywood panels and extends 4″–5″ either side of the butt joint. If the inside joining surface has been fiberglassed, sand smooth with coarse grit sandpaper and apply a liberal application of epoxy with filler. Use glue only to bond the block to the planking, or screw fasten with a minimum of two rows of ¾″ #8, or larger wood screws spaced no more than 2″ apart and 1″ from edges. If the butt joining area has a pronounced curve, it may be necessary to shape the butt block or use thicker applications of epoxy-filler.

type of joint when properly made is every bit as strong as the solid panel or the scarf joined panel. In fact, for the inexperienced amateur, this type of joint is probably preferable from a strength standpoint since the quality of the joint is more easily controlled than the scarf joint. For most, the butt joint method is also easier to make.

It can be difficult to conceal a butt joint, especially if it is located at a point along the hull where the lines are curved or contoured. Using the butt block tends to make a flat spot along the hull, and for this reason, such a joint should preferably be made at as a flat or straight an area as possible.

The butt block can be installed in two ways. The plywood panels to be butt-joined can be roughly cut to shape and the butt joint made before the planking panel is assembled to the framework. The other method is to put one panel on the boat, fasten in the butt block, and then butt and fasten the other panel to the one initially applied. Both methods are satisfactory, one seeming as good as the other. One disadvantage of the pre-butt-joined panel is having to fit the butt block around various longitudinals.

There are two methods of fitting butt blocks around a batten. One method is to fit them between the battens. That method is best if the planking is applied one sheet at a time and the butt joint is made on the hull. There is a possibility of leaking at the junction of the butt block with the battens over the butt joint, but this chance is eliminated if the hull is covered with fiberglass. The other method is to cut or notch away the battens enough to recess the butt block in them, thereby making the butt block continuous over the butt joint. This

method can be used to eliminate the possibility of leaks at the joint if the hull will not be covered with fiberglass. This method weakens the battens, however, and consequently the battens should be reinforced on the back side of the joint with material of the same size located between the frame space, or otherwise lapped well beyond the joint each side on the batten.

The butt block used for joining panels is generally the same thickness as the joining panels, but seldom less than ¼″ in thickness. The butt block should lap each side of the butt joint by a minimum of 4″ and preferably more, especially with thicker panels. In assembly, the butt joint is coated liberally with glue and fastened with at least two rows of screws spaced not more than 2″ apart. The length of the screws should equal the combined thickness of the butt block and the joining panels. On larger hulls, machine screws of the flat head type can be used in lieu of screws. On very small boats, ring nails can be used, clenching the points that protrude through on the inside.

STEAMING OR SOAKING PLYWOOD PLANKING

Though seldom required, steaming of the plywood can be done as one method for easing the bending of plywood planking that is too stiff to make the curves. Steaming plywood panels in a steam box of the type sometimes used in conventional wood boatbuilding would require a box considerably larger than most builders would have or care to make. However, live steam can be applied directly to the panel by any suitable means. Steam can be generated in a sealed can filled with boiling water over a fire with an outlet hose as the only release for the steam. The hose should be as short as possible to eliminate the tendency of the steam to condense. Then too, there are steamers sometimes used to remove wallpaper from the walls of homes. Or a steam iron or portable steamer used to remove wrinkles from fabrics might also be used. Since the area of the plywood panel that will require steaming will be limited, any of these devices can be used. Because the outside of the curve of the plywood is under tension, and the inner surface is under compression, only the outer surface of the panel will require the application of steam.

The same principle applies if water is used also. Soaking the panel with water will help make the bending easier, and by using hot water for this soaking, most panels will limber up thereby making steam unnecessary in most cases. When hot water is used on a planking panel, it is best to retain some of the water and heat over the stressed area. Hot water can be poured over heavy rags laid on the stressed area while fitting or fastening the panel into position. Pouring hot water directly over the panel without rags makes quite a mess and may not be possible in some working areas. The panel could be soaked with hot water away from the work area, but retention of heat in the stressed area is helpful; otherwise the builder would have to work swiftly.

Application of water or steam can cause the Douglas fir plywood panels to check and raise the grain after drying out. If the boat is to be covered with fiberglass, this is not a particular disadvantage. However, if the hull is to be

painted directly onto the plywood, additional primer and possibly a thick putty coat will be required to achieve a smooth surface. Structurally, however, such a condition is not important.

FASTENING PLANKING TO FRAMES

In the SHEET plywood planked boat, it must be emphasized that fastening of the plywood planking to the athwartship frames, either on the side or the bottom, is NOT recommended. This may come as a surprise to many, but after the following explanation, the reasoning should become clear. Note that the statement above refers specifically to "sheet" plywood, and not to the other methods of plywood planking that are covered later.

Perhaps an analogy will describe the situation that exists with the flat plywood planking panel. Imagine that the sheet of plywood is a sheet of common corrugated cardboard with the corrugations running longitudinally. If we took this sheet of cardboard and laid it around the framework much like would be done with the planking, it would no doubt conform to the frame members just like the plywood planking would do. In fact, we could theoretically "fasten" this cardboard to all the longitudinals without any problem.

But what would happen to our cardboard if we "drilled" a series of holes for fastenings across the sheet thereby perforating the cardboard at each of the frames? Obviously, the cardboard would crisply fold and even possibly fracture right across this perforation. Now imagine doing the same thing to a plywood panel put under a lot of stress by laying it over our hull. While the plywood may not actually "fold" or even break like the cardboard, nevertheless, a localized weak point would be set up by the screw holes placed across the panel at each of the frames. It may be that such a panel would hold. But it cannot be denied that the panel has been weakened, and if such a panel were overstressed just once (and it need not be necessarily at that exact point), the panel could fail in use.

Of course, this situation is worse where the bending is most severe. But even in the flat areas of a hull, the practice of fastening to the frames should be avoided. On the properly designed plywood boat, there are enough longitudinal members in the structure to receive fastenings, making the few that could be driven into the frames simply not necessary. While the frames, and especially the side frames in many boats, are used to give contour or shape to the planking, the planking should still not be fastened to these frames. In fact, in many cases, it is not even desirable for the frames to actually contact or mate to the inside surface of the planking. In many cases, such a contact will protrude severely against the planking, thereby forming a sort of stress concentration, or "hard spot" as it is called, and could eventually cause the panel to fail. A possibility of a void in the plywood panel at this point could cause a fracture at the first time the stress is too great. In short, fasten the planking ONLY to the longitudinals (and at the ends of panels of course), but NOT to the athwartships frames. Relieve any frames during fairing which protrude unfairly against the planking.

TRANSITION JOINTS

The vee-bottom boat of conventional form has the bottom planking lapping the side planking except at the extreme part of the vee. The hull, as viewed from the side after being planked, would show the end-grain of the bottom plywood in the aft sections. This exposed edge or end-grain of the panel as it progressively approaches the bow becomes greater, due to the angularity caused by the vee in the bottom of the boat. It would be impractical to continue lapping the bottom planking over the side planking at the extreme bow of the boat. When the exposed end-grain of the plywood planking becomes excessive, the lap should be discontinued and a transition made. From that point forward, the bottom and the side planking will butt join or butt together. The point of the transition can be varied along the chine to a great extent.

When a boat has a flat bottom or a very gradual vee, a transition joint is not required. In this case, the bottom planking will overlap the side planking for the full length of the chine joint.

It is possible to use a butt joint between the side and bottom planking throughout the entire chine length on any boat. This junction, as shown in Plate 19-B (lower right), is an excellent one. A rabbet plane will be required to make such a joint between the side and the bottom planking panels. With this method, either side or bottom planking panel can be applied first. The initially applied panel is left overhanging and the rabbet plane used to bevel the planking. The amateur will find that attempting to fit a large panel of plywood accurately along such a continuous butt joint will be extremely dif-

FIG. 19-2—This shows the side planking just applied at the transition joint. Forward of the point, the side planking has been fitted along the break in the chine.

FIG. 19-3—In this view the projecting plywood planking has been trimmed flush with the chine, ready for the bottom planking. After application of the bottom planking, the joint will appear similar to that shown in Fig. 19-4.

FIG. 19-4—Here the bottom planking mates in a butt joint forward of the transition point, and is left overhanging the side planking aft of the transition point.

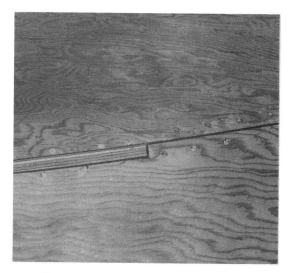

FIG. 19-5—The transition joint is clearly indicated after the planking has been finally trimmed. At the left is the aft portion of the boat where the bottom planking is lapping the side planking. The forward portion shows the joining of the bottom and sides in a butt joint.

FIG. 19-2 to 19-5—These four photos show examples of the method for joining the bottom and side planking in a typical plywood hull. This is the much discussed transition joint, changing over from the bottom lapping the side in the aft portion of the hull, to the side and bottom butting together in the forward portion of the hull.

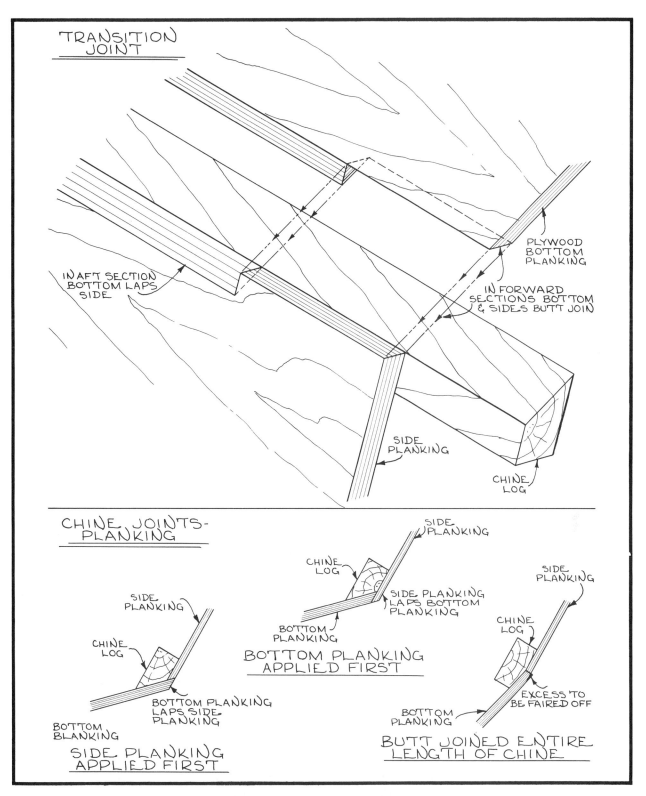

TRANSITION JOINT

PLYWOOD BOTTOM PLANKING

IN AFT SECTION BOTTOM LAPS SIDE

IN FORWARD SECTIONS BOTTOM & SIDES BUTT JOIN

SIDE PLANKING

CHINE LOG

CHINE JOINTS- PLANKING

SIDE PLANKING

CHINE LOG

BOTTOM BLANKING

BOTTOM PLANKING LAPS SIDE PLANKING

SIDE PLANKING APPLIED FIRST

SIDE PLANKING

CHINE LOG

BOTTOM PLANKING

SIDE PLANKING LAPS BOTTOM PLANKING

BOTTOM PLANKING APPLIED FIRST

SIDE PLANKING

CHINE LOG

EXCESS TO BE FAIRED OFF

BOTTOM PLANKING

BUTT JOINED ENTIRE LENGTH OF CHINE

PLATE 19-B—Side-bottom planking junctions over chine log, including transition joint

175

ficult. For that reason, for the plywood planking up forward on vee-bottom plywood boats, most amateurs and professionals utilize the transition from a lap to a butt joint.

SIDE PLANKING

As previously stated the side planking is usually put on first. Many novices think that a paper pattern for the cutting of the planking panels is desirable. However, experience has shown that for the most part using such a pattern is a waste of time and effort. It is easier to lean the plywood panel against the side of the hull and scribe the contour to rough size around the extremeties. Then the panel can be removed and sawn to rough shape and applied. In this manner there is no need to lay out the pattern, transfer it to the planking panel, and then check for fit as would be required with the paper pattern. The "pattern" is exactly provided by the actual hull framework instead.

After the planking panel has been fitted and sawn to shape, relocate the panel on the side of the boat. Use several locating screws through the planking into the chine member. This will give a positive position for the panel and enable it to be relocated in the same position each time it is fitted and replaced. It is not important to fit the planking panel accurately along the sheer, transom, stem, and most of the chine. The planking can be left ½" or more oversize along these areas and trimmed off after the planking is permanently fastened in place. In fact, at the ends of the panel, such as at the transom, leave plenty of length beyond the required

size and cut to be flush with the transom after fastening. This will prevent splintering along the edges where the screws will be driven.

The transition point previously described is selected by making it at any convenient point where the exposed end-grain of the plywood planking bottom panel would become excessive. From the transition point forward, the side panel must be fitted along the break of the chine. The break of the chine means the dividing line that was used to delineate the portion of the chine on which the bottom and the side planking panels would be fastened. This is covered in Chapter 18. It is not necessary to remove the plywood panel to fit that portion that will butt join with the bottom planking. The aft portion can be left positioned on the side of the boat, and the forward portion sprung out sufficiently to allow the fitting to be done. Fitting the side planking panel in the forward portion is shown in Fig. 19-7.

After all of the fitting has been completed on the side panel, the screw holes can be drilled, eliminating the possibility of getting sawdust behind the planking panel and its adjoining member. Such pre-drilling is not absolutely necessary if a clamp is used adjacent to the point where the hole will be drilled in the panel when the surfaces have been glue-coated. In the final gluing, the planking panel and its mating member must have no sawdust between them.

After all preliminary fitting and marking, the panel is removed from the side of the boat and checked to the opposite side. The panels should be interchangeable. If they are not reasonably the same contour, a further check should be made, as an error has undoubtedly been made in the setting up of the boat. The initially fitted side planking member should then be marked to the plywood panel that will be used for the second side.

After a side panel has been preliminarily fitted and later reapplied to the boat, often it will not fit. This is particularly true in the case of a long thin plywood panel being fitted to the side of a hull. This problem is caused by what is known as "edge setting." It is also possible to change the contour or the amount of bend in a panel by this method. To explain this "edge set" condition, let us assume that a side planking panel has been fastened at the bow. As the panel is bent around the hull form, it is possible to move the aft portion up or down to some extent on the side of the boat. This movement causes minor buckling, although the condition would possibly not be noticeable. To eliminate this condition, always fasten the plywood panel at its midpoint for fitting. Having at least two people fitting a planking panel will also tend to eliminate this problem.

All of the mating surfaces for the plywood panel should be coated with glue. As indicated in Fig. 19-9, using a small paint roller will speed up the application of the glue. Work as rapidly as possible, particularly if the weather is warm, as the glue tends to set faster as the temperature rises. With the assistance of a helper, locate the panel on the side of the boat. Usually, a single locating screw at a midpoint along the chine is driven in first. The portion of the side planking that will butt-join the bottom planking is then fastened in position. This is the only part of the panel that need be fitted closely. It is very easy to vary the position of the side planking on the chine at this point, so it should al-

ways be located and screwed first.

The screws are next driven along the chine, working aft. It is good practice to check the sheer and either clamp or fasten the flared portion of the boat forward of midships. If not fastened at the proper time, this portion may have a tendency to bow out. When a boat has a severe tumble-home or roll at the transom, fasten along the chine and then work progressively along the sheer line, eventually pulling the roll or tumble-home to the transom. Recommendations for fastening sizes and spacings have been given in Chapter 6.

The side planking can now be faired along the chine aft of the transition point. This is the area where the bottom planking will lap with the side. Careful fitting must be done, as the lap joint must firmly fit both the chine and the side planking along the entire area. The excess side panel can also be trimmed along the transom and the stem. Observe in Fig. 19-12 that the side panel is filed flush with the stem contour at the bow. This second side panel will lap the initially applied panel. This situation is typical of almost all plywood boats, except possibly the very round-nosed type. In this case, use a back saw to saw the panel on the centerline of the stem. The second side to be applied will be butt-joined to the first-applied side panel over the centerline of the stem. When trimming an overhang of Douglas fir plywood, be very careful not to splinter the plywood. Use a fine-tooth saw in such a manner as to score the outer or tension surface of the panel first. This is illustrated in Fig. 19-11.

It is good practice to apply the other side-planking panel immediately after applying the first. This tends to equalize the strains and stresses on the

Boatbuilding With Plywood

FIG. 19-7—The side panel is temporarily relocated to the side of the hull. Several screws should be driven in to locate the panel as each fitting is made. The builder is fitting the part forward of the transition joint that will join with the bottom planking in a butt joint. The overhang aft of this point is clearly shown.

FIG. 19-9—The mating areas for the planking skin should be thoroughly coated with glue. The builder is using a small paint roller to facilitate the application of the glue. Note that the builder is not skimpy with the glue, and that it is being applied evenly.

FIG. 19-6—The plywood panel is leaned against the side of the completed framework and the contour marked around the chine and sheer. It is then removed and roughly cut to shape with a fine toothed hand or power saw.

FIG. 19-8—If the side panel is a close fit, or if it is desirable to obtain both panels from a single width sheet, a paper template may be used to determine the approximate contour of the planking as shown. The first side fitted should always be checked to the other side of the hull and marked to another sheet of plywood to eliminate the rough cutting and fitting.

178

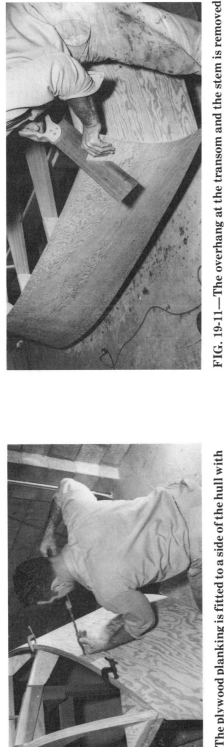

FIG. 19-11—The overhang at the transom and the stem is removed with a saw. The builder is scribing the outer surface of the panel with the saw first. Particularly with the roll in the side of the boat, as indicated here, the panel would have a tendency to tear the top lamination if this were not done.

FIG. 19-13—After the second panel has been applied similarly to the first side, the overhang is again trimmed off along the bow and filed to a smooth finish. Capping of the area can then be done after.

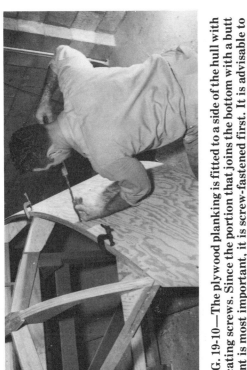

FIG. 19-10—The plywood planking is fitted to a side of the hull with locating screws. Since the portion that joins the bottom with a butt joint is most important, it is screw-fastened first. It is advisable to use a clamp adjacent to, or near, the position at which the screw is being driven.

FIG. 19-12—The initially applied side panel is filed flush with the stem contour. The second panel will lap the first at the stem.

FIG. 19-15—The bottom planking panel is clamped along the centerline of the keel and positioned with several locating screws. Rough-mark and cut away the excess portion at the point where the bottom will mate with the side planking. Doing this will make the panel easier to work.

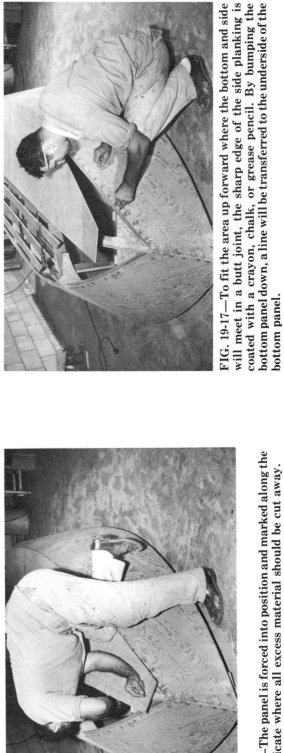

FIG. 19-17—To fit the area up forward where the bottom and side will meet in a butt joint, the sharp edge of the side planking is coated with a crayon, chalk, or grease pencil. By bumping the bottom panel down, a line will be transferred to the underside of the bottom panel.

FIG. 19-14—The overhang along the chine aft of the transition joint is planed flush. Great care must be taken in this operation, just as with the fairing, to eliminate the possibility of humps and hollows.

FIG. 19-16—The panel is forced into position and marked along the stem to indicate where all excess material should be cut away.

FIG. 19-19—After preliminary fitting the first half-bottom, it is scribed to another panel for the opposite half of the bottom.

FIG. 19-21—From the forward section, the builder works progressively aft, sinking the screws as rapidly as possible. The power screwdriver shown will speed this process.

FIG. 19-18—The fit for the transition joint will still need to be done by hand. Note that the builder is using a plywood washer block to hold the bottom planking in position as he progressively fits the panel.

FIG. 19-20—The panel is clamped in position and located with the locating screws. Hot water is being used to make the panel bend easier. The first part fastened is the area along the transition joint.

framework of the boat. After the second side is applied, it too is trimmed along the chine, and the overlap portion of the bow and transom finished off. The overhang along the sheer is left long until the hull has been completely planked and is righted.

BOTTOM PLANKING

The rough-fitting of the bottom panel is done similarly to that of the side planking. The straight edge of the bottom plywood panel is aligned along the centerline of the keel, fitting to the centerline if required, and fastened with several locating screws. If the boat has considerable vee in the bottom, it is preferable to bevel the edge along the centerline of the keel to match with the vee in the bottom of the boat. In most craft, it is easier to leave the edge crisp on the initially applied panel and bevel the edge of the other bottom planking panel.

As shown in Fig. 19-15, the excessive overhang of the bottom plywood panel is rough-marked along the chine and cut away. In a boat with considerable vee up forward, the builder may feel that it is impossible to spring the panel into position. To make the bend easier, cut away as much excess material as possible in the forward sections. The bottom planking panel aft of the transition joint can be left about ½" long. This is easily trimmed flush with the side planking after the bottom panel has been permanently fastened in place.

The area up forward where the bottom planking will butt-join with the side planking must be carefully fitted. A method of obtaining an approximate fit is illustrated in Fig. 19-17. As shown, the sharp edge of the side planking up forward is marked with a grease pencil, crayon, or chalk. The bottom planking, still clamped in position, is bumped down to transfer the mark to the underside of the bottom planking panel. Cut away from this line slightly, as hand-fitting will be required. Start the fitting of the panel to mate with the side planking at the transition point. Progressively fit the joint, working forward, as shown in Fig. 19-18. As an area is fitted, drive a screw with a plywood washer block to temporarily hold the planking panel to the chine. When the vee at the bow of the boat is considerable, it is imperative that washer blocks be used. Without them, a screw may pull through the plywood panel. The block distributes the pressure over a greater area. The area around the stem need not be closely fitted. The overhang can be removed after the bottom panel has been permanently anchored in place. After fitting the panel, either pre-drill all screw holes or mark the location of the longitudinal members. A marking gauge that can be used along the chine to determine the area into which screws can be driven is shown in Plate 19-C.

After all fitting and marking, remove the bottom planking panel and mark the outline on the other plywood panel that will be used for the second half of the bottom. All of the mating areas of the bottom planking are coated liberally with a hardsetting glue. The bottom planking panel is aligned along the keel and anchored in position with the locating screws. Since the area up forward of the transition joint is the most critical for fitting, that portion of the panel should be forced into position and

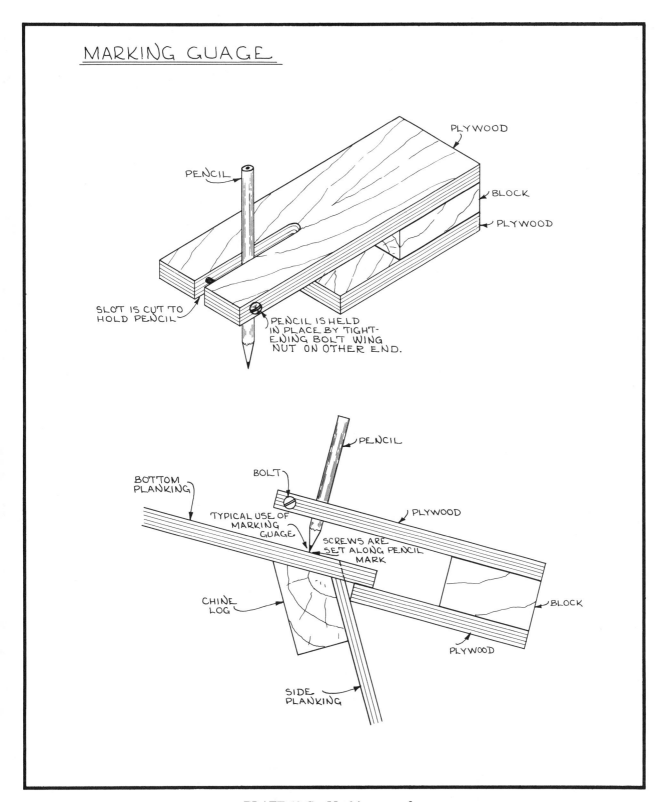

MARKING GUAGE

PENCIL

PLYWOOD

BLOCK

PLYWOOD

SLOT IS CUT TO HOLD PENCIL

PENCIL IS HELD IN PLACE BY TIGHTENING BOLT WING NUT ON OTHER END.

PENCIL

BOLT

BOTTOM PLANKING

TYPICAL USE OF MARKING GUAGE

PLYWOOD

SCREWS ARE SET ALONG PENCIL MARK

CHINE LOG

BLOCK

PLYWOOD

SIDE PLANKING

PLATE 19-C—Marking gage for trimming planking overhangs

fastened first. Several other screws may need to be driven in the aft portion of the hull as the panel will tend to buckle up if too few locating screws are used. After fastening the portion up forward, the remainder of the screws are progressively fastened, working aft. At the transition joint where the side and bottom panels meet in a butt joint (see Figs. 19-20 and 19-21), the butt joint of the side and bottom planking up forward may not always be perfect. A small seam may be filled by rubbing sawdust over the area where the glue is oozing out between the panels. This glue and

sawdust mixture will set up very hard and the excess will need to be ground or filed flush. Optionally, a putty filler of the polyester resin type can be used.

The overhang along the transom and chine should be trimmed. At the junction of the bottom planking panels at the stem, two options are possible. The first would be to butt-join the two panels over the stem. With this method, a back saw is used to cut the initially applied bottom panel over the center of the stem. Careful fitting will be required in applying the second half of the bottom planking. A simpler method, and a more

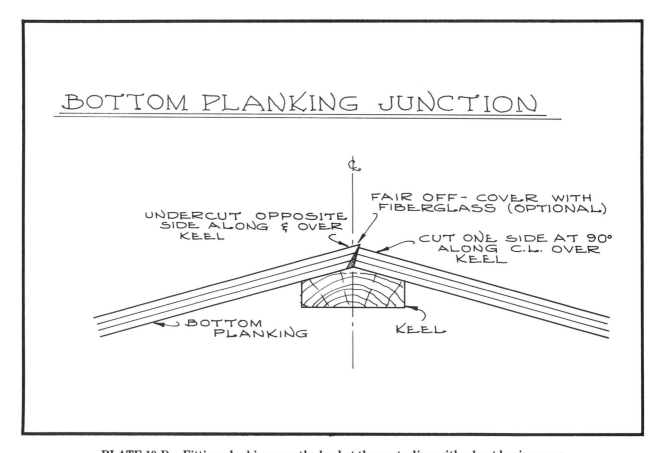

PLATE 19-D—Fitting planking over the keel at the centerline with a boat having a vee bottom. Cut the first half of the bottom planking with a 90 degree edge and install. Then fit an excessive bevel onto the edge of the second adjoining panel. Slide the panel up against the first half tightly and fasten in place. Excess glue will fill into the concealed joint for a tight fit all along. If the bevel is not cut excessively, a gap will exist that must be filled later.

FIG. 19-22—The completed half-bottom. The "smears" over the screw holes are hard-setting wood dough or putty.

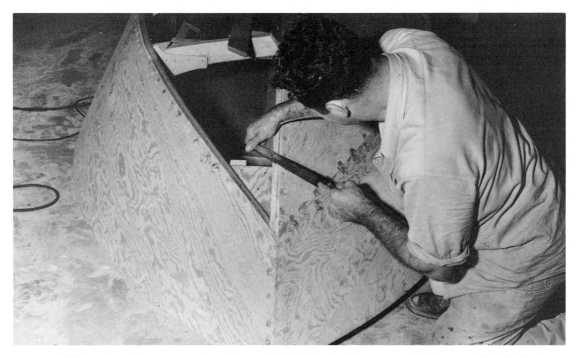

FIG. 19-23—The portion along the bow is filed flush with a rasp so the the second half of the bottom will lap to the initially applied bottom panel.

FIG. 19-24—From a convenient point on the stem, usually near the forward ending of the keel but never directly over it, a transition must be made.

FIG. 19-25—This is the second panel being fitted over the initially applied panel. Note that the second panel will lap the initially applied panel up forward. Aft of this point, the two will meet in a butt joint along the centerline over the keel.

FIG. 19-26—The fitting of this area must be carefully done. Here the builder is using a water soaked rag to facilitate the bending while the fitting is done.

FIG. 19-27—It will be necessary to carefully hand-fit that portion of the bottom planking along the chine that will butt join to the side planking.

FIG. 19-28—A disc sander is just one way that overhanging edges can be trimmed off flush.

FIG. 19-29—All screw holes are filled with a hard-setting putty.

FIG. 19-30—A completely planked hull after sanding all filled screw holes and other imperfections flush. The hull is ready for finish or fiberglass at this point.

common one, is to use a transition joint. In the aft portion of the hull along the keel, the two bottom panels will meet in a butt-joint. The initially applied panel will be lapped over the stem by the second half of the bottom panel. Make the bottom transition point at a location where the straight portion of the initially applied panel is no longer on the center of the keel. Aft of this point, the bottom planking panels will butt-join, and forward of this point, one will lap the other. Such a joint is illustrated in Figs. 19-23, 19-24, and 19-25. Fitting and fastening the second half of the bottom are similar to the method described for the initial bottom panel.

It is common in small boats to use side and bottom planking of different thickness. This practice causes an offset condition up forward where the bottom and side planking will butt-join, as illustrated in Plate 19-E. If spray rails are used, such an offset may be readily concealed. If spray rails are not used, the builder has several alternatives. One solution is to relieve the chine the difference between the two panels. This is accomplished after the side planking has been fastened in place. A rabbet plane is used to recess the chine from the transom forward progressively to the stem. The stem will also need to be relieved to compensate for the difference in thickness between the two panels along the area to which the bottom planking will be fastened.

Plate 19-E shows other alternatives that may be used when the side and bottom planking are of different thickness. One shows a method of relieving the bottom of the plywood on the underneath side. Another illustrates compensating for the different thickness by the removal of the exterior plies of the bottom panel. Both of these methods have a tendency to weaken the joint and to eliminate most of the advantages of the heavier, stronger bottom plywood panel. Feathering or removal of the exterior plies of the bottom panel is definitely not advocated unless the builder is fiberglassing the hull. Another method to compensate for the difference between the bottom and side planking as shown on Plate 19-E, is to use a filler strip on the chine under the side planking. This filler or shim strip is laminated to the chine with glue. After the glue has set the filler strip must be tapered from the transition point forward. In the forward part of the boat where the side and bottom planking will meet in a butt-joint the total thickness of the shim must be the difference between the thickness of the side and bottom panels. The feathered portion does have a tendency to splinter and make a good joint difficult to achieve. Care must be taken in drilling the filler piece so that it will not split. Plywood may be used for the filler strip to eliminate this tendency.

Another method to cover the planking thickness discrepancy is to build up the low area with layers of fiberglass mat or cloth and resin. Then the surface is ground fair and smooth with a disc sander, and the hull covered with fiberglass after.

DOUBLE BOTTOMS

A double plywood sheet bottom means that two laminations or layers of plywood are used instead of just one. Double bottoms are used when the bends are too severe to be made with a single thickness of plywood. Such a

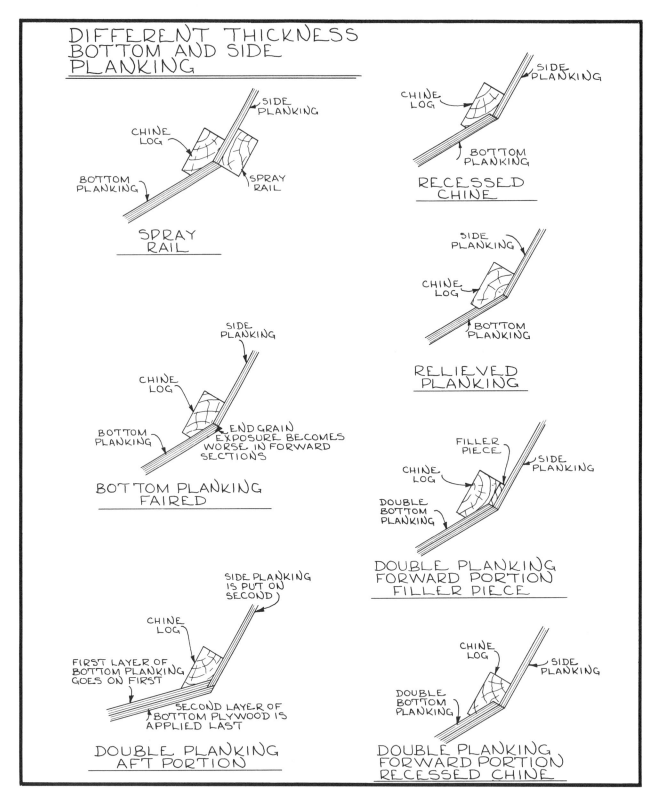

PLATE 19-E—Methods for handling thickness variations between side and bottom planking at junctions over chine logs.

190

double bottom will theoretically be marginally stronger than the same thickness bottom made from just one sheet since there will be at least one additional ply or veneer. For example, a ½″ sheet of plywood is usually made from 5 veneer plies. However, two ¼″ plywood panels would have 6 such plies.

It is preferable to use two laminations of plywood rather than to stress a single panel of plywood to an excessive amount, even if the panels could be eventually forced into place. The double bottom can be used in combination with a single bottom using a butt joint where the two portions mate. This is usually the situation in most vee-bottom boats since the bends in the aft portion of the hull are not so severe as to require the double planking at all areas. However, this choice is up to the builder, and it is possible to double plank the bottom throughout, or to use full length double panels applied at one time over the length of the hull.

Although the application of a double bottom is much the same as with a single bottom, there are some variations. For example, as shown by Plate 19-E, the joint at the chine with the side planking can be made to interlock. In this case, the first panel to be applied would be the bottom. Then the side would be applied, and the final second layer of bottom planking after this. The interlocking joint is desirable since it reduces the exposed edge grain of plywood at this point. However, if the boat is later covered with fiberglass, the regular lap joint with the side planking applied first is satisfactory. A disadvantage with the interlocked joint is the additional work required in fitting the members forward of the transition joint.

The sequence for installing a double bottom is to apply the forward panels first. If double panels are being used throughout the bottom and a butt joint is necessary, the standard butt joint method can be used. An option would be to allow one panel to overlap another, or stagger the ending points. However, this staggered overlapping joint should still be backed up on the inside with a butt block. With a double bottom forward butting to a single panel aft, the standard butt block method is used.

The double bottom planking application must be carefully done to insure a positive glue bond between the laminations. The first layer is fitted and fastened in place on the bottom of the boat. Nails are often used with just enough to hold the panel in position until the second layer is applied. All the mating areas should be coated with glue, and the panel nailed or screwed in place. The second lamination is fitted and readied for fastening. The entire surface of the first layer is liberally coated with glue. A linoleum spreader or large paint roller can be used to expedite the glue application. The second bottom panel is then positioned and fastened, working as rapidly as possible so that the glue will not set up prematurely. Screws are driven through both panels wherever possible in longitudinals below. It is good practice to use a series of weights over the bottom area to apply uniform pressure. A series of small flour sacks filled with sand, or similar weighting devices, can be used for weights. The sand bags are especially suitable in the vee'd portion of the boat since they will adapt to the contour of the hull and stay in place. The application and fastening of a double bottom must be done quickly, and this can require helpers, depending on the size of the boat. Working fast is especially important if the weather is hot, since the glue will set rapidly. On large double bottom boats, a nail gun is sometimes used to speed the application and these are handy if available.

Regardless of the type of bottom planking application if the bottom battens have been pulled down to the building form during the planking application, these must be coated with glue on the surface which will mate to the planking and then released after the planking is in place. Screws or bolts can then be fastened through the planking and into these battens. In rare cases, where battens have not been fastened to a forward frame, such battens may not conform to the frame after the planking has been installed either. When this occurs, fill the void between the batten and the frame with solid blocking and screw or bolt in position from the outside with flat head fasteners of suitable length.

HULL APPENDAGES

Depending on the hull, there may be a variety of members which are secured onto the outside of the planking. As previously noted, spray rails are frequently used along the chine to cap the edge of the plywood and to deflect spray. Sometimes a guard member is located along the side planking aft for docking protection. With some boats, a skeg or deadwood may also be installed after the planking.

On some powerboats, especially of the deep vee high speed type, a type of spray rail known as a lift strake may be required. These lift strakes may number several on either half of the bottom planking depending on the design. Unlike other hull appendages, the lift strakes may be shaped so that the bottom surface will be horizontal while mating flat to the hull. This usually requires that the lift strakes be in a triangular section configuration. Other shaping requirements may be necessary also. For example, the lift strake may require tapering and fairing into the hull lines as well as curving along the hull contours in much the same way as the bottom battens do on the inside. Usually the lift strakes can be pre-cut to the required angle for the most part by use of a table or radial arm saw. However, some hand fitting, usually forward, will be required. As with all the appendages noted here, the lift strakes are installed after covering with fiberglass if this is done.

Bed the lift strakes in resin saturated fiberglass cloth or mat, trimming the edges just before the resin sets up hard. Otherwise, glue these members in position if installed directly on the plywood planking. Lift strakes may be fastened from the outside if they are backed up on the inside with bottom battens. If this is not the case, they must be fastened from the inside of the hull through the planking, taking care to make sure that the screws will enter into a thick portion of the lift strake. A flat head bolt is advised for fastening the ends of the lift strakes to the hull at the forward ends, and the ends should be faired into the hull to minimize drag and resistance. Where lift strakes run aft to the transom, it is common to stop them short of the transom on outboards and outdrive equipped boats in the area of the propeller to prevent cavitation and turning problems. This distance is usually noted on the plans, and may frequently be 4' with higher powered craft.

COLD MOLDED DIAGONAL STRIP PLANKING

A variation of plywood sheet planking is known as cold molded diagonal strip planking. As noted earlier in the text, plywood cannot practically be bent over surfaces which are not segments of a cylinder or cone, or otherwise "compounded" in curvature. However, such curvatures are often desired by the designer for performance or aesthetic reasons, and consequently the cold molded method may be specified.

While some may think that the cold molding process is a new development, such is not the case. This time-proven boatbuilding method was largely developed and perfected during the war years of World War II, where it was a boon to the builders of various small boats such as the famous PT boats and air-sea rescue craft. The cold molding process enabled boatbuilders to rapidly build many duplicate craft using less skilled labor and less expensive materials than would be required with conventional wood boatbuilding methods. Of course, the other advantages of the cold molding process were light weight and dimensional stability in the planking making these boats suitable for drying out without having the seams open up. With the advent in recent years of even better plywoods, glues, resins, and fiberglass sheathing techniques, the cold molding process is even better.

The terminology "cold molding," as carried over from the past, is used to differentiate the process from plywood boats built up from successive glued veneer laminations using a mold where heat and pressure cured the glue. With cold molding, however, no heat is required to cure the glue, and an elaborate mold is not necessary, thereby making the process quite suitable for the amateur builder or small professional yard where only one or a few boats will be built.

There are several variations used with the cold molded process, but basically the cold molded diagonal strip planking procedure using plywood consists of cutting the plywood into longitudinal strips which are then laid diagonally over the hull framework in at least two layers. The first layer applied is usually placed at about 45 degrees to the hull centerline, while the following layers are applied at approximately 90 degrees to each one underneath. In some cases many layers may be required depending on the degree of curvature, size of hull, thickness required, etc. In some boats, this planking application may only be required in the forward portion of the hull. In these cases, a transition to sheet plywood may be made at some point into the aft areas. In other boats, such as round bottomed sailboats, the entire hull may be planked in this manner.

Generally speaking, the larger the design, the more a designer will tend to favor this planking method over sheet plywood, and for several reasons. As noted, the designer may require the use of compound curves for both appearance (such as a broad flaring topside forward), and performance (such as the reserve buoyancy together with spray deflecting qualities of a double curvature forward on power boats). Then again, the cold molded planking method is

FIG. 19-32—As the flatter areas of the boat are reached, less edge fitting is required and the size of the planking pieces can be enlarged as much as is required to suit the hull form. Notice that with this planking method fastenings are used into all hull members, even the athwartship frames.

FIG. 19-34—The second lamination of diagonal plywood is applied at nearly right angles to the first layer as much as possible. Fastenings are used through both layers into all contact members, plus along the plank edges to minimize curling of the edges of the planking strips. Finishing the job from this point on is just like with sheet plywood planking.

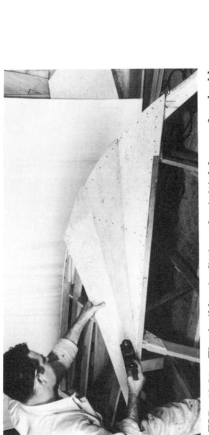

FIG. 19-31—The builder is fitting the initial layer of a double diagonal plywood bottom. Each planking strip must be edge fitted to the preceeding one for a tight joint. While the initial strips can be applied at any convenient point, this builder has begun at the bow. Notice how the pieces fan out in shape for easier bending, as it makes little difference whether the pieces are parallel or more triangular in shape as long as they make the bend and contact the hull members.

FIG. 19-33—As the transom is approached, it is often possible to use a full sheet of plywood. Only the junction with the preceeding planking strip at this point needs special cutting and fitting. The planking at such areas should be fastened the same as for regular sheet plywood planking. The overhanging portion along the chine forward will be trimmed off before applying the side planking.

suitable for making round bottomed sailboats using plywood which could not be done with ordinary sheet plywood. Another advantage, especially for the builder of larger boats, is that it is often easier and cheaper to build with this method. The handling of long and heavy sheets of plywood is not required. Then too, the builder can often get by with smaller plywood sheets, and in some cases lower grades of void-free plywood thereby cutting costs. One worker may easily install strip planking, however, several helpers may be required on a larger design using sheet plywood planking in order to handle fitting and fastening of the plywood sheets.

In general, the cold molded strip planking method will use thinner plywood seldom more than ⅜" in thickness, and perhaps less depending on the hull. Plywood any thicker than this is more difficult to work with and will not usually provide as smooth a finished surface. In many cases builders may substitute solid wood veneers in place of plywood, and usually this is entirely acceptable. However, if solid wood veneers are used in place of plywood, their thickness should be decreased somewhat since they will be more difficult to bend in place than plywood with its alternating grain pattern. As a general rule such solid wood veneers should not exceed ¼" in net thickness, and veneers as thin as ⅛" are commonly substituted. Of course, the larger the boat and the less severe the contours, the thicker the diagonal planking layers can and should be.

If solid wood veneers are used in lieu of plywood, the completed net thickness of the hull should be at least equal to that specified for the plywood planking, together with a comparable number of alternating layers. If the veneers are too thin, however, there may be a tendency for the veneer strips to "flatten" between longitudinals. If this occurs, then either thicker veneers should be used or additional longitudinal members or battens should be installed to narrow the gap between. Whether plywood or solid wood veneers are used, however, the other installation requirements and procedures are similar.

DIAGONAL PLANKING APPLICATION

The first question a builder will usually have about the cold molded method is, how wide are the strips of planking? There is no one answer since the widths will vary with the boat. For example, a hard-chine powerboat with a distinct junction between the side and bottom planking and moderate curvature may be planked with much wider strips than, for example, a round bottom sailboat hull of considerable curvature. As a general rule, the strips should be in as wide of widths as practicable to make the bends and meet at all contact points, but narrow enough to form a smooth and fair hull surface. However, strips must be wide enough to get at least two fastenings across the ends, which means a practical minimum of about 3". In some cases, the designer may specify the widths required. For most boats, plywood strips should not be wider than a foot or so (except in flatter hull areas), although solid wood veneers should not exceed about 6", if used in lieu of plywood.

While the general configuration of applying the various layers is for the first layer to be at 45 degrees to the

FIG. 19-35—In this double diagonal planking application note that the planking pieces are progressively larger in the aft areas. This is common on hard-chine power boats.

FIG. 19-36—In the forward areas the planking strips become narrower in order to conform to the double cuvature bottom often designed into the forward bottom areas of larger powerboats.

FIG. 19-37—The side planking has been applied before the second layer. This caps the edge of both the first layer and the side planking, and makes a tighter junction at the chine. Note the second layer installed progressively from the transom in this case.

FIG. 19-38—The second layer has been installed and the surface sanded smooth with all imperfections being filled. The reverse curved bottom shows clearly, and could not be accomplished with sheet plywood in the conventional manner.

centerline, and subsequent layers then applied at 90 degrees to each other, it is desirable to vary the angularity somewhat between successive layers to prevent or minimize edge joints from falling over edge joints in the parallel layers underneath. It is also desirable for all planking strips to run in continuous lengths from keel to chine, and from chine to sheer, on hard-chine hulls, or from keel to sheer on round bottomed boats. However, on larger boats this may not be practical because of the lengths required, especially at the amidship areas on round bottomed hulls.

If long lengths of material cannot be obtained, then strips can be butt joined or scarf joined, with scarf joining being the preferred method, especially on the final outer layer where appearance may be important. If butt joining is done, the joints should fall at areas of the hull that are as flat as possible. It is advisable to allow only one joint per strip, with the joint staggered a respectable distance from adjoining joints. In the initial layer, butt joints should preferably fall over a longitudinal batten. If not, the butt joint must be backed up with a butt block similar to that used for regular sheet plywood butt joints. On intermediate layers, butt joints can fall over longitudinal members or in between. Depending on the thickness of the planking application at this point, fastenings at butt joints between longitudinals can be driven into a backing block on the inside or simply clenched over on the inside. Some builders use washer blocks or pan head screws for intermediate layers which are later removed after the glue sets as will be covered in the following.

The success and quality of the cold molded planking application is highly dependent on the glue bond between layers. Fastenings are used to hold the layers in place while the glue cures, and theoretically the fastenings could be removed after curing and the planking would stay put forever. In the final layer, the fastenings are usually removed except along the outer planking edges such as along the sheer, chine, and keel. Screws or boat nails can be used for fastenings, but in boats of the larger sizes it is common to fasten the planking layers with a pneumatic powered or electric staple gun due to the tremendous number of fastenings required, and the speed capabilities offered by these tools which is desirable when working with glues that have time limitations.

Some builders advocate using any type of metal for the staples since they state that the only function of the staples is to hold the planking in place until the glue sets. While this thinking is theoretically correct, the practical aspects make such practice questionable unless all the staples will be removed from each successive layer. For example, often staples will protrude on the inside of the hull, and these must be cut off for appearance and safety, and/or convenience on most boats. If such staples are made of steel, they will rust and create quite a mess in the bilge of the boat at some later date. On the outer layers, even on those hulls that may be fiberglass covered, leaching may occur and cause unsightly stains on the hull. Then again, who knows what type of galvanic corrosion problems might be set up with non-marine type fastenings adjacent to more noble metals underwater in such an application? In short, unless the fastenings will be removed after

FIG. 19-39—This photo shows a neat application of the first layer of a double diagonally planked hull. Permanent fastenings are used at the contact points.

FIG. 19-40—This is one way to fit the diagonal planking strips in place. However, not all builders are so lucky as to have a ceiling overhead which can be used to transfer pressure to the planking pieces.

FIG. 19-41—The second layer of this double diagonal application is almost complete. Note the fastenings (in this case permanent ones) used along the edges of the planking strips to prevent curling. The butt joint in the side planking shown here would have been better located farther aft in a flatter area of the hull.

the glue sets, it is questionable practice to use any but non-corrosive (preferably Monel or bronze) staples in cold molding applications, at least in a salt water environment. Using ferrous staples could be penny wise, but pound foolish. While the inital cost may be greater for the higher quality fastening, this will usually be regained in the future with higher resale value for the boat.

When fastenings are to be removed, especially through the final layer, they should be driven in with "washer blocks," or thin pieces of plywood between the staple head and the hull surface. This not only prevents the fastening from going in too far, but also spreads the pressure out over a larger area thereby assuring a better glue bond. The washer blocks also make the fastening easier to remove. Drive plenty of fastenings along the edges of the planking strips to minimize the tendency for the edges to curl. After removing the fastenings, the holes should be filled with a suitable putty or filler. However, if the staple holes are small, and the boat will be covered with fiberglass or equivalent, filling the holes may not always be necessary.

In applying the diagonal strip planking, the planking sequence can begin usually at any convenient point, most often amidships, either working forward or aft. In some cases, the builder may want the planking to show through for appearance's sake, such as might occur when using naturally finished veneers, and perhaps alternating between strips with a different colored veneer. In such an application where appearance is important, more care in the planking application will be required. Regardless of the owner's requirements, a close fit between plank-

ing strips is necessary for a good job, and this will require some spiling or shaping of strips from end to end to maintain both the proper diagonal format as well as providing a close fit at joints. If the boat will be covered with fiberglass and painted, absolute tight fits are not always necessary since any minor gaps can be filled with a suitable putty or filler. However, this should not be considered an excuse for sloppy craftsmanship.

SPILING METHODS

Spiling or fitting of the planking is not a difficult job, but it can be time consuming. There is more than one method for spiling and some of the techniques will be described in the following. Spiling, as a word applied to boatbuilding, is generally not defined in standard dictionaries. Basically, spiling is a method of fitting two adjacent planks on a boat so that the joint will fit closely. When diagonally planking a boat, the initial plank bent around the hull is generally (although not necessarily) of uniform width. The next plank to be fitted against the initial one, however, will seldom fit tightly without a gap except at very straight sections. Even if successive planks did fit tightly, the contours of the hull would be such in most cases that the planks would need shaping from end to end, both to maintain the proper diagonal format, and to provide landing to solid hull members on the ends so as not to run out at some intermediate point. Thus, fitting of each successive plank after the initial one will usually be required.

The method of spiling can be done in

FIG. 19-42—Cold molded diagonal plywood plank-ing application over a round bottomed hull. The thin sheet plywood is cut into strips reaching from the keel to the sheer in one piece if possible. Longitudi-nal battens are used to support the planking strips. The battens must be spaced close enough, and the planking should be of sufficient thickness, to pre-vent forming flat spots between the battens.

NOTE: The photos on this page were provided through the courtesy of the Gougeon Brothers, Bay City, Michigan.

FIG. 19-43—Note the diagonal format in this initial layer over a round bottomed hull. The second layer will be applied over this layer at approximately 90 degrees. Glue is applied to all mating surfaces before fastening the planking strips in place. The slight curvature in this hull allows the use of fairly wide planking strips with a minimum of spiling or fitting.

FIG. 19-44—The planking strips are fastened into the longiudinal battens. Here a pneumatic staple gun is being used for speed and convenience. Since all the fastenings at this point in the application will later be removed, strips of plywood ("washer blocks") are used under the fastening heads so that they can be easily removed after the glue sets. The washer blocks also distribute the pressure more evenly for a positive glue bond.

several ways. Obviously if the gap is minimal, the amount to be removed by spiling from the edge of the plank to be fitted can be "eyeballed" and then fitted using a hand plane. In many areas, however, the gap may be considerable and the progressive hand fitting method more time consuming. When this is the case, the piece to be fitted is butted as closely to the preceeding strip as possible. If the gap between the strips is about ½" or less, a batten of at least the width of the widest area of the gap can be used, butted against the edge of the inital plank and lapping over the top of the piece to be fitted. A line can then be drawn using the edge opposite that butted to the preceeding plank as a guide. The plank being fitted can then be sawn to shape and very likely will fit relatively close. Hand fitting, however, still may be necessary in areas with severe twist curves.

Variations on the use of the batten to spile the plank could be the use of a small block of wood guided by the edge of the initial plank, lapping over the strip to be fitted, and then marking the line to be cut. Dividers can also be used, with the one edge of the dividers riding against the initial plank edge, and the point of the other end of the dividers pricking into the strip being fitted at frequent intervals. The pricked points can then be connected with a batten and a line drawn. Then the strip can be sawn to the marked line.

A simple method that can be used with thicker planking is to coat the edge of the initial or preceeding plank edge with chalk or crayon. The strip to be fitted is then lapped over the initial one and a mallet or the palm of the hand is used to force the edge of the initial plank against the underside of the piece being

fitted to transfer a mark. The plank can then be sawn to the transferred line.

Still another method of fitting adjacent planking strips uses a portable power tool such as a router or panel-type circular saw with a small diameter blade. Instead of trying to fit the planking strips closely and progressively, a series of strips can be positioned, stapled, and glued close to, but not in contact with each other, thereby leaving a small gap between each strip. This small gap is then cut away with the tool to form a wider gap with parallel edges about 2" wide. Pre-cut strips 2" wide can then be used to fill each of the gaps thereby making hand fitting unnecessary.

While this method has been used mainly by professional boat builders, there is no reason why any amateur cannot adopt this method as well. However, certain "tips" should be considered. If a power saw is used, it should have a small diameter blade since the depth of cut will be shallow. Furthermore, the guide used is a special bent or flexible type that will conform to the hull contours, and may have to be improvised by the builder. With a router, the tool is mounted onto a plate with a guide fixed to the underside to control the width of cut. A carbide bit is recommended since some staples will invariably be hit in the process. The guide on the router must not be as thick as the planking layer, and with either tool, the guide follows the edge of the preceeding veneer. The depth of cut must be exactly equal to the planking layer thickness. Needless to say, care should be taken in the process, and eye protection should be worn.

Another method of spiling that is somewhat similar to the preceeding is to apply the planking strips with alternating spaces or gaps between (see Plate 19-F). The planking strips must be parallel edged, and the gaps, especially if solid wood veneers are used, must be narrower than the planking strips. In other words, with the planking strips in place initially, there will be a planking strip, then a gap, then a planking strip, etc. To fit the planking strips to the gaps, a special marking gage is used that the builder can easily make. The gage is run along the edge of the planking strip already in place to scribe a line onto the planking strip being fitted which is laid onto the surface so the edges overlap onto the adjoining planking strips. After scribing, the planking strip can be cut to exact size even though some hand planing will be required in most cases to make a tight fit.

In applying the layers of planking with the diagonal method, plenty of glue should be used with all laminations. However, this can be messy work and the builder should take care to clean up all excess glue. Furthermore, care should be used to prevent accidental bonding where it is not desired. For example, glue may tend to get between washer blocks and the planking skin where the staples are located, and this can be minimized by using sheet plastic or waxed paper under the washer blocks. As each layer is applied, the builder should smooth up the surface as necessary and relieve any irregularities in order to insure a positive bond between layers as well as a smooth and fair outer surface. The use of fiberglass or comparable sheathings over diagonally planked hulls is considered standard practice.

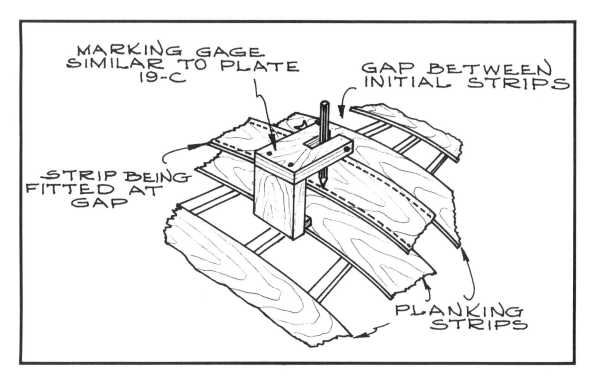

PLATE 19-F—A scribing method for spiling planking strips with diagonal planking

CHAPTER 20 — RIGHTING THE HULL

To complete the construction of a plywood boat, the hull must be tipped right side up, or righted. The manner in which this is done largely depends on the size of the boat. With small boats, there is little problem since sufficient manpower can do the job. However, as the size of the boat increases, so do the problems. In addition to the problem of righting the hull, the builder must consider and plan his construction so that all the various processes such as fiberglassing and finishing the hull are properly coordinated. Therefore, before righting the hull, do a lot of thinking to make sure that everything is ready. It would be a sad thing to go to a lot of trouble in righting the hull and then discover, for example, that the fiberglassing operation, if desired, had been overlooked. Ideally, painting and finishing the hull is completed before righting the hull.

A primary consideration in righting the hull is for the builder to realize that the hull structure at this point will be relatively weak. Before the decking structure and the deck have been added, the hull can easily twist or warp out of alignment, particularly in the case of lightly built boats. Therefore, it is imperative that the hull alignment be maintained before, during, and after the righting operation. Once the hull has been righted and leveled into position both lengthwise and athwartships, it should not be moved until the decking

structure has been installed. If the hull must be moved before this time, it should again be rechecked for alignment before continuing with the construction.

Whenever possible or practical, it is best to right the hull AND the building form together. Doing this will keep the hull rigid and true, besides making it easier to maintain the reference points for completing the inside and easing the job of removing the building form members from the hull. Of course, on larger boats, the weight of the building form would add considerable weight to the hull righting operation, and this should be considered.

The means and devices used to right a hull seem to be limited only by the imagination of the various builders, and consequently there is no preferred or "best" method. Much depends on how much manpower or how much money the builder may have available. Therefore, the methods described in the following should not be considered as the only ways to right a hull. These are merely some methods that can be used, and may not be the most suitable for a particular boat. In picking a method, always take into consideration that lifting the boat up to turn it is usually the simpler part of the task. It is the lowering of the boat down once it has been flipped where the most care and effort must be exercised. On most boats there will be limited ways of holding on to or securing the hull as it comes down right side up.

Most amateurs are usually a little nervous when the righting operation is contemplated. This is probably because the hull may appear to be very large, especially when it might be occupying all of one's garage or yard. However, the typical plywood boat, even though it may seem big and bulky, is usually not as heavy as one would think. For example, the average 20' plywood boat hull on the building form will usually approximate only about 1000 lbs., or only somewhat more than a good sized piano. Consequently, boats up to this size range or slightly larger are most often righted by manpower alone.

The manner of righting a hull using manpower alone will vary depending on the size and weight of the boat. But regardless of the size of the boat, once the hull has been righted it must be set onto something that will hold the boat for the balance of the construction. This can be any sort of jig or cradle that will provide level and rigid support. A cradle on rollers is preferable if possible. Or on the typical trailerable boat, the cradle may be the actual trailer that will be used to haul the boat. This is an excellent way to do the job since it is easy to level and move about such a trailer for completing the rest of the construction. Leaving the wheels off will bring the boat closer to the ground for easier access to the inside.

Obviously, if the boat is so small or

FIG. 20-1—This 17' plywood boat is being righted together with the building form. A total of three men easily performed the task. Notice that one man can support the hull on edge while the others can move around to the other side to let the hull down gently.

204

light that a few people can pick up the ends and simply flip the boat over, not much else need be said except to take care not to chip any paint and to pad any of the forms on which the boat will set. However, on larger boats, more care and thought must be taken. The typical procedure when using manpower alone is to have plenty of room to one side of the boat. Use several old tires on the ground onto which the hull can be rolled since it will not be practical to actually lift the boat as such. Instead, the hull will actually be "rolled" right side up. As noted, the form can be left in the boat. However, if the hull is first removed from the form, be sure that there are some cross braces between the sheer clamps since the hull may be resting with all its weight on a limited area of the sheer momentarily during the rolling.

Gather together as many people as you can find to help in the righting or "rolling" operation. Sometimes a good old "party" with lots of beer will get everyone enthused and help relieve some of the anxiety. Everyone then lines up on the side opposite the clear

area and lifts the boat up to where it is teetering on edge, resting on the sheer, and supported by the tires so as not to damage the hull. Once at an equilibrium point, it only takes a few people to hold it in this position. Then everyone quickly runs around to the opposite side and lets the hull down slowly and carefully onto the tires which should be carefully located to prevent the hull from hitting the ground. The hull can then be lifted or jacked up and the supporting cradle or trailer placed underneath.

A second but similar method can be used and usually applies to the larger craft. All the elements are similar, but instead of using manpower, a light crane is substituted. The crane controls both the lifting and rolling procedure all along, even though some manpower must be used to properly guide the hull. While the use of a crane may seem extravagant, the time required is only brief, and the safety and control, especially where a large, heavy hull is concerned is usually worth the money especially if many helpers are not available.

A precaution should be noted at this

FIG. 20-2—After the hull has been completely planked and righted, it should be securely chocked in the fore-and-aft and athwartship directions. Extreme care should be taken to level the hull about the set-up level or other reference plane. At this stage of the construction, the plywood hull is relatively weak and will tend to distort if not lined up properly. With a hull that is leveled accurately, it will be possible to use a builders square and a level to construct the interior and cabin.

point, and this concerns the righting of large sailboat hulls which may have the ballast installed in or on the hull while it is upside-down. When righting a hull of this type, considerable care must be given during righting because of the leverage such ballast will exert. Once such a hull reaches a certain position, the leverage arm of the ballast could quickly snap the boat over and cause quite a hazardous situation. Therefore, some means of control, such as with lines to the ballast or keel bracing,

should be provided that will restrain this action.

Another method for righting a boat is to use a series of blocks and tackle from a gin pole (see Plate 20). The pole must be long enough for the tackle to reach beyond the beam of the boat when it is on edge. The gin pole is erected approximately at amidships on one side of the hull. The tackle is hooked to a sling around the hull that cannot slip. The pole must be supported with guy wires to the sides so it will not fall. As the hull

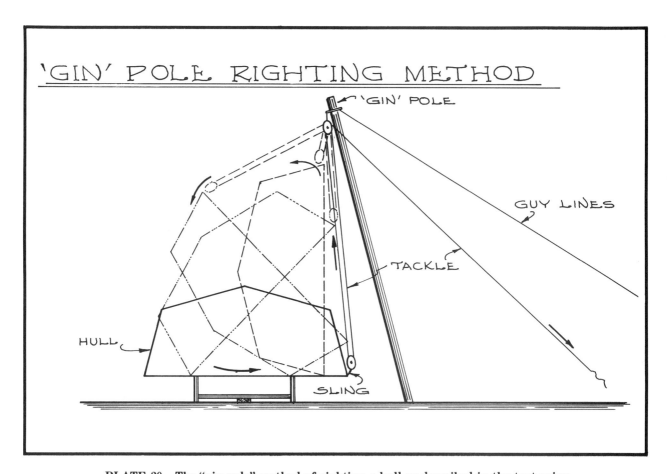

PLATE 20—The "gin pole" method of righting a hull as described in the text using blocks and tackle. A "cradle" can be built around the hull for protection and to provide an automatic "resting place".

is gradually lifted, it must be pulled toward the pole to allow it to come down in about the same area as when it was upside-down. Depending on the size and weight of the boat, several helpers could be required, both to control the tackle, and to guide the hull. The more parts forming the tackle, the easier the tackle will lift the hull, but the slower the tackle will travel through the blocks. On heavier boats, it would be possible to use two such arrangements side by side, however, this could take even more manpower.

A method that can be used, especially on a heavier hull where limited manpower is available, is to jack one edge of the boat up progressively. Use braces to hold the boat on edge while shifting the jack up on supports as the limit of each jack is reached. Once the boat is on edge, use guy lines, preferably from each end of the boat and connect these to the trailer hitch of a car or to a good, stout bumper such as that on a pick-up truck. Locate the vehicle at right angles to the hull approximately amidships so the guy lines form approximate 45° angles with the boat's centerline. The guy lines support the hull on edge, and then the vehicle can be slowly backed to let the hull down on the right side. Care should be taken to ease the fall of the boat and to prevent it from "scooting out" along the bottom as it is lowered. Obviously, with this method there must be considerable room to one side for the vehicle to maneuver.

Finally, a novel method that has been used by some builders is to treat the hull of the boat much like a hunk of meat on a broiler rotisserie. Scaffolding is erected at each end of the hull which is somewhat higher than the hull is wide. The hull is raised off the ground to a height equal to just slightly more than the half-beam. Then a good sized length of pipe is spanned between the scaffolding under the hull and is securely anchored to the hull at several points to form the "spit" about which the hull is then rotated. Lines attached to either side are used to tip the boat and to control the speed of the roll. On heavy hulls, a series of blocks and tackle can be used for greater leverage. After the hull is righted, it is then lowered down into a cradle slid underneath for the balance of the construction.

With some sailboats which have ballast keels, the hull and ballast keel unit are built separately. When the hull is righted, it must be set onto the ballast keel unit. When this is the case, the hull can be righted by just about any of the means described. However, it must be raised high enough to set onto the keel member. In some cases this will be complicated by keel bolts that may have to align and pass through floor timbers on the inside of the hull. This will require that the hull be lifted even higher than the ballast keel itself. While it may be possible to jack such a hull to this height, in most cases a light crane is advised since aligning the hull exactly in position can be more carefully and easily done, and is also much safer.

CHAPTER 21 — DECKING & DECK FRAMING

Once the boat is righted and the formwork removed, the decking is the next procedure in the construction of most boats. Depending on the boat, much of the deck framing members may already be a part of the framework of the hull. In other cases, especially on larger boats, additional members will be required. These members may include deck beams, side deck beams, deck battens, carlings, and strongbacks. The positions and sizes of these members are usually noted on the plans. If the deck beams have not been installed, they must be put in place at this time. Deck beams at frames are fastened with bolts and/or screws as previously described.

Intermediate or auxiliary deck beams are often required between frames on the forward deck or at other points in the hull. The crown of such beams is usually noted on the plans. The crown can be developed by one of the methods given in Chapter 8. It is imperative that preliminary fairing be done along the sheer line to locate the up-and-down position of the intermediate deck beams. The sheer must be a fair, even-flowing line, without dips or hollows. Characteristic of the careless amateur's boat is the humpy or bumpy sheer. Stand back and sight very carefully. If filling is required, by all means fill or shim rather than leave the discrepancy in the sheer line. Although not recommended, such shimming or filling is pre-

ferable to having a defective sheer line, with resultant crude-looking boat.

It is imperative that intermediate or auxiliary deck beams be firmly and securely anchored at their outer extremities, either at the sheer or the carling. Rather than to fit the beam between the sheer clamps, for example, and fasten them into end grain, it is preferable to provide blocking on the sheer. Screws are then driven in through the deck beam into the blocking to provide a secure landing for the beams. Such blocking is shown in Fig. 21-3. Take care in aligning the beams. The deck line must be a smooth, flowing, even curve. Vertical alignment of the beams can be determined by springing a batten fore and aft over the various members, bringing the auxiliary beams to their correct positions.

The longitudinal members forming the extremities of the cockpit and cabin or open area in the boat are called carlings. These members are usually butted to the vertical side of the frame members or to partial deck beams extending from the side frame members. In many cases, it will be possible to make the lower edge of the carling member a straight line. The upper line of the carling, as viewed in profile, must be contoured in a fore and aft direction to the contour of the deck line. This can be accomplished by fitting the carling at the fore and aft extremities. Allow it to project above the side deck beams about

FIG. 21-2—Checking the faired contour of the deck beam to determine the amount of bevel required on the sheer is done in the same way as for the bottom and side planking. Care should be taken in the decking, as humps and hollows will be detrimental to appearance.

FIG. 21-4—Sheet plywood decking is relatively simple to apply. The sheet is lined along the strongback or the dividing points. The builder has painted the interior and installed his steering before application of the decking. This eliminates the necessity of crawling inside the boat to paint the hull.

FIG. 21-1—The overhang that was left at the sheer line when the side planking was applied must be faired. Just as in the application of the planking, the decking must be firmly fitted to all mating areas.

FIG. 21-3—Framework for the decking of a sheet plywood runabout. The longitudinal carling members have been put in place and anchored to the side frames. Notice in particular the blocking at the beam junctions and the landing of the strongback at the stem. Filler blocks have been applied on either side of the strongback to provide a solid bearing over the breasthook area.

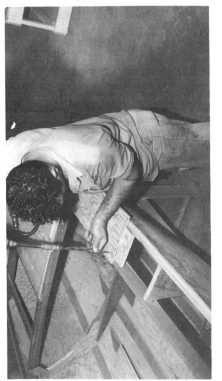

FIG. 21-6—The easiest method of joining the decking is with the simple butt block, although the scarf joint can be used. Note that the builder is making the joint away from the cockpit forward ending.

FIG. 21-8—An inboard runabout with a sheet plywood mahogany center area and raised fir plywood finishing board.

FIG. 21-5—Hatch framework for a small cruiser. Note the fitted piece underneath the strongback to prevent "dishing".

FIG. 21-7—Many unusual types of decking arrangements are possible. This is an overlay method shown in the photo. the raised portion around the sheer will be later radiused to give a rounded appearance before fiberglassing.

½″ at its highest point. To obtain the contour of the side deck for the carling, use a batten sprung over the side deck and extending as far fore and aft as possible. With a pencil, transfer the line of this batten to the carling. The carling is usually set in vertically or canted to some precise angle. Be sure that if vertical, the member is at right angles to the set-up level and, if canted, it is properly angled. If the carling member is a fore-and-aft straight line, as viewed in the plan (from above), use a chalk line and true in the member perfectly. If the carling is meant to be a curved member, as viewed from above, be sure the curve is even, symmetrical, and gentle. Remove or shim the deck beam ends or side frame members so that the carling is either a straight or a flowing line.

The strongback is the longitudinal member running along the centerline of the boat, and notched into each of the deck beams. This member is often heavier and wider than the normal deck battens. It acts somewhat the same as the keel on the bottom of the boat. The fore and aft sweep of the strongback must be a smooth, uniform curve ending on the tip of the stem or breasthook, as the case may be. The breasthook, if used, is often notched to accommodate the strongback or the strongback may be notched over the breasthook. Filler blocking should be used on either side of the strongback over the breasthook to furnish solid bearing for the decking in the forward area of the boat. This blocking should be faired from the sheer to the strongback. If a forward hatch is incorporated in the particular boat being constructed, it is good practice in preliminary installation to allow the strongback to be a continuous member in fore-and-aft length. The decking is

applied over the area and the decking cut away along with the strongback for the hatch area. This will tend to eliminate any flat areas in the fore decking. As shown in Figure 21-5, a vertical fore-and-aft member cut to the contour of the decking may be used to prevent the strongback from flattening out.

Longitudinal deck battens are used on either side of the strongback to give additional strength to the decking area. These members are notched into the deck beams, and carefully fitted against the sheer clamps, or their forward ending points, via blocking.

It is usually not desirable to have the ending of the battens or the strongbacks appear on an exposed beam. This is particularly true in the case of a dashboard in a runabout. Either blocking screwed behind the dashboard or an auxiliary beam can then be used to provide a landing for the battens or strongback.

After all the decking framework members are installed, the entire area must be carefully faired. Just as in the preliminary fairing of the sheer, it is extremely important to shape all the decking areas into smooth, fair curves. Be careful at the ending of a foredeck where it extends along the side of a hull. Do not allow a dip to appear at this point. Spend a lot of time, and stand back often to sight carefully along the lines. Then, when the decking is laid over the framework, it will have a smooth, even contour without humps, bumps, or dips.

Plywood is the logical material for decking or topside covering on just about any type of wood boat, whether the overall construction is plywood or conventional planking. The strength of plywood in all directions, and its low coefficient of expansion and contraction

Boatbuilding With Plywood

make it an ideal material for decking all boats, from runabouts to cruisers. Many variations are possible with plywood decking, and the following paragraphs, photos, and illustrations will cover a few of them.

Although plywood cannot be put on over a compound surface, perhaps this statement should be temered with the realization that plywood panels can be slightly compounded in the decking of a boat. Plywood panels can be applied to almost all decks that are not severely crowned athwartships and in their fore-and-aft direction. If they are radically crowned, it is best to put the fore deck panels on in three or more pieces. To eliminate compounding of the panel, plywood decking almost always requires a joint at the centerline of the boat. In cases where the boat is extremely wide or severely crowned, the joints are made on battens over either side of the strongback putting the decking on in three or more pieces. The plywood panels used for the forward decking should extend as far as possible in a continuous length along the side

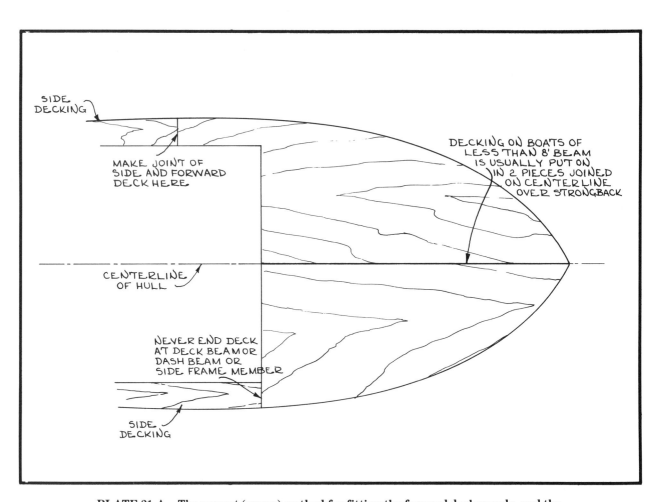

PLATE 21-A—The correct (upper) method for fitting the forward deck panels, and the incorrect (lower) methods. If the foredeck ends at the deck beam as shown, a crack will surely develop in the fiberglass covering and form a weak spot in the deck structure. Continue the foredeck panels aft of this point in all cases.

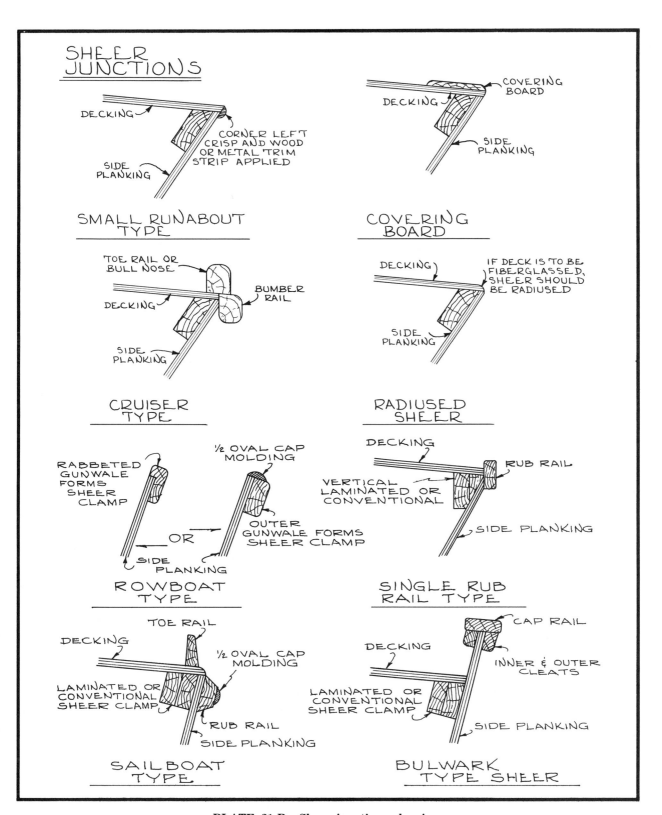

SHEER JUNCTIONS

DECKING

SIDE PLANKING

CORNER LEFT CRISP AND WOOD OR METAL TRIM STRIP APPLIED

SMALL RUNABOUT TYPE

DECKING

COVERING BOARD

SIDE PLANKING

COVERING BOARD

TOE RAIL OR BULL NOSE

DECKING

BUMBER RAIL

SIDE PLANKING

CRUISER TYPE

DECKING

IF DECK IS TO BE FIBERGLASSED, SHEER SHOULD BE RADIUSED

SIDE PLANKING

RADIUSED SHEER

RABBETED GUNWALE FORMS SHEER CLAMP

½ OVAL CAP MOLDING

OR

SIDE PLANKING

OUTER GUNWALE FORMS SHEER CLAMP

ROWBOAT TYPE

DECKING

VERTICAL LAMINATED OR CONVENTIONAL

RUB RAIL

SIDE PLANKING

SINGLE RUB RAIL TYPE

TOE RAIL

DECKING

½ OVAL CAP MOLDING

LAMINATED OR CONVENTIONAL SHEER CLAMP

RUB RAIL

SIDE PLANKING

SAILBOAT TYPE

DECKING

CAP RAIL

INNER & OUTER CLEATS

LAMINATED OR CONVENTIONAL SHEER CLAMP

SIDE PLANKING

BULWARK TYPE SHEER

PLATE 21-B—Sheer junctions showing details at the deck/side planking joint

decks as shown in Fig. 21-6. Ending the plywood panel at the foredeck ending point will create a weak spot that will crack and open up in use. The junction of the side and forward decking is made with either a scarf joint or a butt joint, as shown in Fig. 21-6.

Natural mahogany decks are always attractive and typical of finely finished runabouts. Such decking may be mahogany-veneered plywood. In a runabout-type boat, raised portions can be worked into the deck as shown in Fig. 21-7, with contrasting mahogany and painted finishes. In smaller fast boats, cowls are often used. Finished in natural mahogany sheet plywood, such cowls are attractive when used with a painted deck.

An unusual and attractive finish for a plywood deck is achieved by scoring the plywood panels to make the deck appear as though it were applied in planking strips. These planking strips can be simulated by using a router or a power saw, or they may be painted. In the latter case, the mahogany deck is filled, stained, and varnished. Prior to application of the two final coats of varnish, the decking is striped to the desired contour with a rubber-base paint. A striping wheel can be used for the fine lines required. The two final coats of varnish are then applied over the entire surface. The varnish will not dissolve rubber-base paints, and the finished sheet plywood deck will appear to be planked.

Application of sheet plywood decking is readily accomplished. Usual practice is to align a straight edge of a panel along the strongback or joining portion. The outer contour along the sheer or inner extremity of the cockpit area can be marked and rough-cut. As shown in Fig. 21-4, it is not imperative that the sheer edge or over-hanging edges be trimmed accurately. Plywood decking can be fastened in place either with annular-ring-type nails or screws placed similarly to those in the planking skin. All mating surfaces for the decking should be spread liberally with glue before application. Where appearance is important, take care to prevent marring the decking surfaces. Fastenings should be countersunk or set below the surfaces, and then filled. For naturally finished wood decks, the filler should be to match the wood. More information on finishing is given in Chapter 23.

Covering of decking surfaces with fiberglass or an equivalent sheathing system is recommended for durability, appearance, and a leak-proof covering to prevent water from getting into cabin spaces. On decks where a natural wood finish is desired and durability is not as critical, a lightweight fiberglass cloth sometimes called "deck cloth" is used. Such a material when wetted out with resin makes the weave of the cloth virtually indiscernable. In other cases, a non-skid texture should be provided on the deck covering, and this is covered in Chapter 23. As with other hull appendages, rub rails, toe rails, and similar members are installed after covering the decks with fiberglass.

CHAPTER 22 — MOTOR STRINGERS

Any boat with an inboard engine will require some means of mounting the engine within the hull. The method for mounting will vary not only with the design, but with the type of powerplant system used. For example, with some inboard/outdrive (I/O) units, very little in the way of structural members may be required since the engine may be literally hung onto the inside of the transom in what is called a "cantilever" mount. If the transom is strong enough or if the powerplant is not unduly heavy, such a mounting method may be suitable. But in most instances, it is desirable to mount the engine on members which will distribute the stresses and weight of the engine throughout the hull structure, thereby not concentrating stresses in a localized area.

The longitudinal members to which the inboard engine is mounted are commonly known as motor stringers. Ideally, motor stringers should be as long as possible to spread the strain of the engine over a broad area. However, in some cases, motor stringers may be located only between two bulkheads or frames, especially where the engine is small and low powered such as might be the case in a sailboat auxiliary.

In some cases motor stringers may be made a part of the building form and remain in the hull as shown in Chapter 13. When this is the case, the builder should have a good idea what engine will be used, since the spacing of the motor stringers must be to suit the motor used. Motor stringers which will determine the spacing and location of frame members should be clamped together, laid out while clamped, and cut simultaneously for accuracy. In many cases on runabouts, the motor stringers will require additional notching or contouring in order to support the seat structure, motor, or other adjoining structures (see Chapter 13, Fig. 13-4). In other cases, installing the motor stringers is not done until the hull has been righted and removed from the building form.

One method that is often advocated for mounting the motor is to bolt the motor directly to the motor stringers (see Plate 22-B). With some motors, especially those using a straight shaft with a considerable angle from the horizontal, very wide members or pieced-and-joined members will be necessary to suit the required contour. Such motor stringers may tend to be weak unless reinforced with additional members. But the primary disadvantage with this type of motor mounting method is that aligning the engine is very difficult and tedious if adjustable mounts are not used, especially if the motor is not flexibly mounted at all points including the shaft. Shimming of the engine is usually required with this method, and the alignment must be checked several times before it is perfect.

A better and easier method also uses

motor stringers as the main support members. However, instead of mounting the motor to the motor stringers, the motor is instead mounted to motor beds which side to the inside surfaces of the motor stringers (see Fig. 22-3). The motor can then be carefully aligned while suspended from a hoist, and then once in alignment, bolts are used through the sides of the motor beds into the motor stringers thereby holding the alignment and angularity exactly. The motor beds can be made from solid wood such as oak or Douglas fir, or from galvanized steel or aluminum angles of a suitable size. Because the motor is

mounted to the motor beds and not to the motor stringers, the spacing of the motor stringers will be farther apart for the motor beds to fit between. In some cases, cutting away the motor stringers to clear certain parts of the motor may be required. However, such cutting away must be kept to a minimum to maintain strength. The motor beds with this installation should ideally be at least as long as the engine, and preferably 6" or more longer each way. Good sized carriage bolts no less than ⅜" in size should be used for the motor beds, spaced about 6" apart or at least four bolts per stringer. Lumber used for the

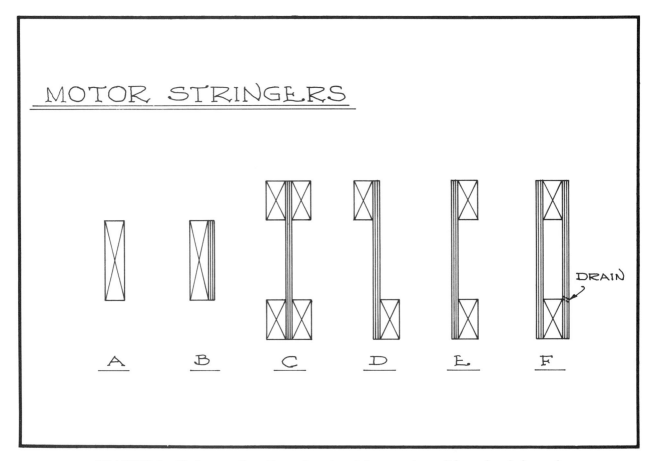

PLATE 22-A—Various sections through motor stringers using solid wood and plywood in combination with solid wood. Types "A" and "B" are most commonly used by the amateur boatbuilder. The plywood web-type ("C" through "F") is often cut away in the plywood area to reduce weight. Type "F" should have limber holes for drainage as well.

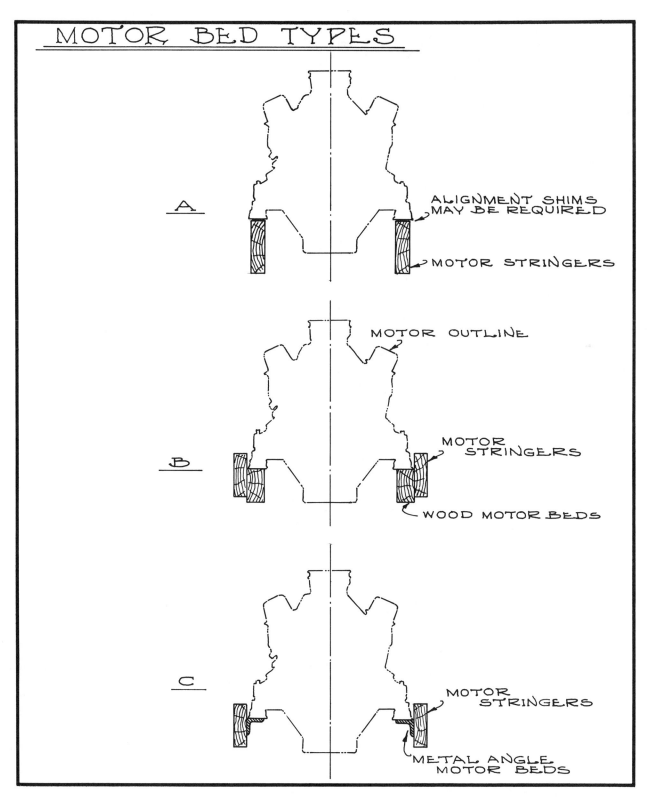

PLATE 22-B—Various motor bed types commonly used. As noted in the text, "B" and "C" are the preferred methods since the motor can be more easily aligned and shimming is not necessary.

FIG. 22-1—Motor stringer blocking is used to transfer the stresses on the motor stringers to the frames as shown here. Wood blocking used here is reinforced with a layer of plywood to prevent splitting. At least two bolts per junction/member are used. Also note that the motor stringers in this boat have been reinforced with a layer of plywood.

FIG. 22-2—At the transom, motor stringers can lap to motor stringer uprights bolted through the transom. Note the additional layer of plywood on the inside of the transom to provide the required thickness to suit the outdrive unit which will be installed later. It is not normally necessary that such a layer extend completely across the transom.

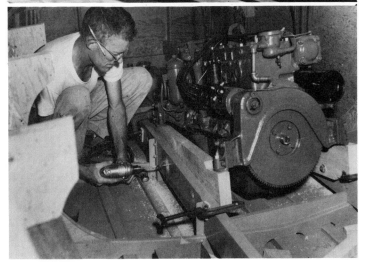

FIG. 22-3—This photo shows the preferred method of installing an engine. The engine is mounted onto motor beds which are in turn bolted to the sides of the motor stringers. This method makes alignment both simple and positive. Note the use of metal angles securing the motor stringers to the frames.

motor beds should not be less than 2″ nominal stock, and considerably bigger with larger and heavier engines. Diesel powered engines require heavier timber than comparably powered gasoline engines, and this should be considered. As a strength adjunct, the sides of motor stringers are frequently laminated with plywood to prevent splitting.

In some designs motor stringers may be made from plywood on edge in conjunction with solid wood members. Such motor stringer configurations form a web structure in the shape of a box section or I-beam section, and can be very strong, considering that the weight would be far less than solid wood members. This type of motor stringer usually ties the bottom of the hull into the motor stringer via solid wood members such as bottom battens, and the motor is then mounted to solid wood longitudinals along the top edge. While this type of motor stringer system has a place on large high speed inboards where weight is critical, it is not common with most amateur built boats as it requires more work and care in fabrication.

With the standard lumber motor stringer system common in plywood boatbuilding, the motor stringers will frequently continue over several frame spaces. Spanning between bulkheads, or a bulkhead to the transom is common practice. In some cases, the motor stringers will be low enough in the hull so that they must be notched over each frame. Such notching must not be excessive, however. In other cases, the motor stringers may be a considerable distance above the top of the frames. Regardless of the case, the motor stringers should not only be structurally joined to each intersecting frame, but also at the ending points such as with a bulkhead or transom. Note, however, that not all designs will necessarily have motor stringers which end at a transom or bulkhead; some may end at frames only. Whatever the case, upright members or blocking are used to tie the motor stringers to the structure. Such blocking can be solid wood or metal angles of either galvanized steel or aluminum. Fig. 22-3 shows an example of metal angle upright blocking methods, while Fig. 22-1 shows wood being used for motor stringer blocking. Fig. 22-2 shows transom uprights used to support motor stringers at the ends. Uprights on transoms and bulkheads can be through-bolted or screwed with large screws through the plywood (as long as the plywood is thick enough) into the uprights. If the plywood is thin, solid wood backing blocks should be used on the opposite side and then fastenings driven about 6″ apart through this, the plywood, and into the upright blocking.

CHAPTER 23 — FINISHES & FIBERGLASSING

The methods and materials used to finish the hull as well as any other portion of a boat's structure will vary considerably. Much will depend on the builder's pocketbook, the use to which the boat will be put, the quality of finish desired, and the amount of work the builder is willing to undertake. The products and technologies in this area are rapidly advancing to such an extent that any aspect that is current can become outdated almost overnight. Consequently, it is difficult to make specific judgements and recommendations on just what may be the most suitable or desirable method to finish out a boat.

For example, most people are familiar with the word "paint", as well as with the procedure of "painting" for the most part. However, the manufacturers of these products prefer to call what is ordinarily known as paint, "coating systems" instead. And when one becomes better informed about their products, the use of this phraseology appears to be justified. Many of the modern coating systems are much more than ordinary paint, and not only is their application more complex, but sometimes very expensive. Of course, expense can be a relative thing, and the durability of some coating systems is so good that ordinary painting, which may be required at closer intervals, could be more expensive in the long run. For the purposes of this book, however, we will speak of coating systems as painting since most individuals are more comfortable with this terminology.

PAINTING

The most important aspect of using any paint is surface preparation. Following this at a close second is following the instructions provided by the manufacturer of the particular product being used. Otherwise, a top quality job that will live up to the manufacturer's promises cannot be expected. For example, if a product calls for a specific grade of thinner, especially where spraying is involved, don't try to save a few bucks by getting a "cheap" thinner that you may think is just as good. Most coating manufacturers spend considerable work and money in researching and proving their products, so take their advice and follow the directions.

The first decision in painting a plywood hull is to decide if the hull will be covered with fiberglass or equivalent sheathing. If such a covering is desired, the surface preparation may be somewhat different since fiberglass must be applied over a clean, dry, unpainted, oil-free, bare wood surface. Therefore, nothing should be applied onto the bare plywood surface that would interfere with the bonding of the resin. For this reason, any putty or filler that is used on the plywood must be of an oil-free type compatible with resin and fiberglass, and it should dry hard with minimal shrinkage.

If the hull will not be fiberglass covered, the following method can be used to finish out the boat if using ordinary marine enamel paint systems. First fill all screw holes, cracks, nicks, and crevices, or other imperfections with a hard-setting putty (see Fig. 23-1 and 23-2). Then sand the surface smooth, but avoid excessive sanding of any plywood surface, especially if of Douglas fir. On other plywood areas, sand only enough to remove surface roughness. Next the plywood surface should be sealed with a suitable sealer. A sealer is used to prevent excessive water and paint absorption thereby stabilizing the plywood. It also means less primer will be used. There are several types of plywood sealers, most of which are usually a very thin, clear liquid resin product. A light sanding after the sealer dries can be done to smooth out the surface. Then sufficient coats of a primer undercoat are applied to hide the grain. This coat can be brushed or sprayed, but if sprayed, the material can be built up to a thick coating in one application. The surface is sanded after drying, re-

moving as much of the undercoat as required to make the surface smooth and to conceal the grain. An undercoat that is a "high-chalk" or easy-to-sand type is preferable to make the work easier. If the surface cannot be made smooth, or the grain of wood not filled after sanding, it may be necessary to recoat again with primer and resand the surface. Any number of coats of primer may be required to obtain the highest quality finishes. After this, two coats of marine enamel should suffice to finish the boat. If a finish color other than white is used, the undercoat can also be tinted to match, thereby making coverage easier.

The above method is a traditional paint method, and it may also be used on surfaces covered with fiberglass with minor modifications. The paint is applied over the fiberglass, and not over the plywood. Since the fiberglass must be applied over a bare wood surface, no sealer can be used on the plywood. But after the surface has been covered with fiberglass, the process is the same; applying an undercoat compatible with a fiberglassed surface, sanding after, then applying the final coats of enamel. The enamel paint system is probably the cheapest system for painting a boat,

FIG. 23-1 (above)—Screw holes and other imperfections or dents filled with a hard-setting putty. FIG. 23-2 (right)—After applying putty, the surface is sanded smooth. While a belt sander as shown can be used, the amount of sanding required is usually minor, and other types of sanders or hand sanding may be preferable. In all cases, excessive sanding of Douglas fir plywood should be avoided.

however, to maintain a fresh appearance, repainting is usually required every season, and sometimes more frequently depending on the color and the abuse the boat will be subjected to. For many, painting is not considered a hard job, especially if the surface is in good shape, and hence this system is often preferred by the individual who will do his own maintenance.

In addition to the enamel paint system, there are many more paint types, some of which are quite "exotic." In many cases, these paint systems are virtually the same types that are used on automobiles. Some of the paint classifications include the epoxy types (both one and two-part varieties), the acrylics, the polyesters, and the polyurethane systems. Most of these are available under various trade names and are especially adaptable to boats covered with fiberglass. In fact, these are the same types of paints often used on fiberglass boats, and in general they are quite durable. For the most part, they are also quite expensive, but since they may last much longer than the enamels, many prefer them, especially where appearance is important.

With many of these special paint systems, a primer undercoat may be optional or even unnecessary. However, the paints will not cover up flaws and surface imperfections, so surface preparation is important. Many of these paints can be applied by brush, but for the most part, spraying will yield better results. Since patching and matching colors is more difficult with many of these paints, be sure that you have all holes that may be required through the hull made and filled with putty before applying the paints. Application requirements may also be critical, so

adhere to the manufacturer's recommendations to the letter. Another precaution is to never "mix" the paint systems of different manufacturers even if of the same paint classification. Stick with one paint manufacturer's system throughout the application.

For boats which will remain in the water for extended periods or at all times, especially in salt water, bottom protection from marine growths and vegetation is recommended. These paints are most often of a type that theoretically never dries completely. They exude toxic substances that kill and prevent such growth from forming on the hull. There are many types of these bottom paints, and some work better in certain areas than others. However, in most cases, bottom paint is renewed at least every season. The best advice on bottom paints is to find out what product is the most popular in the area where the boat will be located, since this is probably the most successful product.

Bottom paints usually require special application techniques. Most are applied directly onto the bare hull surface since they have been known to lift off other paints if applied over a previously painted surface. However, this can vary with the paint, and the manufacturer's recommendations should be followed. Bottom paints are usually applied by brush since spraying may be dangerous. Since the principle of many bottom paints is that they must not dry completely in order to be effective, the boat should be placed into the water almost immediately after application with this type of product.

The bottom paint should be applied somewhat above the actual waterline of the boat in order to provide protection in the event that the boat sinks in the water or trims down at the bow or stern more than expected. The dividing line between the bottom and topside paints is often differentiated by a contrasting paint strip often called the "waterline" but correctly known as the "boot top." This paint is often a special formulation to combat oil and scum discoloration.

To apply a boot top or "waterline," first be sure that the hull is leveled both lengthwise and athwartships. Then mark a couple of points (such as at the stem and transom) where the waterline will be located. The plans should provide this point, or a "guesstimate" will have to be made. Use a level to mark around the hull from these reference points, making the line as wide as desired or as noted on the plans. Mask off the area and then paint. With some boats, the boot top will taper and be wider at the ends of the boat. This is often done for appearance as well as the practical fact that many boats trim down fore or aft.

For fiberglass covered boats which will not remain in water for long periods or where bottom protection from growths is not necessary, painting of the bottom is often not done. Instead, the resin is applied in a clear coat thereby making a transparent surface. While this practice may not appeal to many, it does have a practical reason besides cutting down on work and paint costs. If ever there is a leak in the hull, such as at a crack in the fiberglass covering or other location that could be difficult to track down, the water incursion will leave a tell-tale dark or black trail between the fiberglass and the planking that will be easy to see. Then corrective measures can be localized and made with more positive results. Since the bare resin will not be exposed to sun, durability is not usually a problem.

NATURAL FINISHES & BRIGHTWORK

As with painting, there are many products and methods for applying natural finishes to wood. Again, much will depend on the builder's budget, service requirements, quality of appearance desired, and how much work can be devoted to the job. Since the naturally finished wood surface is almost a marine tradition, such an appearance is often desired, especially by the novice. However, one must realize that it is easy to overdo a good thing. Not only can naturally finished surfaces, especially if of the dark mahogany type, overwhelm the senses when overdone in small cabin spaces, such surfaces can be extremely difficult to maintain, especially when exposed to the elements. So it is a good idea to not become overly ambitious with the use of naturally finished bright-work, especially when it is exposed varnish, unless you enjoy frequently refinishing this sort of surface.

The most basic natural finish, of course, is no finish at all, and this is sometimes used, especially with a wood like teak. Because of the naturally oily nature of teak, some will let the wood "weather" and often speed this process by bleaching the wood. Others may not care for this approach, and instead will apply oil to the wood. Many products can be used for this, and the process is quite simple. The wood is simply sanded smooth, and coats of the teak oil product applied until the wood is thoroughly saturated. Waxing after with a good paste wax is often done but not really necessary.

However, few woods are suitable to these techniques, and hence many will want the protection and appearance of a clear natural finish. Many types of natural finishes are available, including the typical marine varnishes, polyurethanes, and so on, in varying degrees of gloss. As with paints, surface preparation is important, as are the instructions provided with the product. Some products require that the wood be filled, while others can be applied directly to the wood.

Many desire to use wood plugs on natural surfaces in order to conceal or even accentuate the fastening holes. Plugs can be made with a plug cutter, or often purchased ready-made, to suit the size of the screw hole. Either the same wood can be used for matching plugs, or a contrasting wood can be used if the plugs are to show in contrast. In either case the plugs are cut with the grain running longitudinally, and are at least ⅛″ in thickness, which means that the screws must be counterbored at least this far. The plugs are seated over the screw head after coating with glue with the plug grain running parallel with the wood. They can be lightly tapped in place with a mallet. Leave the plug high and trim off with a sharp chisel. Care must be taken, however, as chiseling against the grain is apt to shear the plug off below the finished surface. Leave the plug a little high instead and sand off after to prevent this. Such plugged holes in plywood, however, can be a disadvantage, since the plywood must be drilled too far in for the screw to hold all the laminations as has been noted previ-

ously. Therefore, if plywood is to be plugged it is best relegated to interior work, and then the plywood should preferably be at least ½″ in thickness.

For naturally finished varnished surfaces, the wood is usually filler stained, especially if using mahogany. Because the wood may have varying tones, the filler stain will help even these out as well as filling the open pores which will make subsequent coats of varnish easier to apply. Just about any tone filler can be selected to bring out the grain. Some manufacturers advise a sealer coat directly on the wood before applying the stain, while others are used directly on the bare wood. Either case works out, but follow the instructions. Most fillers are a paste-like substance which can be thinned to the desired consistency. The filler is brushed on or rubbed on to fill the pores, allowed to tint the lumber, and then the excess is rubbed off.

Marine-type varnish is then applied over the filler-stained surface, using a thinned sealer coat first. A second and a third coat is applied over this as a minimum, sanding between coats to a smooth looking surface. More coats are often used for added sheen and durability. Varnish can be sprayed, particularly on the final coat, but may tend to run since the material does not dry too quickly. Such a varnish finish can look extremely beautiful, but to maintain this appearance requires a lot of work, and for this reason many will prefer using another coating such as the polyurethane clear finish. These tend to last longer and are easier to apply, at least initially. Whichever type is selected, stick to the instructions provided.

FIBERGLASSING

The topic of fiberglassing and use of resins is a very broad subject: one that is best covered in a book. Indeed, the material presented here is a condensation from parts of just such a book.*

The term "fiberglass" has become virtually a household word. The dictionary defines it as "a composite material of glass fibers in resin." In this text, we will use the term in reference to the materials used in conjunction with liquid plastic resin, either epoxy or polyester, to sheath a typical plywood boat. There are, of course, materials other than fiberglass that can be used. But, for quite a number of years, fiberglassing has been the method most favored by boatbuilders of all types.

Properly applied, the fiberglass becomes permanently bonded to the plywood and provides a hard, lasting surface that will accept finishes of the highest yacht standards. It must be emphasized that the fiberglass covering described here is applied only for specific purposes. Its advantages are both practical and cosmetic. It improves the appearance and durability of the boat, contributes to ease of maintenance, and helps make a hull leakproof. It is NOT used to increase strength. In a properly designed and built plywood boat, the strength lies in the wooden structure itself. Adding fiberglass for the purpose of decreasing the thickness of the plywood planking is definitely NOT recommended.

*"How to Fiberglass Boats", Second Edition, Published by GLEN-L Marine Designs.

FIBERGLASS CLOTH

Fiberglass cloth is usually a plain square open-weave type. The type of filament most often found in the fiberglass materials used for sheathing boats is known as "E" glass. The lengthwise and crosswise yarns intersect at right angles, much like a basket weave. The cloth is then "cleaned" with a finishing substance, to eliminate ingredients not compatible with polyester or epoxy resin. Although there are many finishing treatments available, the two most common types are volan and silane (or amino-silane).

Fiberglass cloth is categorized by its weight per square yard. Choice of proper weight is important. Cloth thinner than 4 ounces is not durable enough for most boat work, while cloth heavier than about 10 ounces is difficult to wet out and form around corners.

Lightweight 4–6 ounce cloth (usually called "deck cloth") is often used on the decks or hulls of boats, as protection for a natural wood surface. The light fabric becomes very transparent when wetted out with resin, and the weave becomes practically invisible, allowing the true beauty of the surface below to stand out through the clear resin.

For more general applications, such as covering the hull, deck, and cabin top areas, 7-½ to 10-ounce cloth is the best choice. It will provide greater durability and resistance to scrapes and abrasions than the lighter cloth, yet remains quite workable. A single layer of cloth is adequate on sheet plywood hulls, using double lapping seams in critical areas, such as the chine and keel. This laminate will add about 2 or 3 ounces of weight to each square foot of hull cov-

FIG. 23-3 thru FIG. 23-6—These photos show the basic procedures of covering a plywood boat with fiberglass. The "dry" method as noted in the text is being used. The cloth is placed onto the surface, lapping at such areas as the keel and chine. Then the cloth is wetted out with resin, and subsequent coats applied to build up the surface and conceal the cloth. Excess material overhanging the edges is trimmed just before the resin sets up hard.

ered. Two layers of cloth may be preferred on boats planked with multiple layers of plywood or veneers, such as in double diagonal types.

Fiberglass cloth is sold by the yard, and is available in widths of 38, 44, 50, and 60 inches. Fiberglass cloth tape, with selvedged edges, comes in widths from 2 to 12 inches and is ideal for sealing localized areas such as seams.

FIBERGLASS MAT

Fiberglass mat is a reinforcing material. It is made from glass fibers about 1″ to 2″ in length, or from continuous strands arranged in a random swirl pattern, and is formed into a felt-like product. The fibers are held together with a dry resinous binder that is highly compatible with polyester resin. However, there can occasionally be a problem if other resins (especially epoxies) are used, which may be incompatible with mat binders.

Mat for boat use is commonly referred to as "chopped strand mat" or "CSM" and is categorized by weight per square foot (rather than per square yard as with cloth). Like its cloth cousin, mat comes in a variety of weights and widths — ¾ to 1 ounce mat, in 38" width, is ordinarily used for sheathing.

Mat is seldom used alone in sheathing applications. One reason is that the surface does not end up smooth without a great deal of sanding. More importantly, it tends to absorb a high percentage of its weight in resin, and that may cause it to be brittle. The recommended procedure is to use the mat next to the planking, with the cloth over it applied simultaneously. This mat-cloth combination is commonly used over double diagonal plywood or veneer. It can also provide more abrasion resistance at selected hull areas.

A CHOICE OF RESINS

For many years, polyester resin was the principal material used in conjunction with fiberglass to sheath plywood boats. Then along came epoxies, with certain aspects which made them superior to polyesters. As a result, the use of epoxies became widespread. Epoxy resins not only have superior bonding strength, they also virtually do not shrink, and they exhibit a degree of flexibility. They are also more costly than polyesters.

To properly choose which resin is best for his purpose, the user must determine just what his requirements and expectations are for his particular boat. Is the boat worth the extra expense of epoxies? Will the boat be kept long enough to warrant the cost? Does the user want to subject himself to the potential health problems associated with epoxies? Since the application methods are basically the same for both, labor is not really an issue. However, the decision to sheath with epoxy or polyester resin is not an insignificant one, and should be based primarily on the answers to the questions raised here.

In some instances, it is possible to use polyester resin in combination with epoxy. For example, a boat may be assembled with epoxy glues and fastening holes filled with epoxy resin-putty, fiberglass sheathing with polyester resin could be used over such a surface as the majority of the area is bare wood. However, if the entire area has been coated with epoxy in an encapsulation system, sheathing using polyester resin would be a poor choice, as it would not stick well. Conversely, an epoxy resin applied over a cured polyester would bond, but the process wouldn't make sense. The bonding ability of the epoxy would only be as good as the polyester substrate. The two resins would be stuck to each other tighter than they would be to the hull.

POLYESTER RESIN

One of the disadvantages of polyester resins is that they tend to be brittle when unreinforced. This peculiarity can make them unsuitable for coating or gluing. The polyester used in sheathing is catalyzed by a substance called M-E-K (which stands for methyl ethyl ketone peroxide.) The addition of the catalyst creates a heat reaction within the polyester, causing the resin to harden.

The catalyst is a small percentage of the final mix, usually 1% to 2% by weight. However, to be sure of getting the proper amount required, you should follow the directions for the resin being used. The amount of catalyst can be varied, within a range, to compensate for ambient temperature and to control pot life.

Two types of polyester resin are commonly used for sheathing a boat. These are called laminating and finishing resins. Catalyzed polyester laminating resin will not cure completely as long as the surface is exposed to air. In order for the resin surface to cure completely (at least within a reasonable period of time), it must be sealed off from air. This is done with an air inhibitor (most often, wax) that is built into the resin. The resultant product is called a finishing resin.

One frequently-used (and desirable) option is to add a surfacing agent (the wax additive) to the existent laminating resin to make it into a finishing resin. The wax additive or surfacing agent is added before the catalyst, and thoroughly stirred into the laminating resin to convert it to a finishing type.

The advantage of using a surfacing agent is that it can help to eliminate having two different products in separate containers. Converting laminating resin into finish resin gives the builder better control. The finishing resin can be mixed when needed and in the quantity required, thereby eliminating

waste. Having to purchase only the laminating resin, and the wax additive, should also result in considerable cost savings.

During the cure, the wax in finishing resin will rise to the surface and "lock out" the air, allowing the resin to set. This wax must be removed in order to obtain a good bond for additional coats of resin or paint. The cured surface can be washed down with acetone or lacquer thinner, but final removal can only be done by careful sanding. The usual procedure is to apply laminating resin for the preliminary coats and finishing resin for the final one, eliminating sanding between coats, except to smooth out nubs, runs and major imperfections. Laminating resin can be sanded, but does tend to gum up sandpaper very quickly.

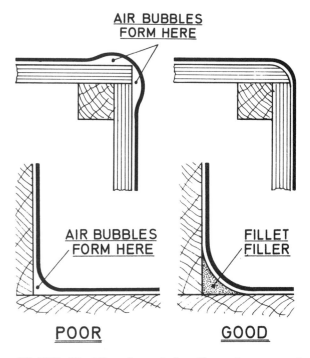

PLATE 23 Fiberglass cloth will not form around interior or exterior crisp corners. The material will lift from the surface and an air bubble will form. This is why all edges should be radiused and all interior hard corners filleted with wood or resin-putty.

Polyester resins are usually brushed or rolled on the fiberglass surface. However, by thinning the resin about 5%–10% with styrene and usng a pressure-pot type spray gun, spraying may be feasible. A note of caution: spraying is best done by those well experienced with the process. Catalyzed resin has a limited pot life and, if the spray gun is not cleaned in time, the gun can be ruined. Repeated coats of resin can be sprayed on, but only so long as the surface does not set up. Spraying resin, while easier in some ways, has its drawbacks. It spews a lot of objectionable fumes into the air, which can be dangerous if the worker is not adquately protected and in a proper workplace.

EPOXY RESIN

The materials for sheathing with epoxy consist of two parts: the resin (usually called part "A"), and a curing agent or "hardener" (usually called part "B"). Proportions of resin to hardener may vary, depending on the product, but ratios of 1:1 to 5:1 are common. Hardeners are categorized as "fast" or "slow," indicating the speed with which it causes the resin to set up. Selecting the proper hardener allows the builder to accommodate the ambient working conditions. Higher temperatures shorten the time available to work with the resin before it starts to jell. As the quantity of hardener should NEVER be varied, different hardeners are used to control pot life.

Unlike polyester resins, all epoxies are tenacious bonding agents and can be used as a glue. However, it should be noted that, for many conditions, micro-spheres, silica, fiber fabrics or other products may be added to more effectively fill gaps.

Only one epoxy resin need be used throughout the sheathing process. There are no separate laminating or finishing resins as there is with polyester resins. This means that successive coats of epoxy can be applied with little or no preparation of the surface between applications (assuming, of course, that the previous coat is smooth enough).

There is one qualification to this statement, however. Epoxy coatings which have completely cured have a by-product, usually caused by ambient temperature variations. Called "amine blush," this wax-like substance is quite normal and can be removed easily. First, it should be wiped down with water, often with a little ammonia added. Then it is sanded. The film may not occur when the resin is in a semi-cured state and subsequent coats are added without further surface preparation. Remember, however, that epoxy resin should NOT be applied by spraying, due to its toxicity. The recommended method is to use a brush, roller or squeegee.

PIGMENTING RESIN

Both polyester and epoxy resins can be pigmented, but there are considerations the builder should be aware of. Resins are not paint products, so the finished surface may not be as high quality as some may desire. Coloring does not provide the opaque quality, depth or brilliance of paint. Since the final surface will require sanding, a certain amount of gloss and color intensity is lost. Often the surface ends up splotchy. However, using pigment to color the resin to match the final paint coating is often done. This can provide a subsurface to the final finish and help make abrasions less apparent. When coloring resin, use only the amount and type of pigment recommended for the particular polyester or epoxy product being used.

THE WORK PLACE

A critical factor in working with resins is heat. The ideal temperature to use either epoxy or polyester resin is about 70 to 85 degrees F., Do not attempt to use polyester below 60 degrees F., although some epoxies can be used down to the 40 degree range. In most cases, temperatures above 100 degrees F. are impractical for resin application. Don't work in direct sunlight or where moisture from fog, dew or rain may settle on the surface overnight. Have plenty of ventilation, but avoid forced air circulation devices or windy conditions which may dry solvents in the resin too rapidly.

Don't come up short in the middle of the job. Be prepared. Have all the necessary supplies and tools on hand. You'll need a tape measure, razor knife, scissors (preferably two), squeegees, brushes, close-nap foam paint rollers (with frame), a paint tray, measuring cups, stirring sticks, mixing containers, a staple gun and/or masking tape. To handle sanding, you'll want a power sander or a drill with disc sander, and varying grit sandpaper. To keep track of everything, a well-organized workbench is useful, as is a shelf to store

things. For cleaning your hands and tools, have a solvent (such as lacquer thinner or acetone) and a bucket of hot water with some strong detergent and/or household ammonia on hand. However, DO NOT use the solvents to wash your hands as you would use soap. Serious dermatitis can be caused by repeated and excessive use of such solvents. A good waterless hand cleaner with lots of paper towels is much safer for cleanup.

SAFETY

READ THIS SECTION CAREFULLY . . . THEN READ IT AGAIN

* * *

Epoxy and polyester resins, and especially their catalysts and hardeners, are chemicals that are very DANGEROUS if not handled properly. READ ALL SAFETY INSTRUCTIONS (both on containers and in supplemental literature from the supplier) and FOLLOW THEM.

* * *

ALWAYS use protective glasses, goggles or face mask when using these chemicals. NEVER handle them without gloves. Use protective clothing and a GOOD respirator when sanding or handling filler materials such as silica or microspheres. Consider using barrier cream and hand cleaner.

* * *

Keep ALL materials away from children and animals.

230

DO NOT work in any area with an open flame and DO NOT SMOKE when working with these products.

* * *

Disperse partially jelled resin over the ground; concentrated batches of partially cured resin can give off enough heat to ignite combustibles.

* * *

If epoxy or hardeners come into contact with the skin, WASH IMMEDIATELY. Epoxy resins can cause severe dermatitis in some people and if a rash develops — STOP — see a physician and explain the chemicals being used. Fiberglass fibers are an irritant that may cause minor skin rash. However, this usually disappears in a day or so and is more of an itch but clothes contaminated with these fibers are best disposed of.

* * *

If you do TAKE CARE with resin and related materials, treat them with the respect they deserve and use good safety practices, you should have few problems or hazards to contend with.

SURFACE PREPARATION

Preparation of the plywood hull prior to fiberglassing is very important to the success of the job. Fiberglass must be applied over a dry bare wood surface free of dirt, oil or grease if the cloth is to adhere properly. All screw holes, cracks and other indentations should be filled with hard setting oil-free putty. One such putty can be made from resin, either epoxy or polyester with suitable additives. For best results, use the same resin that will be used to fiberglass the boat.

Common additives are microspheres, silica, milled fibers or even sawdust. Microspheres are tiny beaded hollow spheres and are quite easy to sand when made into a resin-putty. Silica alone tends to be somewhat harder to sand. Another approach is to use a combination. A mixture of microspheres with a little silica tends to retain most of the sanding ease and makes the resin-putty easier to apply. Consistency can be varied by adjusting the ratio of resin to additives. Usually a 2-½ to 3 parts filler to 1 part of resin (by volume) is a good starting point for a microsphere and silica filler.

After puttying all imperfections, the surface should be sanded flush. Avoid excessive sanding on rotary cut plywood, such as Douglas fir. It isn't necessary (or desirable) to sand the entire plywood surface. Just be sure it is cleaned of all sawdust prior to applying the fiberglass covering. Edges and corners should be generously rounded, as fiberglass will not adhere to sharp edges.

Appendages such as lift strakes, outer keels, spray rails and similar items should be put on after the fiberglass is applied. They should be bedded in a resin-putty mix or attached with a layer of resin-saturated fiberglass acting as a gasket. Once installed in such a manner, the appendage is there to stay. If there is any likelihood that removal will be desired, substitute marine mastic or bedding compound. Fittings such as a strut or a bow eye through the stem, should be pre-assembled to the boat prior to fiberglassing, then removed and the fiberglass applied. Once the hull is finished, the fittings are refastened in place.

FIGURING THE MATERIAL REQUIRED

Fiberglass cloth comes in varying widths, generally from 38 to 60 inches. Judicious selection of sizes to best match the hull can result in cost savings. Applying cloth lengthwise is common, but it can also run across the boat or even diagonally. In smaller craft, such as canoes, the cloth may cover the bottom and sides from keel to sheer, or even from sheer to sheer, in one piece. In most boats, however, hull junctions and corners such as along the chine, keel and stem are double-lapped. It is best to have as few joints as possible, with all junctions lapped from 2 to 4 inches.

When figuring widths and lengths of fiberglass cloth required, be sure to take lapping distance into consideration. The square footage of coverage per gallon of resin varies. However, assuming the use of three coats, most resins should cover about 50 to 60 square feet per gallon. Thus, after determining the cloth required, multiply width times length (both in feet) and divide by the square footage factor of 50 or 60 to obtain the approximate number of gallons of resin required.

Obviously, any calculation regarding resin use must be based on the premise that it will not be wasted. Don't mix more resin than you can use before it jells. Usually a quart of catalyzed polyester resin, or epoxy with hardener added, is about as much as a person can handle in normal temperatures. To eliminate waste, pre-measure the catalyst and polyester resin (or the epoxy and hardener) in separate containers. Have a helper ready to mix the ingredients together on demand. In this manner, resin loss will be kept to a minimum and a ready supply of new resin will be available for continuous application.

Polyester working time can be controlled to a certain extent, by varying the amount of catalyst. By the same token, fast or slow hardeners will alter pot life of epoxies. Both polyester and epoxy will cure more slowly in cooler temperatures. To provide more pot life, pour catalyzed resin in a large pan, such as a paint tray, and set the container in ice water. Conversely, to shorten pot life, set the container in warm water.

APPLYING THE FIBERGLASS

There are two methods of applying fiberglass: one called "wet" method and the other "dry" method. The wet method lays cloth over the plywood surface to be covered in a wet layer of catalyzed resin. The dry method applies cloth on a bare wood surface with resin forced through the cloth weave onto the plywood surface. Except for vertical or overhead surfaces, the wet method is seldom used for typical plywood boat sheathing.

Don't confuse the terminology. Epoxy resin can be applied to bare plywood prior to fiberglassing, BUT this coating may also have been pre-applied prior to either building the hull or to sheathing, and thoroughly cured. Pre-coating with polyester and allowing to cure is NOT advised.

When the wet method is used, the fiberglass cloth is roughly pre-cut to size and rolled onto a cardboard tube or dowel for later application. The hull is then coated with catalyzed resin, either epoxy or polyester laminating type. Any area that appears to absorb resin rapidly and looks dry is recoated. The fiberglass cloth is unrolled from the tube right onto the wet resin surface. Wrinkles will appear and should be smoothed out by lifting and stretching the cloth. The builder can also use glove-covered hands to force the cloth to the plywood. The surface may have white spots in areas that are not completely saturated with resin. If so, additional resin should be immediately applied (before resin starts to jell) and spread with a roller or squeegee, as described in the following section on the dry method.

In the dry process, fiberglass cloth is stapled, or taped into position over the surface, just enough to hold it in place. The average person, working alone, can cover about 20 or 30 square feet, at 70°F. before resin starts to set up or jell. So, if the surface is larger, either get a helper or do the task in segments. Catalyzed resin, either epoxy or polyester laminating type, is poured onto the cloth surface and spread with a squeegee or a short-napped plastic foam paint roller.

Areas not completely coated with resin will appear white or "milky." More resin is then applied, or pushed over from another area. Use the squeegee and work the cloth from the center toward the edges, forcing the air and white spots from the surface. Add more resin if required. Remove the tape or staples as soon as practical. Don't apply an excessive amount of resin, only enough to wet the fiberglass cloth and make it bond to the plywood. At this stage, the cloth weave should be apparent and the surface free from bumps and runs. Watch for "resin-rich" areas, which will be indicated by a glossy surface.

White spots, indicating an air pocket or a resin-starved area, frequently appear at edges and must be eliminated. This is done by reworking the area with a brush, squeegee, or roller. If, by some chance, the resin sets up with surface white spots, rework the area again. First, it must be ground down to bare wood. Then, a patch of fiberglass is applied, lapping over the solid laminate by a couple of inches or so. The patch is then feathered into the solid fiberglass area.

After the hull is covered, trim the cloth at the overhanging area. This should be done before the resin sets up hard, but not too soon. If done too early, the cloth will be pushed around and the bond may be ruined. If done too late, the razor or utility knife will not cut the cloth, and the edge will have to be ground or sanded off. Try a small area at different intervals in order to determine the exact time to trim.

It is possible to continue applying additional coats of resin over fiberglass cloth without stopping until the weave is filled. However, when the resin begins to jell, STOP and allow the surface to harden. A fiberglass surface coated with polyester laminating resin will be somewhat tacky. At this point, only the nubs and rough spots need be knocked off before applying further coats. Use a final coat of finishing resin to seal the surface from the air. Epoxy resins will set up hard, but an amine blush may come to the surface. This must be removed before sanding or the application of subsequent coats (see the section on EPOXY RESIN above). Once the surface has been built up with sufficient resin, sand it smooth in preparation for applying the final finish.

Joints and overlapping fiberglass areas are "feathered" or tapered to prevent a hump or unfair appearance. After curing, the first layer is tapered to the hull surface. Subsequent layers lap over and are ground flush with the first layer in a gradual taper. An alternate method of feathering the initial layer is to use resin-putty (mixed as mentioned previously) to taper from the cloth edge to hull surface. Make the taper gradual by applying the mixture with a wide putty knife or drywall tool. This works especially well with epoxy resins.

If two layers of cloth are required, the second layer can be applied right after the first is wetted out, finishing the process as described in the foregoing section. When using a layer of mat and cloth, usually with polyester resin, the two can be put on simultaneously by working rapidly. Polyester laminating resin should be catalyzed to allow as much working time as possible, and the job should be done in mild temperatures.

The weight of cloth and mat is also critical. Do not attempt to use mat heavier than 1 ounce or cloth over 10 ounces. Resin applied directly over mat cannot be spread by brush, roller, or squeegee, since the glass fibers tend to pull apart. A special serrated "mat roller" is made for this purpose, and should be used if laminates of mat and cloth are applied separately.

To apply mat and cloth simultaneously, rough-cut the material to size. Mat junctions are butted together, not lapped. Tear the edges at the junctions, rather than cut with scissors. This will provide the best means to interlock the mat sections. Then lay a section of mat in position, and fold it back onto itself. Pour or daub generous amounts of resin onto the mat surface that will contact the hull. Then, unfold it over the area to be covered, so that the resin will wet the mat from the backside. Use glove-covered hands to manipulate the mat

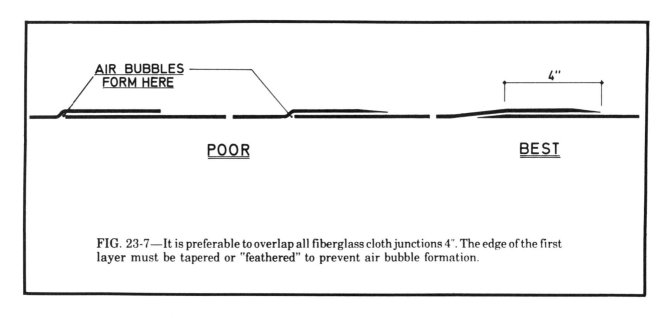

FIG. 23-7—It is preferable to overlap all fiberglass cloth junctions 4". The edge of the first layer must be tapered or "feathered" to prevent air bubble formation.

into position, and pour on more resin. Once the mat is in place and wet with resin, immediately apply the cloth. Use a squeegee, with firm pressure, to smooth out the mat and cloth simultaneously. Apply more resin as required and keep working the material until the surface becomes transparent without white spots. The remainder of the job is done in the same fashion as a single-layer fiberglass sheathing application.

OBTAINING A TRANSPARENT SURFACE

Many desire a natural finish over woods such as mahogany or similar types of plywood veneers. Such surfaces can be covered with lightweight 4-6 ounce fiberglass cloth. The weave will be virtually invisible, particularly with the lighter material. The wood surface must be carefully prepared, leaving no sandpaper scratches or other apparent imperfections. Fiberglass resin will darken the surface considerably and will usually give the rich appearance desired. It is also possible to stain the wood to the desired color, prior to fiberglassing, with certain types of oil-free products.

Lightweight cloth is applied by the dry method, preferably without seams. Where seams are required, cloth is lapped slightly and the two layers of cloth cut simultaneously with a razor knife running against a straight edge so cloth edges will mate in perfect butt joint. The knife must cut cloth only, not plywood. The exact time of the cutting may also be critical. Cut too soon the cloth will roll up on the blade; too late and the wood to cloth bond may be broken.

Lightweight cloth should be applied with an epoxy resin for best results. Finishing coats of resin are used to completely fill the cloth weave. The surface is then sanded smooth with very fine grit sandpaper, preferably wet or dry type. This will dull the surface, but several final coats of clear marine finish with ultra-violet inhibitors will bring it back to a high sheen.

FINISHING

When applying sheathing materials, use only as much resin as necessary to saturate cloth, bond the surfaces together, conceal the weave, and provide a sanding base. Excess resin can lead to cracking, and thick buildups will not be properly reinforced by the sheathing material. More resin does NOT mean more strength. The final coat of resin should be no thicker than necessary to develop a smooth, even surface.

The amount of sanding required depends on the surface quality acceptable to the builder. Bear in mind that gouges, deep sanding marks, or other surface imperfections will not be concealed by the final coat of resin. These imperfections should be resin-putty filled or further coats of resin added and then sanded until smooth.

Another method is to sand the surface as smooth as possible, though not necessarily totally free of minor gouges or sanding marks. A high-build primer can be brushed, sprayed, or rolled on the surface to fill minor defects and then sanded for the final finish. Sanding primer is much easier than sanding a hardened resin surface.

CHAPTER 24 — INTERIOR JOINERYWORK

The cabinetry, or interior joiner-work as it is called in the marine field, will vary considerably depending on the type of boat. A small open boat will require little if any such joiner-work, whereas a large cruiser could have considerable joiner-work inside the cabin and cockpit areas. Plywood is the ideal material for much of the joinery material, but an exterior or marine type must still be used even though the cabinetry members may be located within a cabin. In some cases, depending on the type of boat and the conditions under which it may be used, some compromises can be made with the quality of the fastenings and glue, but the lumber and plywoods used must not deteriorate under marine conditions. Non-corrossive fastenings are still recommended, especially in saltwater conditions.

The prime rule with all interior joiner-work is to keep the members as light in weight as possible. While this may be more critical in certain types of boats, the rule should still be adhered to if only for economy reasons. A lighter boat is always cheaper to run, and a sailboat will perform better if it is not overloaded with deadweight. In most cases, the interior joiner-work will be nonstructural in nature, and consequently, heavy structural members and overly strong building methods won't be necessary. In fact, with most boats, the interior joiner-work could be removed from the boat and the hull would still be a completely integral strength unit. However, there are some exceptions to this which will vary with the design. For example, some bulkheads which are strength members may be a part of the joiner-work. It is also true that the joinery, especially where it is attached to the hull, will impart considerable strength and rigidity even though this extra reinforcement is not absolutely necessary to the strength of the boat. Therefore, if extensive modifications are desired to the boat being built (or even an existing boat for that matter), it is advisable to contact the designer for advice if in doubt.

Throughout the joiner-work, all junctions should be glued with a hard-setting glue. An exception to this would be in areas which may require access, where the removal of certain members would therefore be necessary. Plastics can sometimes be substituted for metal hardware items with good results, such as for door and drawer pulls.

Throughout the installation of the joiner-work, the builder should constantly consider the ventilation of the interior hull spaces. All cabinets and closed-in spaces should be fitted with vents that will insure an adequate and positive flow of air through the boat at all times. Dead air when coupled with moisture and high temperatures can promote mildew and rot, not only to the boat, but to its contents as well. Doors and drawers of lockers should be fitted with vent holes, screens, or louvers. On taller locker doors, an upper and a lower vent should be fitted, or the entire door of any locker could be of the louvered type. Ventilation to the bilge spaces must also be provided, and this is often done by deck-located intakes and outlets with tubing leading to the enclosed spaces. It is common to install a powered ventilator in line with such tubing at some point.

In joiner-work, the amateur tends to use heavier material than is necessary. With the exception of some structural bulkheads, vertical joinery bulkheads such as locker sides and facings can usually be from ¼" to ⅜" plywood. Structural bulkheads usually range from ⅜" to ½", with ¾" plywood sometimes used on larger craft. Tops of lockers and counters are frequently ½" plywood, as are berth tops and seat tops. The thicker ¾" plywood is usually only used on countertops which will be used in heavier service or for table tops. Countertops are often covered in plastic laminate or linoleum to suit.

Plywood cabin joinery is framed with solid wood members at all the junctions. These solid wood members provide the solid backing for the various fastenings and add strength. At corners, the solid wood members can be rabbeted for the plywood which will then conceal the exposed plywood edge. Or the plywood can lap over the solid wood blocking, and the exposed edge later covered with a suitable molding or trim strip (see Plate 24-A). Either practice is suitable as long as the edge of the plywood is protected from damage. Such junctions are also more attractive and stronger than just a simple lap.

FIG. 24-1—Fitting floorboards in a runabout or small cruiser is done by using a guide block as a marking gage to the side of the hull. In this particular instance, the floorboards bear on the frame members.

FIG. 24-2—The floorboards being fitted into position. In many instances, the floorboards will be in several pieces, with a joint over a longitudinal batten. In many cases, the outer floorboards are screwed in place, although not glued, so that future removal is possible. The center section should have hatches at critical points or be removable for bilge inspection and access.

FIG. 24-3—The beginning of a cabinet in a small cruiser. Note that the construction is being carried on before the cabin sides are put into position. This will simplify much of the fitting if all similar structures are put in before the cabin sides and roof.

FIG. 24-4—The construction of a vee berth in the bow of a small cruiser. The berth tops of ⅜″ plywood are in two parts joined over a batten on the centerline. Note the blocking on the chine logs against the planking to support the berth tops.

FIG. 24-5—A bulkhead in position in a small cabin cruiser. Note the ledge or cleat fastened on the bulkhead to provide a landing for the cabin sole, and the notches for supporting battens under the sole.

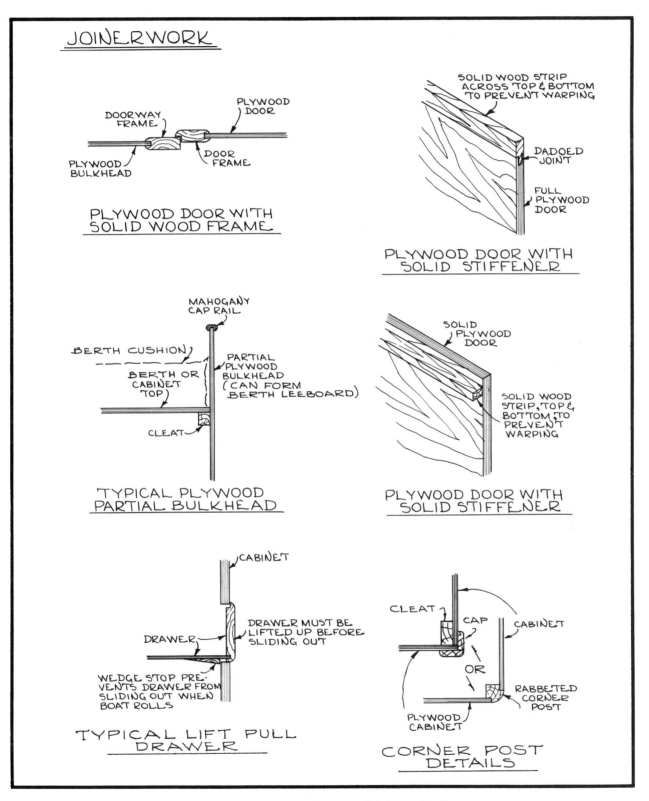

PLATE 24-A—Typical plywood joinery details

Junctions at cabinet and countertops are handled in a similar manner. However, on boats of any size, such as cruisers, raised rails called "fiddles" or lee rails should be fitted to all such tops to keep items from sliding off when underway. Such fiddles may be used to cap the plywood edge. The height that fiddles protrude above the surface will vary with the type of boat, but an inch or two or even more is not unusual in a typical large boat. Openings, at least at one corner, should be provided with all fiddles so that the top can be cleaned off with ease (see Plate 24-B).

Throughout the interior joiner-work, the exposed plywood edge should always be covered, and ways to do this with the cabinetry have just been noted. However, other situations crop up such as cabinet doors and berth leeboards. If cabinet doors are made from sheet plywood, there are at least two ways to cap the edge. One way is to dado or rabbet a solid wood strip around the perimeter (see Plate 24-A). Another way is to cap the edges with thin strips of plywood or "wood tape" glued to the edges using contact cement. Note that plywood doors, especially if they are

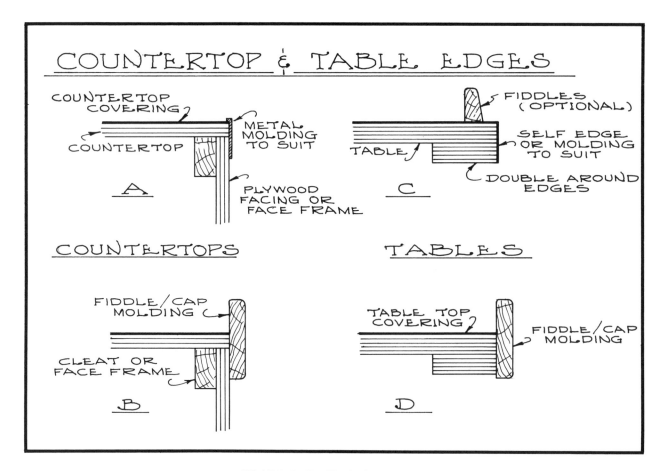

PLATE 24-B—Typical counter-
top and table top edge details

240

large, a backing strip or batten on the inside of the door may be required to minimize warping. Berth leeboards (which keep the crew members from falling out of their bunks) are often an extension of the berth facing plywood. A simple wood cap can be grooved or rabbeted for the plywood to conceal the exposed edge of the plywood and serve as a stiffener in this case (see Plate 24-A).

A lighter type of cabinet door is the panel and frame type. Doweled and/or splined junctions are used at the corners, and thin plywood panels, which can be of a decorative type, are fitted in the rabbeted frame. Natural wood is often used for the frame, stained and finished to suit. The edge of the door is frequently rabbeted to utilize a standard off-set type hinge. Cabinet doors as well as drawers must be held positively in position when underway. Positive catches (and not the regular friction or magnetic catch found in houses!) can be used for this purpose. The cheap hook-and-eye does the job well, if not as pleasing to the eye. With drawers, the lift-and-pull type is recommended as shown on Plate 24-A. In some cases, sliding cupboard doors are used. If these are not fitted fairly tightly in their grooves, or equipped with a catch, especially when located athwartships, they will tend to slide back and forth, spilling the contents of the locker in the process.

As noted, the "floor" in a cabin or cockpit on a boat is called the "sole". The thickness of plywood used for the sole can vary with the boat, sometimes being as thin as ⅜" plywood on small boats, or up to ¾" plywood on larger boats. The thickness depends both on how the sole is framed, and just what degree of flexibility is acceptable. On the larger cabin-type boat, ¾" plywood is often used even

though it is heavy, since it requires a minimum of framing for suitable stiffness. Various hatches should be provided in the sole of a boat at critical areas for inspection and access purposes. Such hatches should be flush with the surface and can be built as shown in Plate 24-C. Depending on the situation, these hatches can be permanently screwed in place, or held with hinges and catches, or simply set in position (although this latter practice is not advisable on certain types of boats such as high-speed powerboats or large sailboats). Some will desire the cabin sole to be decorative by using natural wood coverings. This can be accomplished by using an underlayer of plywood, about ½" thick, and then covering with teak strips caulked between or fitted with contrasting wood filler strips such as holly. Others will simply use a synthetic yarn carpet or linoleum covering.

In the cockpit area, the plywood cockpit sole can be covered with teak strips also. Or the surfaces can be covered with fiberglass or any of the suitable deck covering materials available. Some may want to use ordinary linoleum, however, this surface is quite slippery when wet. Non-skid material (such as ground walnut shells or fine sand) is often mixed into the paint for providing slip resistance to cockpit soles and deck areas.

The vertical and horizontal joinery panels must be attached to the hull at many points. In some cases the sole is installed first, running out to where it junctions with the inside surface of the planking. But in other cases the vertical members may be set in first, sometimes bearing onto the bottom planking, and then the sole is fitted and blocked between these uprights. The joinery members can secure to the hull by a variety of methods. For example, they can junction with various structural members such as frames and longitudinal battens. In other cases, they can junction directly to the inside of the hull planking, other bulkheads, or to other joinery members. At all such junctions, the members are blocked in position and preferably screw fastened. These blocking members are commonly known as "cleats" and any suitably sized wood can be used to make the necessary cleats. Such cleats can be continuous or spaced at intermittent intervals; whatever is necessary to make the structure solid at the attaching junction.

Many cabin boats have vee-berth arrangements in the forward portion of the boat. An easy way to make these berth tops is to use two panels of plywood, one on each side of the centerline and butt joining over a batten or strongback notched into cross beams. While the berth top can extend out to the planking, this is not absolutely necessary in most cases. Instead, a batten can often be notched along the inside of the side frame members, and

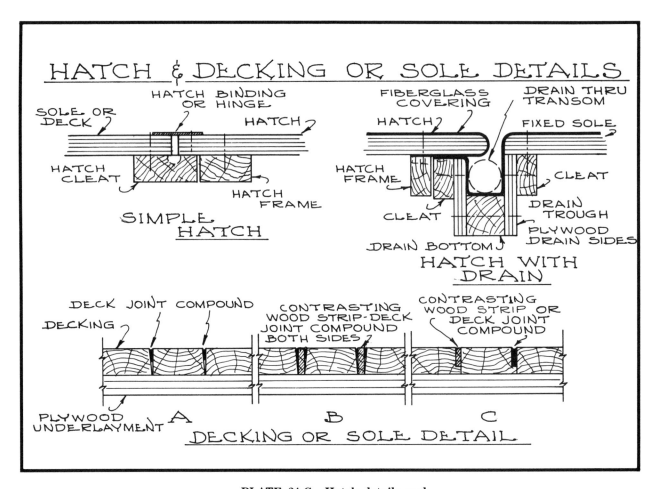

PLATE 24-C—Hatch details and
planked deck or sole methods

then the edge of the berth top can be supported on the batten. Such a procedure does assure a positive flow of air to the enclosed spaces under the berth, and the small gap usually does not detract from the usable space of the berth cushion.

Where it is desired to conceal the exposed side frames and other structure on the side planking inside the boat, sheathing members called "ceiling" can be used. Where the joinery already conceals such areas, the ceiling is not necessary. But in other areas, such as at berths, dinettes, and settees, the ceiling is preferably made of small slats of wood which can be fastened to the inside edges of the side frame members. These slats are often decorative, being of natural finished wood. The slats are spaced to have a gap between each of them for air circulation, and they make an excellent back rest. Solid ceiling of plywood can be used in some cases, but the space being covered must allow for air circulation by gaps at the top and

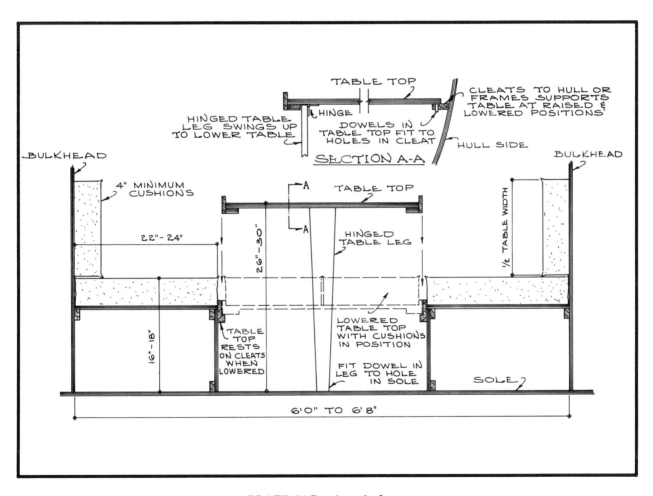

PLATE 24-D—A typical convertible dinette used on boats

bottom.

Many cabin boats include a dinette or settee that converts to a berth. The typical dinette arrangement (see Plate 24-D) uses a seat on either side of a table. The table is arranged to lower where it is supported along the edges of the seats. Then the seat back cushions are placed on the lowered table to make the berth. Many methods can be used for retracting the table, including folding legs and removable table legs such as are often used in recreational vehicles (although these latter are not suitable aboard all types of boats). With settees, it is common for these to slide out and form a larger berth, with the back cushion being used to form the wider berth. Aboard a boat, the synthetic-type foam of a density to suit is recommened for berth and seat cushions since it is lightweight and not damaged by marine conditions. A thickness of 4″ is considered a minimum for good comfort, although smaller boats may require less thickness for headroom and space considerations.

Cockpits on boats, especially of open runabouts may require special considerations, such as on those with exotic seating arrangements and luxurious upholstery techniques. Many builders have the necessary skills to perform the upholstery operations required, however, others will hire this out to specialty shops. Whichever is the case, the seating arrangements are usually made from sheet plywood, usually ⅜″ or more thick, assembled as required. Then these are upholstered to suit. Note that with this process, the builder must make allowances for the thickness of padding when building the seat. If the work is hired out, the shop may want to build the seating, and the builder should check first on this. In other cases, stock seating can be purchased and installed ready-made. Many types for various purposes are available from marine supply outlets.

Cockpits located above the waterline can be made self-draining as well as watertight to the rest of the hull. If this is desired, any hatches installed in the sole must be watertight or made self-draining via scuppers or drain troughs around the hatch openings (see Plate 24-C). Drain holes (preferably with plugs or valves) through the transom or other part of the boat will allow water to drain out of such a cockpit without entering the bilge spaces. However, a bilge pump is still necessary equipment, and at least one manual and one powered type is recommended for most boats. The manual one can be used in the event of power failure, while the powered type is often an automatic pump that actuates whenever the water level reaches a certain point. In small boats the cockpit sole will consist merely of plywood floorboards screwed in position.

CHAPTER 25 — CABINS

Basically, the cabin structure on any boat is a more-or-less stylized "box" or group of boxes. The main purpose of the cabin is to provide room for the accommodation spaces on a cruising type boat, whether sail or power, and to protect the crew from the elements. In many boats, the cabin is not structurally related to the hull, and therefore could be omitted completely without weakening the boat. In other cases, the cabin structure must support other members, such as a flying bridge or sun deck, and therefore considerable additional strength may be required for the cabin structure, and perhaps the cabin structure may even tie in with the hull structure.

In many instances, a builder may wish to modify the plans of a boat in the cabin area. For example, more headroom may be desired, or the cabin length may need changing to suit the builder's requirements, or a flying bridge may be desired when one is not shown. Admittedly, such modifications are part of the pleasure of building your own boat, and perhaps it is the only way to get the boat the way you want it. However, some important considerations should be applied to any such modification. For example, will making the cabin higher to get full headroom make the boat completely out of proportion and create an "ugly duckling"? On boats under about 25' it is extremely difficult to build a cabin with full headroom on a boat not intended for it with-

out making a very awkward looking craft. Another case is adding a flying bridge without considering its effect on the stability of the boat or the weight being added on the cabin top. Such an addition could be extremely dangerous as well as ungainly looking on some boats.

Nothing singles out the "funny looking" amateur built boat quicker than a superstructure where the builder has "gone creative", completely destroying the lines of a boat. A professional designer probably worked many hours to achieve proper eye balance and proportion on the original design. So if you plan on modifying the cabin from that shown on a given design, make some sketches on tracing paper over the original plans first. Try to consider what the boat will look like in three dimensions, and what affect your changes will have on the stability and performance of the boat. If doubt exists in your mind about your proposed changes, contact the designer for his advice. Most designers realize that the boats they have designed will not meet everyone's exact requirements, so they are not necessarily "emotionally involved" with their designs to the point where you might "upset" them with your changes. But do consider that your boat is in effect the designer's form of "advertising". Make sure that your changes are a credit to his design as well as to your craftsmanship. In the long run, it will pay off.

CABIN STRUCTURE

The primary cabin structure members are the cabin sides. The cabin sides must not only be strong, but they must prevent water from entering the cabin. Consequently, they cannot simply be "tacked and glued" in place on the decks like a "box", they must tie in with the hull structure for strength and watertightness. The members running longitudinally under the inboard edge of the side deck and supporting it are called carlings. These are the members that transfer the cabin side stresses to the hull. A simple way that this can be done is to lap the cabin sides to the carling. Such a joint can be sufficiently strong, however, it will not be watertight, at least in the future. Such a junction (see Plate 25-A), will inevitably swell and crack along the junction letting in water from the sea as well as rain. While a trim strip bedded in fiberglass and resin will help, the basic fault of such a joint remains.

The preferred method of joining the cabin sides to the hull is also shown in Plate 25-A. Here the cabin side rests directly on the side deck over the carling member. Ideally, the cabin side is bed-

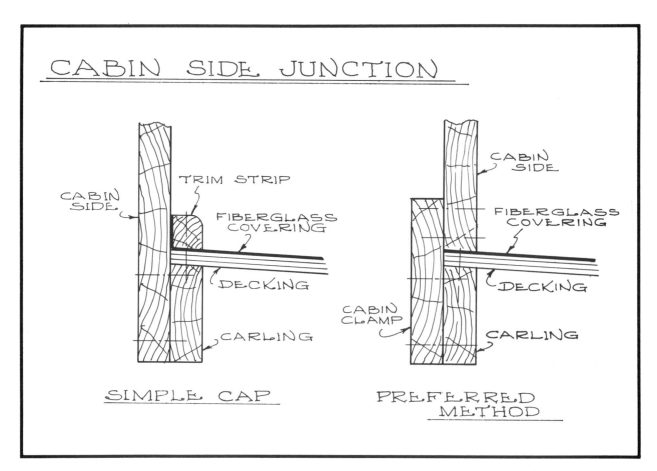

PLATE 25-A—Typical cabin
side junctions at the deck edge

ded in fiberglass and resin, or a flexible marine sealant. Siding against both the carling and the cabin side is a facing member called the cabin clamp, and this member ties the carling and cabin side together. With this junction, the only way water can enter is along the lower edge of the cabin side, and since this is well bedded, this is not likely. The cabin clamp acts as a baffle to keep the water out as well. On many boats, the cabin clamp members are left naturally finished since they are often visible within the cabin. The screws can be counterbored in this case and fitted with wood plugs, or chrome oval head screws with beauty washers are frequently used for appearance purposes.

Because the carling is the determining member for the cabin sides and cabin clamp, its position is critical. In some boats the cabin sides will be vertical as well as straight lines in plan view. Consequently, the carling will be straight and vertical as well. In other cases, the cabin sides may be inclined inboard from the vertical and perhaps in a curve when viewed in plan view, in which case the carling must correspond. Whichever is the case, the members must be sized to conform to the plan and profile contours. Often the cabin clamp as well as the cabin sides may be laminated members in order to ease the bend required by the curvature. Because the contours of the cabin clamp and the lower edge of the cabin side are already determined by the deck edge at the carling, there is little difficulty in fitting these members as they can simply be leaned to the contour, marked, and cut to fit.

The cabin side can be made from plywood or solid lumber depending on the boat and the builder's desires. Obvi-

ously, wide cabin sides are best made from plywood since single widths of wide lumber are usually not available, and if available, may tend to warp or "cup". It is possible to glue up several narrower widths of solid stock to make a single cabin side, but this requires more work. If done, stock at least ¾" in finished thickness is advised, doweled no more than 12" apart. If the builder does not have the doweling facilities, the work can be done by a cabinet shop, and often such facilities have the equipment to sand or surface the completed cabin side to be smooth and flush. One of the main advantages of using solid wood for the cabin sides is that there are no exposed edges of plywood that should be concealed or covered. It is also easier to fit windows and to join to other members.

However, on many designs, plywood cabin sides are the most practical. On long cabin sides, standard lengths of plywood must be joined to form the cabin sides, and the butt joining method is most frequently used. The butt joint may occur over solid framing members in which case the butt block may not be required. With plywood cabin sides, it is common to install the entire piece of plywood on the boat, and then cut openings for the windows afterwards. However, this may vary with the design. The biggest disadvantage of plywood cabin sides is the exposed edge grain of the plywood, especially at window openings and cut-outs. If the windows will not conceal this, then moldings or other devices must be used to protect the edge. Unlike the solid wood cabin side, the plywood cabin side will require solid wood framing members along the edges where the cabin sides are to junction with other cabin members. These are

247

usually fastened to the inside of the plywood, but sometimes may be on the outside. In other cases, the solid framing members may be the actual window frames and may require a rabbet or groove for the window which will later be installed. In building the cabin variations in the design must be planned for by the builder.

Bulkheads in the boat usually tie in with the cabin side structure, and if these are plywood also, good sized corner blocking must be used to back up the junctions. Bulkheads often are used to determine the crown or curvature of the cabin roof, and such a crown must be cut on the tops of the bulkheads initially. In other cases, the crown of the roof will not be known when the bulkheads are installed. When this occurs, the tops of the bulkheads are left long and later cut to suit the crown of the roof when it is fitted.

Various upright stanchions or posts are sometimes specified to support the cabin side or the cabin roof, and in some cases these must be installed early in the cabin structure. Sometimes stanchions will be used to support the weight of the sundeck or flying bridge above, and will run down to hull framing members. In all such junctions, ample screws and bolts must be used for rigidity, plus glue at all joints.

WINDSHIELDS & CABIN FRONTS

Besides the cabin sides and bulkheads, the other member which usually completes the upright members of the cabin "box" is the windshield or cabin front. Many types of windshields and cabin fronts exist, and the main reason for the wide variety is usually pure "style". There are "vee'd" windshields, three-part windshields, straight ones, vertical types, and those which are inclined either fore or aft. Some windshields have openable sections while others are fixed. Some have "windows" (which generally makes them a "windshield"), while others have no glass (which generally makes them a "cabin front").

The windshield or cabin front that is straight across the boat and vertical to the deck is usually the easiest (although maybe not the most attractive) to install. The more complex the configuration, the more difficult it is to both fit and make a windshield. Many desire to have a windshield (or at least a portion of it) that is openable. Admittedly, this is a nice feature, however, such openable windshields invariably seem to leak at least at some point in time, no matter how carefully made. A detail for such a window is shown on Plate 25-C.

The construction of any vee'd or multi-sectioned windshield or cabin front that is inclined from the vertical is a rather difficult problem. To layout such a windshield or cabin front in full size or to scale is quite complicated and usually beyond the abilities of the amateur. Sometimes full size patterns are available for this portion of the boat, but since the pattern can only be given for contour, the bevels for all joining members must be plotted to the work to make up for the thickness of the members used.

For the average builder, it is better to use a large sheet of cardboard or plywood or pieces of lumber tacked together as a template to facilitate fitting to the required contours. After the contours have been determined, the mock-

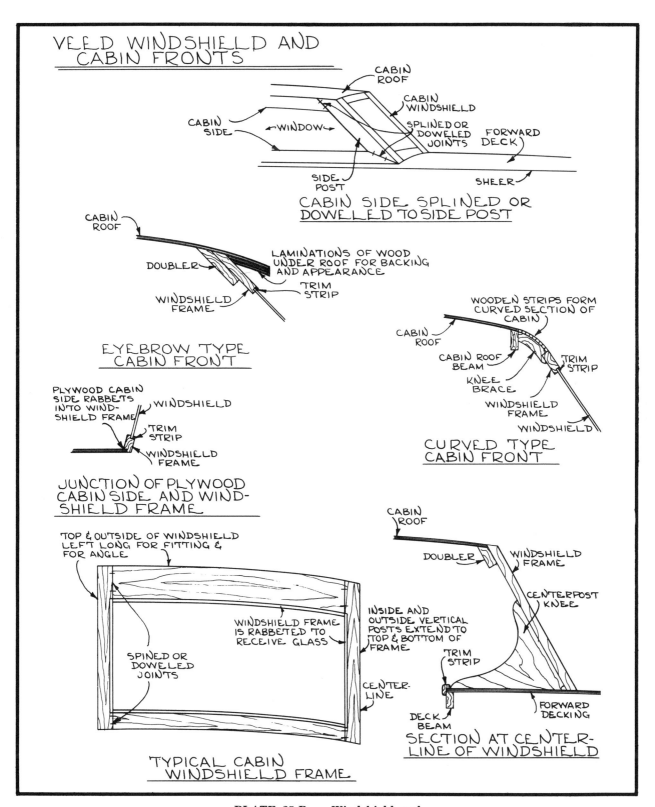

VEED WINDSHIELD AND CABIN FRONTS

CABIN ROOF
CABIN WINDSHIELD
CABIN SIDE
WINDOW
SPLINED OR DOWELED JOINTS
FORWARD DECK
SIDE POST
SHEER

CABIN SIDE SPLINED OR DOWELED TO SIDE POST

CABIN ROOF
DOUBLER
LAMINATIONS OF WOOD UNDER ROOF FOR BACKING AND APPEARANCE
TRIM STRIP
WINDSHIELD FRAME

EYEBROW TYPE CABIN FRONT

WOODEN STRIPS FORM CURVED SECTION OF CABIN
CABIN ROOF
CABIN ROOF BEAM
KNEE BRACE
TRIM STRIP
WINDSHIELD FRAME
WINDSHIELD

CURVED TYPE CABIN FRONT

PLYWOOD CABIN SIDE RABBETS INTO WIND-SHIELD FRAME
WINDSHIELD
TRIM STRIP
WINDSHIELD FRAME

JUNCTION OF PLYWOOD CABIN SIDE AND WIND-SHIELD FRAME

TOP & OUTSIDE OF WINDSHIELD LEFT LONG FOR FITTING & FOR ANGLE
WINDSHIELD FRAME IS RABBETED TO RECEIVE GLASS
SPINED OR DOWELED JOINTS
CENTER-LINE

TYPICAL CABIN WINDSHIELD FRAME

CABIN ROOF
DOUBLER
WINDSHIELD FRAME
INSIDE AND OUTSIDE VERTICAL POSTS EXTEND TO TOP & BOTTOM OF FRAME
CENTERPOST KNEE
TRIM STRIP
DECK BEAM
FORWARD DECKING

SECTION AT CENTER-LINE OF WINDSHIELD

PLATE 25-B — Windshield and cabin front construction methods

up can be used as a jig to construct the members. Plate 25-B shows a windshield frame (as opposed to a solid cabin front) with the outside posts running up and down the full length. These are doweled or splined to the cross members. Angles for fitting to the deck can be taken directly from the work and usually band-sawed after the frame has been assembled. Knees or up-rights are used to back up the junctions of the windshield sections, and in some cases these members tie in with the cabin roof framework. It is preferable for the windshield to overlap the cabin sides at the corners. The fit of the windshield to the deck should be a tight one, and the members should be well bedded in mastic or fiberglass and resin. While it is possible to fasten from under the deck and up into the windshield frame, it is better to fit solid blocking or doublers to the deck surface beveled as required for the windshield especially if the cabin front is made from plywood. This blocking should be bedded in mastic or fiberglass and resin also, and either screwed from the underside or bolted (see Plate 25-D). If desired, the blocking can be rabbeted for the windshield, or the windshield can mate to the deck and against the blocking. Best practice calls

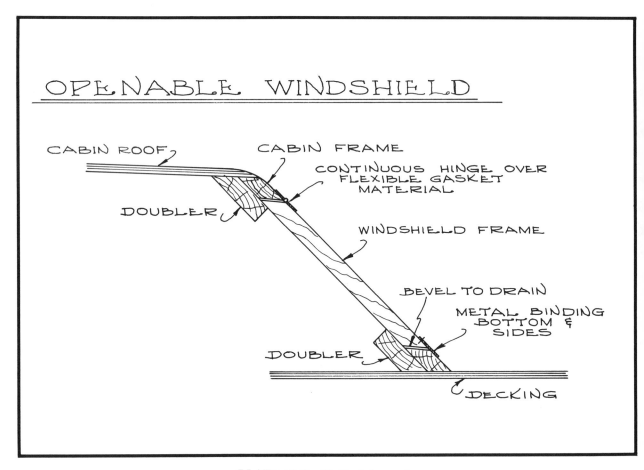

PLATE 25-C—Method for making an openable windshield

for fastening the windshield to the doubler as well as fastening into the lower edge of the windshield frame from under the decking, if of solid wood.

CABIN TOP STRUCTURE

Framework for the cabin top may consist of many members, or perhaps none at all, depending on the design. In some cases, the cabin top framing will run athwartships in the form of various beams, while in other cases, such members may run longitudinally. With

cabin roofs not having any structure, the roof may be supported only by the cabin sides, cabin front, and aft bulkhead.

The main problem with cabin roof frame members is that they tend to reduce the headroom within the cabin causing any number of raised welts on the heads of crewmembers too tall for the cabin space. This is one reason why some boat designers stick to the philosophy that if full standing headroom cannot be provided in a design, then only enough headroom for full sitting clearance above the seats and berths should be provided. In this way,

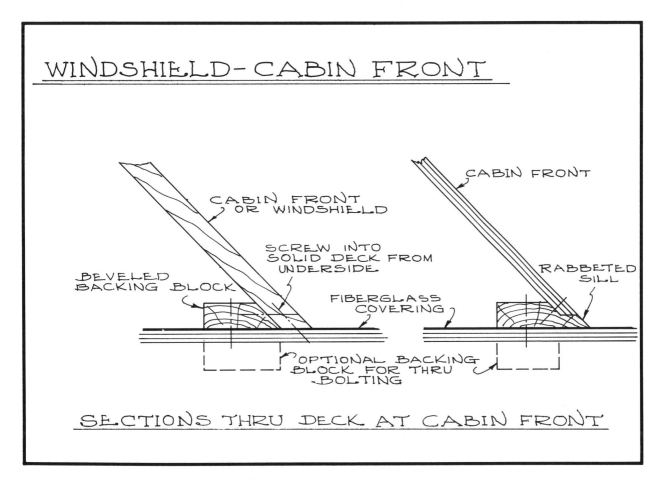

PLATE 25-D—Windshield and cabin front junctions at deck

FIG. 25-2—The junction of the cabin side with the windshield. The junction of the cabin side and the upright is a splined joint. Also note the windshield grooves and centerpost.

FIG. 25-4—The finished cabin structure. The appearance has been enhanced by the use of a painted trim and natural mahogany, together with gently radiused corners for soft lines.

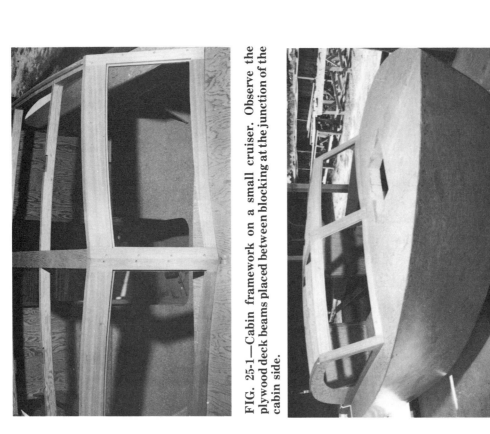

FIG. 25-1—Cabin framework on a small cruiser. Observe the plywood deck beams placed between blocking at the junction of the cabin side.

FIG. 25-3—The complete roughed-out cabin structure. This cabin side uses plywood joined to a mahogany coaming member.

the crew will be conscious of the restricted headroom, thereby always keeping on guard about getting up and smacking one's head on the overhead.

Like the deck areas, the cabin roof will almost always be crowned or cambered. Such a camber not only causes any water to drain off and increases strength, but also provides more room inside without upsetting the proportions of the boat too much. The camber of the cabin top may be noted on the plans, or may be provided in the form of full size patterns for the members, or the camber may be developed automatically as a result of the method of framing for the cabin top (see Plate 25-E). On some boats, camber is not used for one reason or another. There is nothing wrong with this if intended by the designer, but the roof should slope in some

direction so that water will not accumulate on the cabin top.

The typical cabin using cross beams may use joining methods such as shown by Plate 25-F. Not only do such cross beams provide strength for the cabin top, but they also tie the cabin sides together to prevent them from bowing outboard. Beams which run longitudinally are usually fewer in number since the cabin top plywood will run across the boat from side to side. In this instance, the beams are usually located somewhat higher than the cabin side and thereby form the required camber to the roof when the plywood is laid across. Cabin beams can be sawn to shape or laminated from several layers of thin wood or plywood laid flat (see Plate 25-G). In this latter case, a series of beams can be prefabricated. For

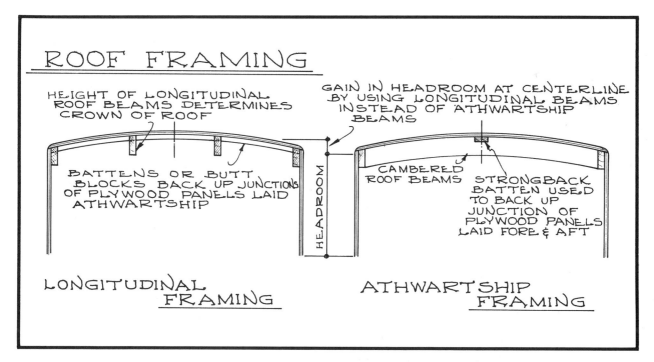

PLATE 25-E—Cabin roof framing can be oriented either fore and aft (at left), or athwartships (to right). With fore and aft framing, the height of the beams determines the camber of the roof and provides more headroom at the center of the boat without raising the profile.

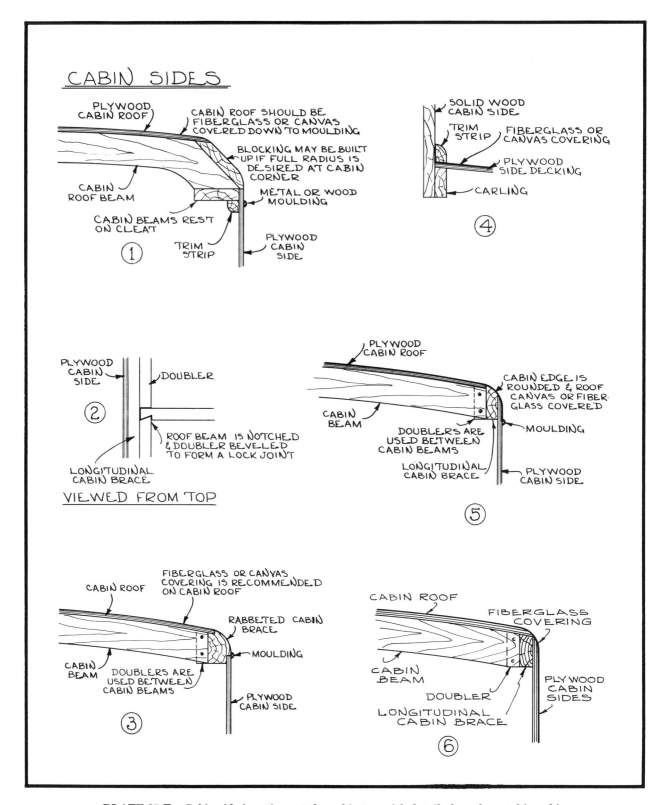

CABIN SIDES

① PLYWOOD CABIN ROOF — CABIN ROOF SHOULD BE FIBERGLASS OR CANVAS COVERED DOWN TO MOULDING — BLOCKING MAY BE BUILT UP IF FULL RADIUS IS DESIRED AT CABIN CORNER — CABIN ROOF BEAM — CABIN BEAMS REST ON CLEAT — METAL OR WOOD MOULDING — TRIM STRIP — PLYWOOD CABIN SIDE

② PLYWOOD CABIN SIDE — DOUBLER — ROOF BEAM IS NOTCHED & DOUBLER BEVELED TO FORM A LOCK JOINT — LONGITUDINAL CABIN BRACE

VIEWED FROM TOP

③ CABIN ROOF — FIBERGLASS OR CANVAS COVERING IS RECOMMENDED ON CABIN ROOF — RABBETED CABIN BRACE — MOULDING — CABIN BEAM — DOUBLERS ARE USED BETWEEN CABIN BEAMS — PLYWOOD CABIN SIDE

④ SOLID WOOD CABIN SIDE — TRIM STRIP — FIBERGLASS OR CANVAS COVERING — PLYWOOD SIDE DECKING — CARLING

⑤ PLYWOOD CABIN ROOF — CABIN EDGE IS ROUNDED & ROOF CANVAS OR FIBERGLASS COVERED — CABIN BEAM — DOUBLERS ARE USED BETWEEN CABIN BEAMS — MOULDING — LONGITUDINAL CABIN BRACE — PLYWOOD CABIN SIDE

⑥ CABIN ROOF — FIBERGLASS COVERING — CABIN BEAM — DOUBLER — LONGITUDINAL CABIN BRACE — PLYWOOD CABIN SIDES

PLATE 25-F—Cabin side junctions at the cabin top with details for athwartship cabin top framing.

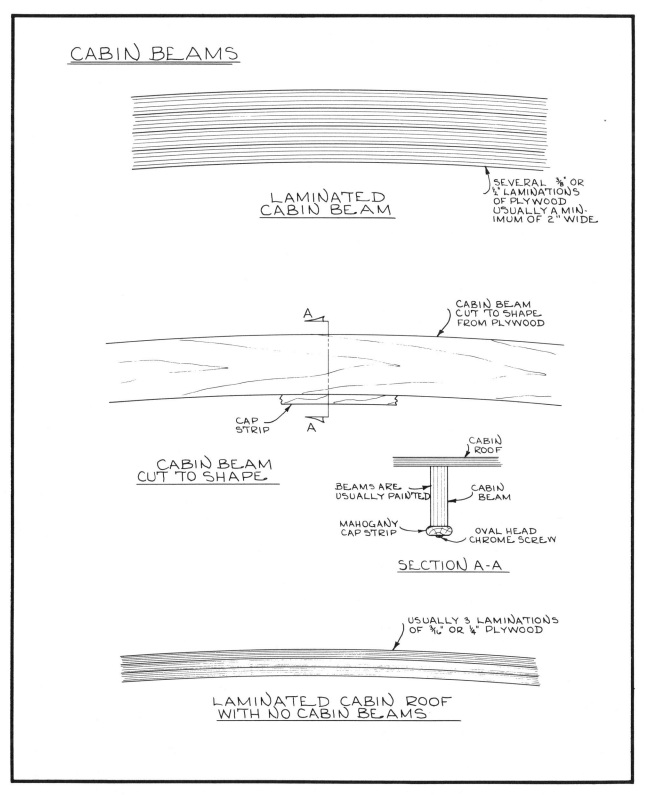

CABIN BEAMS

LAMINATED
CABIN BEAM

SEVERAL ⅜" OR
½" LAMINATIONS
OF PLYWOOD
USUALLY A MIN-
IMUM OF 2" WIDE

CABIN BEAM
CUT TO SHAPE
FROM PLYWOOD

A

CAP
STRIP

A

CABIN BEAM
CUT TO SHAPE

CABIN
ROOF

BEAMS ARE
USUALLY PAINTED

CABIN
BEAM

MAHOGANY
CAP STRIP

OVAL HEAD
CHROME SCREW

SECTION A-A

USUALLY 3 LAMINATIONS
OF ³⁄₁₆" OR ¼" PLYWOOD

LAMINATED CABIN ROOF
WITH NO CABIN BEAMS

PLATE 25-G—Cabin roof beams made by laminating plywood or solid wood, and sawn plywood beams.

example, if six beams 2″ wide are required, glue laminations together to a width of a little more than 12 ″. After these laminations have been set on a form and glued to the required camber, they are ripped to the desired width. This assumes that all the beams are to the same camber. Plywood sawn beams are sometimes used, however, these do not hold the cabin top fastenings too well, and the exposed edge grain inside should be concealed for best appearance. Such a plywood roof beam will have only about half the strength of a solid wood beam of the same thickness. The longitudinal beams are often heavier than typical cross beams, and may require intermediate support via stanchions or bulkheads. The ends of the beams are supported by knees or uprights at the ends to bulkheads or windshields. With either type of roof framing (athwartships or longitudinal types) various battens may be laid flat and notched into the frame members. Sometimes these battens are used to back up the joints in the roof plywood or to back up fastenings from other members such as cabin top handrails, etc.

Plywood is an ideal material for making the cabin top since the joints will be kept to a minimum to prevent leaks, and the material can make a strong roof. Often a cabin top will be made from plywood in a single thickness as thin as ⅜″. This is practical on some boats as long as the supporting structure is sufficient. One must remember that even in the smallest of boats, some stranger may jump aboard your craft right onto the cabin top even though you and your crew may know better. Hopefully, the cabin can take this sort of inconsiderate treatment, since even a rough sea can toss tremendous amounts of water onto the cabin that may equal or exceed the weight of a person, Much, however, will be dependent on the use of the boat. If a designer has designed a boat for sheltered or protected waters, or for the cabin to support nothing other than its own weight, and you are going to change the intended use of such a vessel, you had better consider the cabin structure. It would not be fair to blame the designer if the cabin fails from a freak wave while on an offshore passage or when everyone aboard decides on sunbathing on a too-thin cabin top not intended for this activity.

Other methods for making the cabin top include the laminated sheet plywood roof and the laminated sandwich type of roof. Either type can be made over the cabin framework structure, or they may be made up in place over a temporary structure that will be removed after the roof has been fabricated. Considerable strength can be developed for example, by three laminations of ¼″ plywood glued in place progressively over a cambered form. Little if any intermediate support may be necessary, depending on the size of the area, and butt joints between panels can be staggered thereby eliminating the need for a butt block. With the sandwich roof, an outer and an inner layer of plywood are used, separated by a "core". The core can be in many configurations or materials. The first inner layer of plywood is placed over the temporary or cabin framework members. Then the core material is placed over this. The core can be strips of wood (such as 1″ x 2″ pieces) spaced about 12″ apart spanning over the cabin sides. Insulation can be fitted in between these strips if desired. Other core materials can be various honeycombs, rigid synthetic foams, or

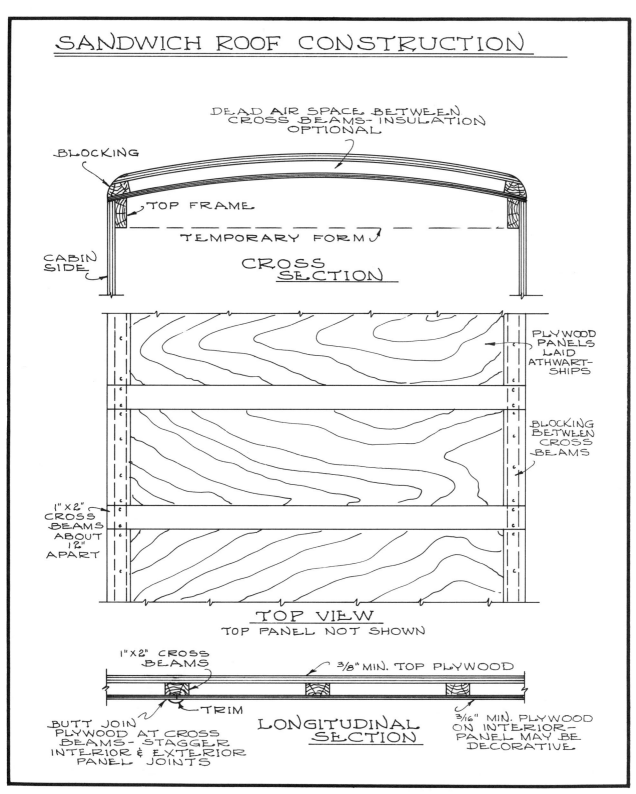

SANDWICH ROOF CONSTRUCTION

DEAD AIR SPACE BETWEEN CROSS BEAMS- INSULATION OPTIONAL

BLOCKING

TOP FRAME

TEMPORARY FORM

CABIN SIDE

CROSS SECTION

PLYWOOD PANELS LAID ATHWART-SHIPS

BLOCKING BETWEEN CROSS BEAMS

1"X 2" CROSS BEAMS ABOUT 12" APART

TOP VIEW
TOP PANEL NOT SHOWN

1"X2" CROSS BEAMS

3/8" MIN. TOP PLYWOOD

BUTT JOIN PLYWOOD AT CROSS BEAMS- STAGGER INTERIOR & EXTERIOR PANEL JOINTS

TRIM

LONGITUDINAL SECTION

3/16" MIN. PLYWOOD ON INTERIOR- PANEL MAY BE DECORATIVE

PLATE 25-H—Sandwich roof construction method without roof beams, built over a temporary formwork.

balsa core. However, these are some-what "exotic" materials for the average amateur plywood boatbuilder to pur-chase and work with, and are more ex-pensive. Next the outer plywood roof (which can be as thin as ⅜", although somewhat thicker plywood is preferable where there will be heavy use) is ap-plied over the "core". Temporary frame members (if any) can then be removed, and the resulting roof will be strong, and have both sound and heat insula-tive qualities. With both the laminated and sandwich roof methods, the first inner layer of plywood can be a decora-tive type to enhance the interior decor. Openings for hatches and the like, how-ever, must not be cut into these roofs until after they are fabricated and framed for such openings. In the sandwich roof, blocking may be re-quired at many points for such items as winches, handrails, and other members which require solid material for back-ing up fastenings, and hence such a roof should be carefully planned.

Depending on the design, the roof may or may not have overhangs. If there are no overhangs, the edges are usually radiused to suit. If there are any over-hangs, these are frequently built up with extra layers of plywood or solid wood to give a hefty appearance to the edge. Don't "short-cut" giving the cabin the proper treatment at cabin edges and overhangs. The designer when he de-signed the boat probably enhanced the appearance by various devices that the novice will often overlook only to won-der why his boat doesn't look like the "picture" shown on the plans. These de-vices may include a well-radiused cabin edge, or the dark shadow line provided by a generous roof overhang, or the con-tinuity of a long, horizontal line by vir-

tue of a critically located trim strip. The waterfront is crowded with boats built by over-anxious builders who either forgot these subtleties, or ignored them. These craft are easily spotted by their hard-cornered "boxy" cabins devoid of overhangs or other appearance-en-hancing design devices.

CABIN SHEATHINGS

Years ago just about every boat cabin was covered with canvas that fre-quently had to be renewed and that often led to rotting cabin and deck struc-tures. While canvas may still be used, other materials and processes have taken over. The reason that cabins are covered with these materials is the same as for the hull. However, there are several different materials available that, while suitable for the cabin areas, are not suitable as a hull covering. Just like the hull, the various appendages are always installed after the cabin has been covered.

Not all people desire to cover the cabin, at least completely. There may be some areas which are to be left natural, and the methods for finishing these areas have been covered in Chapter 23. If only a portion of the cabin is to be left natural, then the area that will be cov-ered should be done first before apply-ing the natural finish. Accent strips or moldings used to differentiate between the two areas can be used to cap the raw edges of the covering materials.

One of the most popular cabin cover-ing materials is fiberglass. This mate-rial was also covered in Chapter 23, and the application on the cabin, for all in-tents and purposes, is the same as for

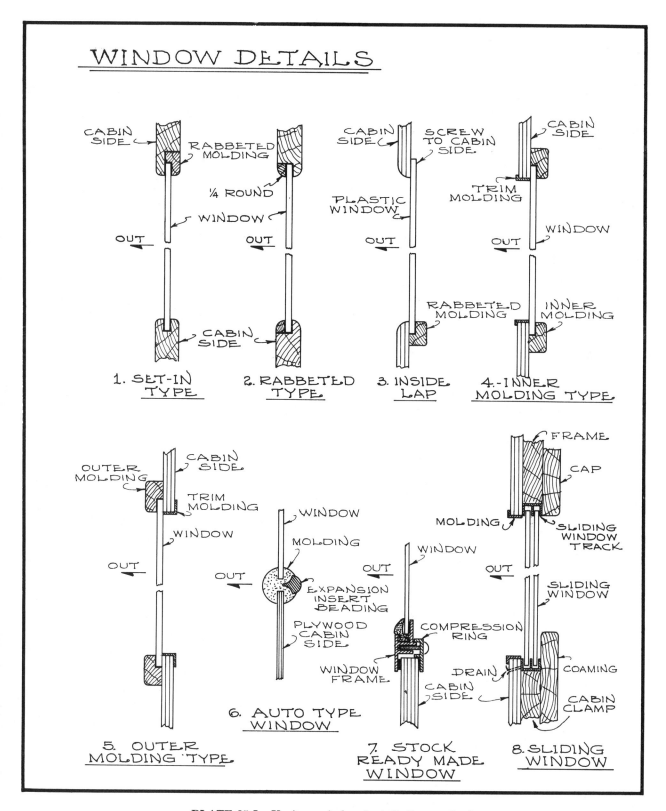

PLATE 25-I—Various window installation methods

the hull. The text also describes many other materials that are alternatives to fiberglass coverings, and are beyond the scope of this book. In addition to the fiberglass and related sheathings, other materials often used are the various fabric-backed vinyls or upholstery-like materials. These are bonded to the cabin surfaces with suitable adhesives and "stretched" over the cabin contours. These vinyls adhere nicely to contoured areas and seem to be versatile and durable. Trim strips are needed at the edges to secure the material since the vinyl will tend to shrink somewhat. No painting is required, and many colors and textures are possible. Note that with just about all cabin sheathings, rounding of the various edges and corners is important to the application. This is all to the good since the rounded corner approach is important to the appearance of most boats.

One difficulty of covering a plywood cabin with fiberglass (or for most other materials as well), is sheathing up to the window openings. Obviously, it is impractical to form the fiberglass material wet with resin right up to and around the edge of a window opening such as shown by Plate 25-I. It is possible to bring the cloth around onto the edge and then cap it with a molding, but the fiberglass will make a very poor bond at such a junction as water will usually creep in at some point. A better method is to end the fiberglass at the edge of the opening. Then use metal or wood trim moldings to cap the junction and plywood edge which also adds to the appearance of the boat as well.

WINDOWS

Many types of windows can be made as well as purchased ready-made. Three types of glazing material are generally used on boats, including laminated glass, tempered glass, and clear plastic types. With glass, there is some argument about which is the best glass to use on a boat, and there are good and bad points about both.

The laminated "safety" glass consists of a thin plastic layer laminated between layers of glass. If the glass breaks, this plastic layer supposedly "holds" the glass pieces together so that the window does not disintegrate completely upon impact. The laminated glass window tends to break into long sharp shards of glass radiating out from the point of impact. Some feel that this type of window on a boat if broken by a sharp impact would hold together enough to keep the sea out. The touted advantage of laminated glass is that it will not "shatter" on impact. However, a fist or a head, for that matter, that is unfortunate enough to become impaled through such a window just might be severely lacerated or even removed upon sudden withdrawl.

With tempered glass the glass is put under stress by heat treatment. This makes the glass very strong (depending on the thickness and manufacturing variations), but any nick or chip can send the entire window into scattered pieces and fragments. Such pieces however, are more like pellets of rock salt and not like sharp sliver-like pieces.

While a wave could conceivably come through a window of this type that was broken and shattered, the thin plastic layer holding the laminated glass together after impact would probably fail just as quickly if it were hit with a wave also, and with much more dangerous pieces of glass. The choice is up to the builder, but one or the other should be used if the windows are to be of glass.

If clear plastic is used for the windows, there are several types available, and in several degrees and colors of tinting. Many types of clear plastic tend to scratch, and some are worse in this respect than others. The installation of clear plastic glazing materials is important. The plastic should preferably be installed at the ambient temperatures at which the boat will be used to minimize excessive expansion and contraction. Leave space around all edges of the plastic for expansion, and bed in a flexible marine-type mastic. Where fastenings are required through the plastic, use only round head screws, drilling the holes somewhat oversize for the screw shank. Never use flat head screws which require countersinking since this tends to fracture the plastic. Note that with curved cabin sides where windows will be located, plastic glazing material is a "must" since glass will not bend. Also note that where weight is important, use plastic since even the thinnest of glass, which should not be used on a boat, is very heavy in comparison.

Sliding windows are often specified on a design to be fabricated by the builder. Tracks are available for such windows which are preferably a non-corrosive material lined with felt or equal weatherstripping. The lower window tracks should be located below the level of the cabin clamp or coaming

on the inside of the cabin to prevent water from getting into the cabin. Small drain holes should be drilled into the bottoms of the tracks connected with small tubes through the cabin side to allow water to drain out of the tracks. The sliding windows, if in two sections, must have the forward section overlapping the after section to prevent water from being forced into the slot between the two while underway. Sliding windows in a curved portion of the cabin side must be made from clear plastic also.

A type of window often referred to as a "bus" or auto-type window can be used for fixed windows. The design principle of such windows is also used for installing some ready-made windows. These windows are installed in an opening that is larger than the actual window opening by so many fractions of an inch. The window is mounted in place by a rubber mounting strip all around the opening that has a separate beading strip which fits into a groove in the mounting strip. When the beading is forced into the groove, it forces the mounting strip to form a tight grip to both the window and the cabin side (see Plate 25-I). Such a window must have radiused corners to suit the rubber mounting strip, and the cabin side plywood must be thin enough to suit the strip. Only fixed windows are possible unless one of the ready-made aluminum windows is selected that use this method of mounting via a flange surround.

Other ready-made windows include ports and windows, usually made from metal or plastics. Fixed and openable types are available. If of aluminum, the material should preferably be anodized for corrosion resistance. Many types have screw-in flanges for easy surface mounting, while others use what is called a "compression ring". Windows of the latter type are placed into the opening with the flange bearing against the cabin side. The ring is located on the inside of the cabin and screws are used to "compress" the ring to the window with the cabin side between for a tight fit. With all these windows, appropriate sealant must be placed around the mounting flanges to prevent leaks. The standard marine portlight, whether of the fixed or openable type, is also frequently used, and can be made from metal (such as bronze) or synthetic plastics.

HATCHES & OPENINGS

Most boats with accommodations will have a hatch somewhere for foredeck access, either in the foredeck itself or through the cabin trunk forward. Such a hatch is usually hinged aft, but not always, though some prefer double hinges so the hatch can be opened either way. This latter situation is desirable since it allows the hatch to be opened while underway in fair weather or while at anchor for best ventilation in warm climates.

Some methods for making a foredeck or similar hatch are shown in Plate 25-J. The basic type of hatch is easy to build and will suffice on many small boats, especially those that are trailerable and will not be subjected to extreme offshore conditions. The other types are intended for more rigorous duty. Note that the hatch coamings are arranged so that they can be securely fastened to the deck framework to pre-

vent leaks around the base of the hatch. A good seaworthy type of hatch is the double coaming type. Even though water may pass the first coaming, it will be slowed to such an extent that the water will drain harmlessly out the scuppers. Compression gaskets around hatches can work well as long as the material does not become hardened and the devices used to secure the hatch have sufficient strength to hold the hatch in place. Making a good foredeck hatch that does not leak is difficult, and consequently many elect to purchase one of the ready-made types that are available. These fasten to the deck much the way a ready-made window fastens to the cabin side, being well bedded in mastic. They are expensive but the savings in time and materials plus guaranteed results may more than offset the high cost. Hatches can be sized to suit, however, a 14″ x 18″ opening should be considered the minimum size on any boat, with 18″ x 18″ being more suitable if access is desired. A 24″ square hatch is preferable on larger boats where escape may be necessary, and a 30″ x 30″ square hatch is advocated for sailboats by some. However, the hatch should not be so large that the foredeck or cabin top is weakened severely. The covering on a hatch must be at least as heavy as the foredeck since people will walk on it with their full weight. Plywood or clear plastic can be used, and some prefer to have diffused plastic, instead of the clear type, for privacy. From a watertight standpoint, the hatch should be well above the deck level even though this may be an impediment to the crew and perhaps spoil the looks of the vessel for some.

Sliding hatches are used in many situations, especially on sailboats. It is extremely difficult to prevent leaks from occuring in such hatches since there are just too many places for the water to work its way in. However, they are a necessity on some boats and the type shown by Plate 25-J is just one example. Some build a covering shroud of wood or fiberglass over such a sliding hatch when it is in the open position which tends to deflect water on the deck

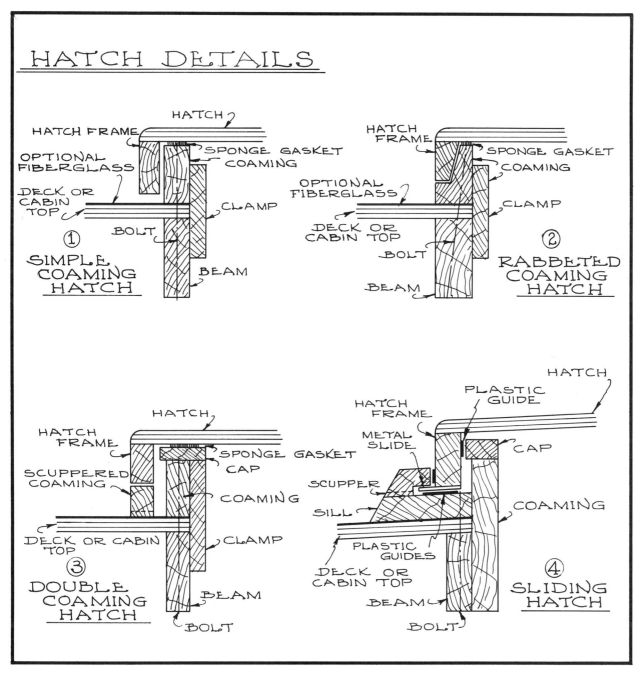

PLATE 25-J—Various deck and cabin hatch construction methods, both hinged and sliding types.

Boatbuilding With Plywood

or cabin top and keep it from entering along the forward opening of the hatch. However, such a shroud must have drain holes at the corners so water that may enter will drain out when the hatch is slid closed.

Exterior cabin doors may be of several types depending on the boat. Some cabin doors must be designed to work in conjunction with a hatch above. Basic

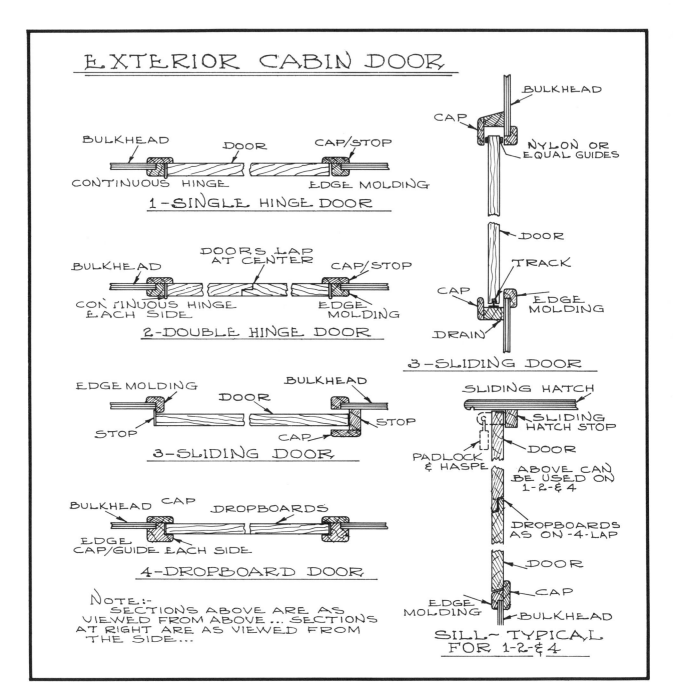

PLATE 25-K—Exterior cabin door details

264

types of doors are the single hinged type, double hinged type, sliding type, and dropboard (see Plate 25-K). The single hinge door works like the one at home, being hinged along one side. This requires an area to the hinged side at least as large as the door so it will open flat against the bulkhead. Note that all doors on a boat should open out from the direction of egress for safety. The double hinge door is a door in two halves that joins in a slight overlap at the middle. This type of door is used where space is limited, but it also has the advantage of being able to remain half open for ventilation. The sliding door is used where space does not allow for the swing of the door, or some other interference prevents using a hinged door. Such a sliding door usually fits into troughs around the door to prevent water from entering. The fit of a sliding door should be fairly tight, and positive devices should be provided to secure the door in the open and closed positions. Dropboards are common on sailboats. The boards are in sections that fit together with overlapping joints between the boards, with the boards fitting into slots along the door jamb. These dropboards can be a nuisance since they tend to jam, get kicked around, and are not convenient. However, they do allow for controlled ventilation below by varying the number of boards in place and keep water out of the cabin. With all cabin doors, the door frame is usually intended to also stiffen the door opening as well as cap the plywood edges of the bulkheads. Continuous hinges are frequently used to minimize the affects of warping on the wood doors and reduce leaking. If plywood is used for the cabin doors, the edges must be capped or otherwise sealed from exposure.

FLYING BRIDGES

Probably no other element of powerboat design has gained such popularity as the flying bridge control station. However, the flying bridge does have limitations that many people ignore or do not consider, especially when they decide to fit one on a craft not originally intended for one. The main problem with any flying bridge is that everyone aboard the boat wants to ride on the flying bridge even if there isn't room. This may seem harmless, but consider these two elements: weight and stability.

Under normal running, the structure may very well be capable of supporting the load on the bridge, even if there are more people than there are seats. However, consider for a moment a boat crossing a good sized wake or running in a light afternoon chop. As the boat comes down off the "humps" the hull may very well be capable of taking the stresses of some degree of pounding, and in fact the crew may not even be aware of the pounding. But what about the flying bridge and the cabin structure that is supporting it? The accelerating forces caused by a boat underway in these conditions can be many times the normal loadings, and is especially severe when the boat is in a turn and banking inboard. Here the stress is down as well as sideways, making things even worse.

Next consider the stability of the boat, especially in rough water conditions. With a load of people on the flying bridge, the center of gravity of most boats is raised considerably, and hence the boat will be much more "tippy" than normal. With loadings concentrated high up on the boat, the rolling from side to side is often increased and amplified to the point that not only is the roll pronounced but quite snappy; in fact it could get violent enough to throw members of the crew overboard. Hence, don't overload the flying bridge if you have one, and make sure that the one you add, if you plan on having one, is strong enough to do the job.

Another element directly related to the above is that the flying bridge structure should be kept as light in weight as possible. Plywood in ¼" to ½" thicknesses can be made amazingly stiff and strong with the proper placement of solid wood backing members. As with the cabin front, the bridge may be straight across, vee'd, in several sections, or sometimes curved to contour. Inherently, the latter type is strongest by virtue of the curved plywood used to

make the flying bridge sides (called the "dodger").

Sometimes the flying bridge is a continuation of the cabin sides. In other cases, the flying bridge structure is a separately mounted unit on the cabin top. Whichever is the case, the control console and seating areas are frequently tied in with the dodger to make a strong structure. Drains are usually required through the dodger at several points so that water on the cabin top can drain off. Like the cabin structure, all plywood edges should be capped or covered, and the exposed plywood surfaces are usually covered with fiberglass or equivalent sheathing. Seating configurations vary, however, the back-to-back type is popular. A sturdy ladder and sufficient hand-holds or grab rails should be provided for safe access.

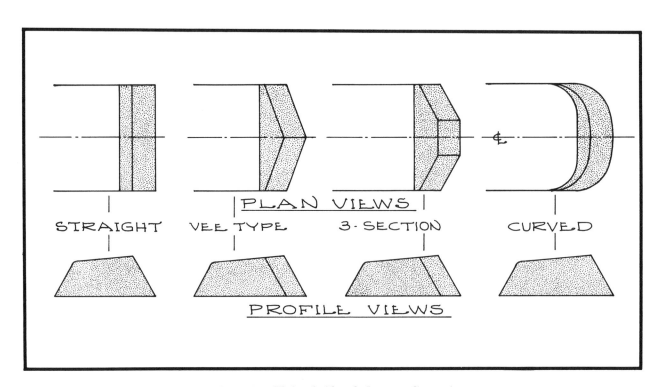

PLAN VIEWS

STRAIGHT   VEE TYPE   3-SECTION   CURVED

PROFILE VIEWS

PLATE 25-L—Flying bridge dodger configurations

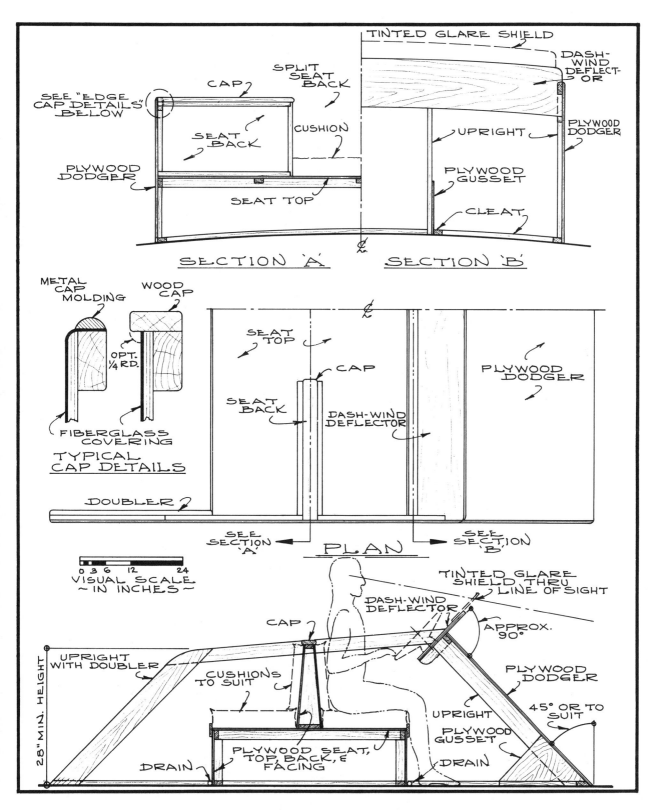

PLATE 25-M—Typical flying bridge details

A problem with flying bridges is keeping the wind out of the faces of crew members. Some elaborate "venturi" devices are often used with the idea of increasing the flow of wind upwards directly in front of the helmsman in the hopes of restricting the wind flow from straight on. These may work, more or less, but an easier way to achieve similar results is to fit a deflecting wind screen, frequently made from tinted clear plastic to reduce the glare, and canted forward from the forward dodger. These tend to deflect and minimize the wind (and sometimes spray), and raise it over the heads of the crew, at least to some degree. However, those sitting too far aft tend to get blown from the breeze as it tends to flow back to its normal pattern. Of course, full height windshields can be resorted to, however, on most boats these tend to spoil the appearance of the boat due to the additional height. They also increase windage and drag.

When installing a flying bridge, consider how the controls will be routed for the engine and steering. There must be a means of getting these aft to the rudder or outdrive as well as to the engine. The problem is even more critical if dual control stations are desired. Some types of controls of the dual type require a connection to the lower control station. This is often done in a duct that can double as a cabin roof support stanchion. In some cases, a window is placed in the cabin roof above the lower control station so the helmsman on the flying bridge can at least read the instruments below thereby requiring only one set of instruments.

CHAPTER 26 — DAGGERBOARDS, CENTERBOARDS, & RUDDERS

Any object floating on the water will tend to be blown across the water in a leeward direction, or away from the direction which the wind is blowing. To prevent this from happening to a sailboat, and to enable it to sail more in a direction into the wind, a daggerboard or centerboard is often used. A daggerboard or centerboard is a thin vertical plate sticking out the bottom of the boat (usually along the center) which gives the boat a "grip" on the water thereby preventing or at least minimizing leeward movement. Contrary to popular believe, the daggerboard or centerboard does not keep the boat from "tipping over", unless there is sufficient ballast included in the board, which is not common.

A variation of the centerboard is the leeboard which is similar except that these are hung onto either side of the hull outboard. They must be attached to the hull with special fittings that allow raising and adjusting the boards. A variation of the daggerboard is the bilgeboard, and this member usually works just like a daggerboard except they are usually located in pairs, one on each outboard side. Leeboards do not require a trunk, however, bilgeboards are usually mounted in some sort of case just like a daggerboard. For practical purpose, leeboards and bilgeboards are similar in construction to centerboards and daggerboards, and are not as common as the latter types, although their

function is the same.

Rudders on sailboats are frequently of the outboard or transom-hung type, and together with daggerboard and centerboard components, may be all or partly made from plywood. In all cases where plywood is used, it should be at least exterior grade. Descriptions on how these components are frequently made will follow, although it is not practical to cover all the possible variations.

DAGGERBOARDS & CENTERBOARDS

What's the difference between a daggerboard and a centerboard? Well, a daggerboard can be likened to an actual dagger which fits into its sheath or "case". The case in the instance of the daggerboard is referred to as the daggerboard trunk. The daggerboard slips in and out of the daggerboard trunk, usually in a vertical direction only. The purpose of the daggerboard trunk is to provide bearing for the daggerboard and to keep water out of the boat. Once the daggerboard is in the trunk there is little movement and little adjustment with most daggerboards. Once it is down in position, the position can only be varied up or down.

Sometimes the daggerboard is made from metal (usually a piece of aluminum sheet), but this is somewhat costly and usually no more efficient or effective than those made from wood, which is the most common and practical material for the amateur builder. The fit of the daggerboard within the trunk and where it passes through the hull should be fairly tight, not only to minimize resistance at the slot below the water, but to prevent the board from banging around in the trunk. However, the fit must not be so tight that it is difficult to raise and lower the board. If this occurs, there will be excessive wear on the board and/or the trunk.

A centerboard is different from the daggerboard in that it is hinged at its forward portion by a centerboard pin. The centerboard pin is basically a bolt or rod about which the centerboard pivots up and down in the centerboard trunk or casing. The centerboard trunk is much like a daggerboard trunk, but unlike the daggerboard, the centerboard remains in its trunk at all times, whereas the daggerboard is removable out the top of the trunk. While the daggerboard moves up and down in its slot, the centerboard "swings" about its pin. Because it can swing, the centerboard is infinitely adjustable to suit varying sailing conditions, and can be used to vary the balance of the boat on the helm. However, technically there is more resistance along the longer slot required for the centerboard. A daggerboard is much less complex than a centerboard, however a drawback of the daggerboard is that should the boat sail into shallow waters or accidentally come up onto a beach, the daggerboard will not pivot back and up into the trunk like a centerboard will. The damage to the boat in such a situation could be extensive, but on the centerboard type boat, there will be virtually none. This

is one reason why daggerboards are usually only found on small daysailer-type boats.

When daggerboards and centerboards are made from wood, there is a tendency for these to float up and out of the water. To prevent this the boards can be made out of metal, and in some cases this is specified on the plans. However, if wood for these members is specified or recommended, there are several methods to prevent the boards from floating up. With daggerboards there are spring stainless steel "clips" available which fit onto the board making the fit tight enough in the trunk that the board cannot float up, but can still be raised easily. Another method is to use an elastic "shock cord" across the top of the trunk secured to eye straps or screw eyes. With both daggerboards and centerboards, a removable "pin" can be used through the trunk sides and board which will "lock" the board in position (see Fig. 26-1). By providing a series of holes in the board, the pin can be used to lock the board in various positions to suit sailing conditions. On centerboards of wood, a common method is to put a weight on or in the board. This can be a lead weight built right into a hole in the board, or a specially fabricated casting designed to fit the bottom of the board. Used in combination with the pin, the weight will pull the board down into position, and the pin will lock the board in place.

Daggerboards and centerboards can be made from solid wood or plywood. The solid wood is preferable, however, when the board becomes too large, plywood can be used in preference to gluing up widths of solid lumber. Because daggerboards are most often long and narrow, solid wood is most frequently used for these. Covering such solid wood members with fiberglass cloth and resin can be done, but since these members are frequently left naturally finished, such covering is seldom done. However, on boards made from plywood, fiberglass covering is recommended, although this is not applied until the board has been faired to shape.

To minimize the resistance underway, the portion of the board below the bottom of the boat should be faired to an "airfoil" shape (see Plate 26-A). This shape is also applied to wood rudders below the waterline. The thickest portion of the member will be about ⅓ aft of the leading edge. The edges are radiused, with the aft edge being finer or "sharper" than the forward edge. Fullness to the contour free of concavity is important or else "chattering" or vib-

ration of the rudder at speed will occur which can be nerve-racking. This "chattering" is caused by the water moving over the board surfaces at such speed that it " pulls away" from the board surfaces causing "eddies" or turbulence.

Making a centerboard or daggerboard is usually simple. Often full size patterns are provided, or dimensions are given for the contours. The patterns can be transferred to the material, or the dimensions laid out directly to the material. Then the member can be sawn to shape. With centerboards, be very careful in locating and marking for the centerboard pin. Various wood rasps and surface forming tools (such as the "Surform" group of patented tools) are excellent for fairing these members. A template of cardboard to the "airfoil" shape can be made which can be frequently checked to the work. When plywood is used for the members, the various plywood laminations denoted by the glue lines can be used to check the amount of material removed. Such glue lines should be straight if the contours are the same all along the surface. After fairing to shape along the edges, the board can be finished or covered with fiberglass.

DAGGERBOARD & CENTERBOARD TRUNKS

With the exception of locating and installing the centerboard pin, the fabrication and assembly of daggerboard and centerboard trunks is basically similar. Sections through typical trunks are shown by Plate 26-B. The trunk sides are made from sheet plywood, and in most cases these protrude through the

FIG. 26-1—To prevent the daggerboard from floating up and out of the trunk on this boat, a pin hooked to the trunk with a small length of chain passes through the trunk side and daggerboard.

keel member and past the bottom planking. The slot through the keel member must be to suit the net size (both length and width) required for the trunk. On small boats using a dagger-board, the slot can be cut after the keel member is in place on the building form prior to applying the planking. Usually four locating holes can be drilled into the keel at the trunk extremeties and then a saber saw is used to cut the slot into the keel.

The slot for a centerboard can be handled in similar manner. However, on larger boats or those with thick keels, it may be more convenient and accurate to make the slot on a table saw using a blind cut. To do this, first determine where the slot will be located along the keel member, either from dimensions provided or taken directly from the work by temporarily locating the keel. Then clamp the keel to the table saw against the fence with the

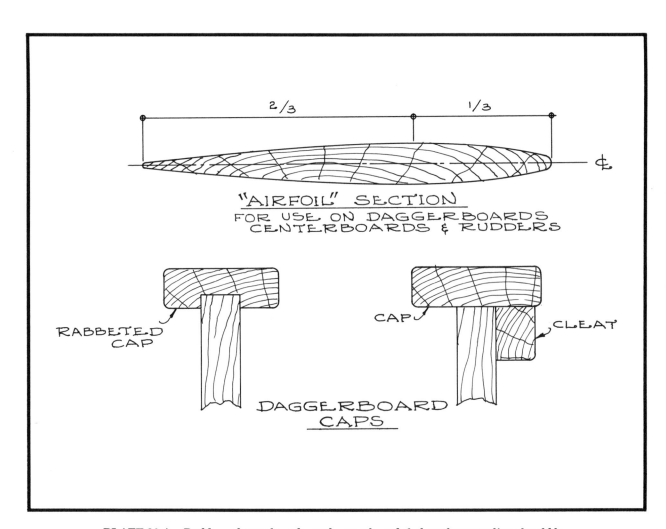

PLATE 26-A—Rudders, daggerboards, and centerboards below the waterline should be faired to minimize the resistance to the flow of water. The "airfoil" shape is best suited to this requirement, proportioned as shown. The tops of daggerboards can be capped by either of the two methods indicated.

blade lowered. Turn on the saw and gradually raise the blade to make the cut to the correct points, repeating this procedure until the longitudinal cuts are completed. A saber saw can be used to cut out the ends of the slot after this. Regardless of the methods used to cut the slot, whether for a daggerboard or centerboard trunk, the fit with the trunk sides should be as tight and accurate as possible to prevent leaks from occuring.

As with the daggerboard or centerboard, the contours of the trunk sides may be determined from dimensions given on the plans or by full size patterns. Depending on the design, the trunk may require fabrication and locating on the formwork before the keel can be located, or the trunk may be installed after the keel is positioned over the framework. The solid wood members located on the outboard sides of the trunk along the keel are called

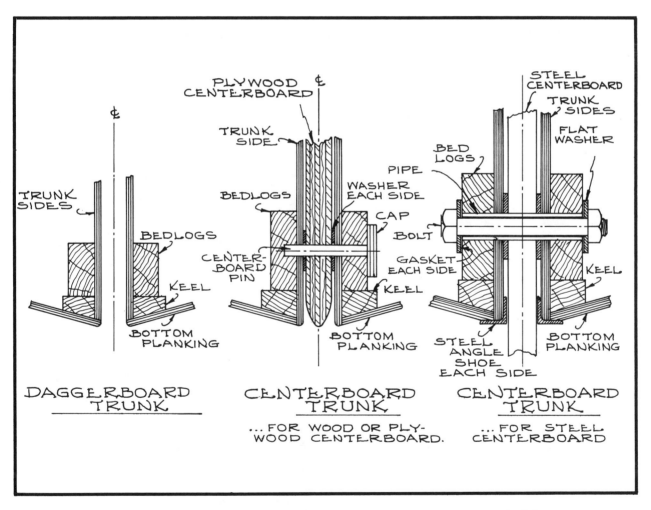

PLATE 26-B—A typical section through a daggerboard trunk is shown at the left. A section through a centerboard trunk using a plywood centerboard is shown at the center, while to the right is a section through a centerboard trunk using a steel plate centerboard.

FIG. 26-2

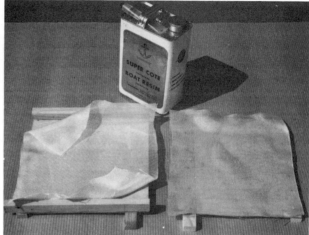

FIG. 26-3

FIG. 26-4

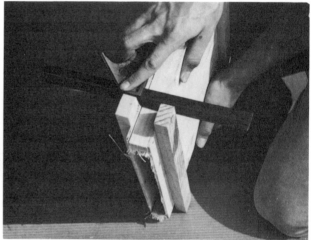

FIG. 26-5

FIG. 26-2 thru FIG. 26-6—The construction, fiberglassing, and installation of daggerboard trunk. The two halves are covered with a layer of fiberglass cloth and resin, and then assembled. FIG. 26-5 shows a square being used in the assembly to check accuracy. FIG. 26-6 shows the completed daggerboard trunk installed into the keel slot.

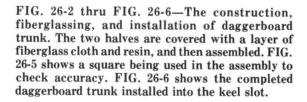

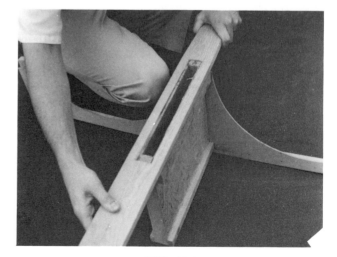

FIG. 26-6

bed logs, and these provide solid bearing of the trunk against the keel. Therefore, they must match the keel contour in profile view and may vary somewhat to suit the net thickness of the keel member used. Each half of the plywood trunk sides is fastened to the bed log members as well as to the solid wood members or blocking at the top edge. For centerboard trunks, the two halves with the bed logs in place are clamped together and the hole for the center-board pin is drilled. If possible, a drill press or other drilling device that will assure the hole being located at 90 degrees to the surface, should be used for accurately making the hole. If the hole is not accurate, it will probably leak and perhaps skew the centerboard so that it does not operate smoothly within the slot.

Spacing blocks of thickness to suit are then fastened to one half of the trunk on the inside surface. Then the two halves can be again temporarily clamped together for pre-drilling the screw holes. On smaller trunks, this step may not be necessary since nails may be used to fasten the two halves. If the trunk will not be covered with fiberglass, paint and finish the exposed portions of the trunk sides that will be inside the slot once it is assembled.

Fiberglass or equal sheathing methods however are advised for the trunk and should be done at this point. Cover both halves separately. The half without the spacing blocks is covered so the material extends to the edges of the trunk where it is trimmed off flush. On the side with the spacer blocks, it is best to fill the inside corners with a resin-type putty such as "microballoons" (see Chapter 23) in the form of a radiused fillet so the fiberglass will not lift and

form air bubbles at the corners. Also radius the spacer block corners. Apply the fiberglass to this half and trim flush with the edge of the trunk side. Completely sand the fiberglass surfaces of both halves to the desired degree of smoothness, but do not apply any paint.

The trunk halves are now ready for assembly. With some centerboard trunks, provisions must be made before assembly for various centerboard components such as the centerboard pennant (the line which raises and lowers the centerboard) and the centerboard pulleys that may be a part of the pennant tackle. The trunk halves can be assembled with screws being recommended for larger centerboard trunks, and with nails or screws for daggerboard trunks. If the trunk will not be covered with fiberglass then glue applied liberally can be used at the junction between the two halves. If the trunk has been covered with fiberglass, bed the trunk halves in strips of resin saturated fiberglass cloth or mat to act as a "gasket" to bond the members and prevent leaks.

Accuracy in aligning the trunk halves is critical. Use a square to bring the edges of the trunk into alignment and clamp or nail to hold in this position (see Fig. 26-5 and Fig. 26-10). The bed logs must be parallel with each other so that when the trunk is installed on the keel, it will assume a 90 degree angle with the keel to be exactly vertical in the hull.

The completed trunk is inserted through the keel slot with the trunk sides protruding through the keel member a sufficient amount to pass through the planking to be installed later. Use long screws to fasten through the keel and into the bed logs at close

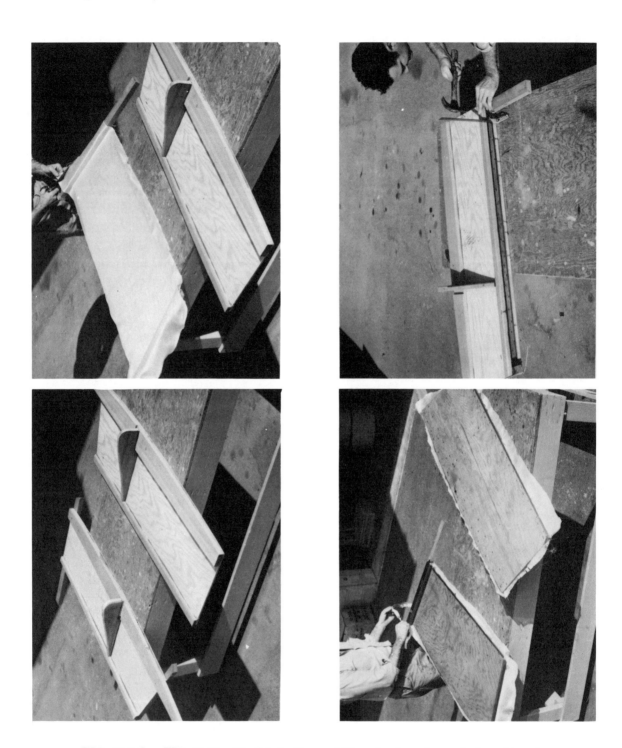

FIG. 26-7 thru FIG. 26-10—The fabrication and fiberglassing of a centerboard trunk.
FIG. 26-7 shows the two trunk halves with all members assembled in place. Note the
knees on the sides which will lap to partial frames that butt to the trunk bed logs. FIG.
26-8 illustrates fitting of the fiberglass cloth, while FIG. 26-9 shows the layer of cloth
being saturated with the resin. On trunks up to about this size, the two halves can be
brought together while the resin is wet and immediately assembled, thereby making it
unnecessary to apply a separate gasket layer of mat and resin as could be necessary with
a larger trunk where the resin would set too quickly. FIG. 26-10 show the builder using a
square to check and maintain accuracy in assembling the trunk halves.

276

intervals after gluing in place. Be sure that liberal amounts of glue are used at this junction as well as where the trunk sides lap the keel. Where possible, drive fastenings angularly through the trunk sides at close intervals into the keel along the slot. The trunk will often intersect with other hull members and require fastenings. For example, the trunk may butt to frames at one or both ends, or half-frames may butt to the bed logs. Use ample fastenings and glue at all such junctions with blocking where necessary, being sure that the trunk is exactly vertical in the hull and not skewed to one side or otherwise distorted. With daggerboard trunks, this completes the installation.

With centerboard trunks, the centerboard must be inserted into the trunk. On small boats with light wood boards, this can be done while the boat is upside down on the form (preferable), or after the hull has been righted as long as access is provided underneath. With heavier boards or those made from steel that may serve as ballast and cannot be easily handled, it is possible to install these while the hull is upside down, however, many will prefer to right the hull and set it directly in place over the centerboard.

Whichever procedure is used, usually washers are located on each side of the board at the pin hole to serve as spacers. These washers are taped in place on the board to hold them while the board is fitted. Two details at centerboard pins are shown by Plate 26-B. One is a lighter type for use on smaller boats using wood centerboards. This pin can be made from a bolt or rod and does not pass through both bed logs. One consideration of centerboard pins is that they have a tendency to leak at any through-

joint area. Hence, by stopping the pin half way through the one bed log, the leaking problem is minimized. With this pin, the weight and swing friction is taken directly on the pin, However, it will be relatively easy to remove the pin (as well as the board) for replacement or maintenance.

With the heavier duty pin (often used for steel centerboards), the friction is taken on a section of pipe which also supports the weight of the board. The bolt is tightened down to provide a watertight junction, and hence the reason for the washers and gaskets. The hole for the pipe should be a very firm fit, and the length of the pipe somewhat shorter than the assembled trunk thickness.

The junction of the trunk sides through the keel and bottom planking can be handled in different ways depending on the design. In most cases, the bottom plywood planking will butt to the trunk sides where they protrude through the keel. The corners along the slot are then radiused and fiberglassed along with the bottom, running the material up into the slot as far as practical. It is a good idea to apply at least a double lamination of fiberglass and resin at this point. Fill the slot or tape it closed to prevent resin from running down inside the trunk.

On boats using steel centerboards of considerable weight, guides, usually in the form of angles or flat bar, are fastened along the slot to cover this junction. If the boat has a vee bottom, fair the bottom off for these guides so they will mate flat, and then apply fiberglass. Metal guides are best fastened in place after the application of fiberglass, bedding them in a marine-type sealant. After the hull is righted and the centerboard pennant installed, the trunk can be capped per the plans. If the boat will remain in the water at all times, antifouling paint may be desired. This can be applied within the trunk by sealing the slot with a board having a hole in it which can be corked shut. Pour an ample amount of anti-fouling paint into the slot to coat all the surfaces that will be in contact with the water. Remove the cork and drain the excess paint back into the container.

RUDDERS

Rudders on sailboats are often made from solid lumber, however, plywood is sometimes used. This is practical if a good grade of plywood is used and the rudder is thick enough. Like daggerboards and centerboards, the portion of the rudder below the waterline should be faired to the airfoil shape if there is

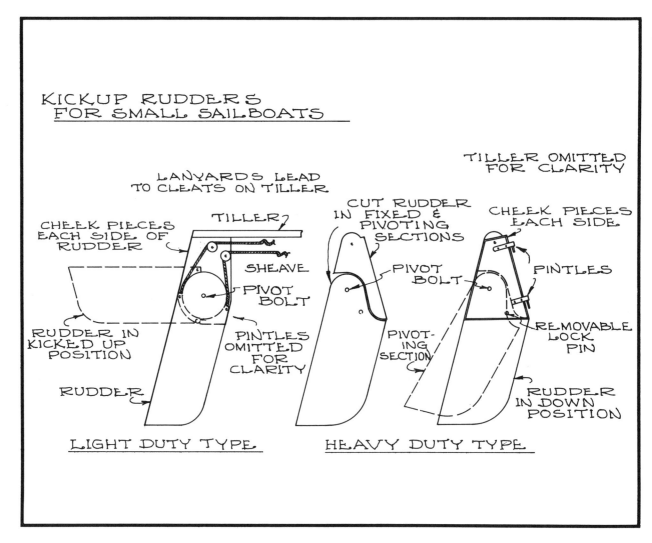

PLATE 26-C—Two types of kick-up rudders can be made by the builder. The rudder to the left is a light-duty type held up or down by lanyards. The rudder to the right uses a pivot bolt which can be tightened, as well as a removable lock pin to hold the rudder down for somewhat heavier duty use.

no keel, skeg, or deadwood ahead of the rudder, or tapered to the aft end if there is a keel, skeg, or deadwood leading the rudder.

As with daggerboards and centerboards, solid wood rudders are frequently left naturally finished without fiberglass. However, those of plywood are preferably covered with fiberglass. The shape or contour of the rudder is frequently given by a full size pattern, or dimensions are noted on the plans. The fittings for hanging the rudder to the hull should be through-bolted into the rudder, and bolted or screwed to the hull. Since wood rudders can float, there must be some type of rudder stop incorporated to prevent the rudder from floating up and out of its fittings when underway.

On small sailboats which will run up onto the beach, a kick-up type of rudder is desirable. Two types that can be made are shown on Plate 26-C. With kick-up rudders, the device should be capable of holding the rudder down in place with plenty of strength, and there must not be an excessive amount of free-play or "slop". The first type shown is limited to small boats since the lines or lanyards used to hold the rudder down will have limited strength, and there is no way of exerting pressure against the rudder between the side or "cheek" pieces. The other method uses a wing nut to provide pressure against the rudder through the "cheek" pieces as well as a pin through the rudder which holds it in the "down" position. The only disadvantage with this rudder is that the pin must be removed before the boat hits the beach or else some damage could be done.

CHAPTER 27 — "STITCH AND GLUE

AUTHOR'S NOTE: I would like to thank Sam Devlin, Tracy O'Brien, and John Marples for sharing their experiences and opinions during the compilation of this chapter.

An alternative approach that may have considerable appeal for the first-time boatbuilder, particularly if one is working on a small craft, is called "stitch-and-glue." Also sometimes known as "sewn-seam," or "tack-and-tape," stitch-and-glue is a method of joining plywood panels by using resin-putty, usually epoxy, and multiple laminates of fiberglass or similar products. As we shall see here, this is one of the simplest methods yet developed for building a boat, requiring only rudimentary skills and equipment. Even the rankest amateurs should feel confident that stitch-and-glue construction is well within their abilities.

The stitch-and-glue method is not exactly a new process. The idea was widely publicized during the 1960s, when the "Mirror" dinghy was developed in England. Thousands of these boats were built in this fashion. However, despite their popularity, stitch-and-glue construction was not considered a really viable building method until epoxy adhesives became available. Although polyester-type resins can be used, the properties of epoxy are far superior for stitch-and-glue construction and will be the resin discussed in this chapter. While it is generally used on flat-bottomed sheet plywood hulls, the method is also capable of handling more complex shapes. Its most popular application has been for smaller boats, usually under 20 feet,

but many larger craft have been successfully built using this method.

The chief merit of stitch-and-glue construction is that it is lightweight. Its simplicity leaves the interior of the boat with a clean look, as very little (if any) internal framing is necessary. Internal backing members, such as chine and stem, are not used. The labor of bending longitudinals into place, and the subsequent fairing or shaping for plywood planking, is eliminated.

Another advantage is that very few tools are required. All you need is a portable saw to cut the plywood to shape, a pair of pliers, and an electric drill for driving the few required screws and for drilling the stitching holes. A power sander is another useful addition, helping considerably to lighten the labor of finishing.

Canoes, kayaks, and similar craft can be made extremely light by using thin plywood and eliminating internal ribs and framing. Flat bottom craft usually have the bottom planking lapping the side planking. This is shown in Plate 27-A-1, while an optional junction at the chine is shown in 27-4.

Larger boats, or those intended for rough usage, are frequently double planked on the bottom to make the bends easier. Heavier bottom planking may be used to overcome the flexibility caused by the elimination of the longitudinals normally found in conventional construction.

FIG. 27-1—Building this small dinghy is easy with stitch-and-glue methods. Only two sheets of 1/4" plywood plus a few solid wood pieces are required to build the boat.

FIG. 27-2—Seat uprights, a bow, and transom are used as forms to shape the side planking. The hull takes shape quickly with wire stitches holding the parts together.

FIG. 27-3—The bottom planking is stitched with copper wire through predrilled holes. Full size patterns, with stitching holes indicated, are furnished for all parts.

FIG. 27-4—Seats form watertight compartments with resin-putty used at interior junctions to assure a leakproof bond. Such seams are then sanded smooth and covered with fiberglass laminates.

Stitch-and-glue construction uses sheet plywood planking that has been precut to the proper contour and then bent into the boat shape. Junctions or seams alone the chine, stem, and keel are held together temporarily by means of wire stitches. A bonding fillet of glue (epoxy resin-putty) is then used on the interior of the seams. This is followed with laminations of epoxy resin-saturated fiberglass cloth or tape, both inside and outside of the joint. Typical seam junctions are shown in progressive sequence in Plates 27 A-C.

Generally, the joints are sewn together with wire stitches, but how the seams are held together initially is inconsequential. Filament or duct tape has been used as well as finishing nails. If the boat is built over a form, the plywood panels can be held in position by using temporary fastenings driven through the plywood into the form members. This may eliminate any need to hold a seam together by other means. Still, wire stitching the joints is the most common method by far, as the name "stitch-and-glue" suggests.

PLANKING

One problem with stitch-and-glue construction is determining the shape of the plywood planking panels. As you may recall from Chapter 4, plywood cannot be shaped into a compound curve, but it can be bent into a cylinder or cone. Planking panel shapes can be determined by mathematics, using a computer, by creating a small model, or by building a full-scale hull. The latter requires a mold to wrap the panels around in order to determine their shape. Unfortunately, this process can be fairly time-consuming, enough so that many of the advantages of the stitch-and-glue method are lost, unless several hulls are to be constructed.

Ready-made plans are available for many types of stitch-and-glue boats. Some plans require scaling, or laying out planking from dimensions. Full-size patterns for planking can eliminate this often tedious task. Blueprinted patterns, showing stitching holes, reference lines and scaled layouts showing how parts are obtained from sheets of plywood are a boon for the neophyte. Using patterns results in cost saving and makes building with stitch-and-glue easier yet.

The outlines of the planking panels and other critical parts are first laid out on the plywood, either drawn from dimensions or traced from a pattern. Then the parts are carefully cut to shape. If two or more parts are the same, clamp or tack the sheets together with nails and cut both simultaneously. A power saber saw is handy for cutting panels to shape, although a small circular hand saw is ideal for gradual curves and straight lines. Parts can be rough cut on a band saw and then machined to shape with a collar shaper or router from master templates if several boats are to be built.

The cut surfaces of all parts should be smoothed with coarse sandpaper or hand planed. Edges which will contact other parts should be given a generous radius. The edge of the plywood need not be perfectly smooth, but curves should be gentle and fair. Sawn fir plywood tends to splinter, so rounding the edges is important. Be careful. Always mark reference lines to the plywood where given and required. If you are

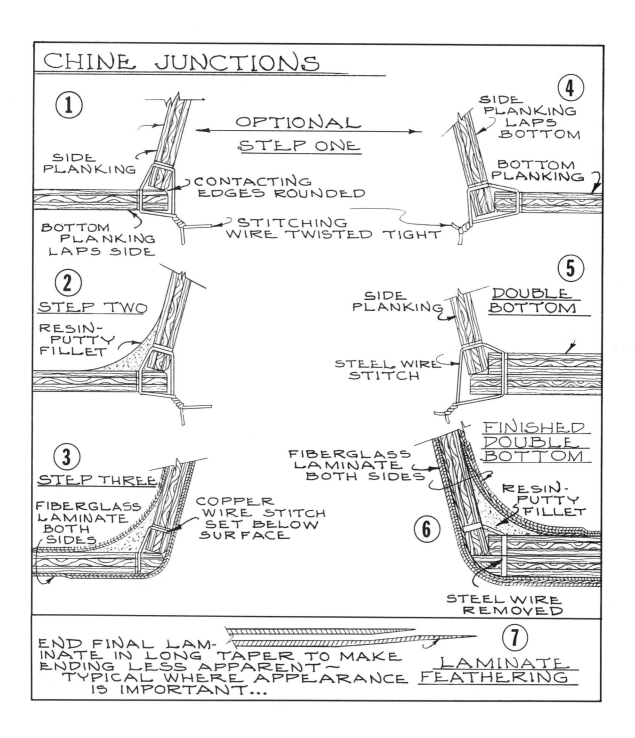

CHINE JUNCTIONS

① OPTIONAL STEP ONE

SIDE PLANKING

BOTTOM PLANKING LAPS SIDE

CONTACTING EDGES ROUNDED

STITCHING WIRE TWISTED TIGHT

④ SIDE PLANKING LAPS BOTTOM

BOTTOM PLANKING

② STEP TWO

RESIN-PUTTY FILLET

⑤ DOUBLE BOTTOM

SIDE PLANKING

STEEL WIRE STITCH

③ STEP THREE

FIBERGLASS LAMINATE BOTH SIDES

COPPER WIRE STITCH SET BELOW SURFACE

FIBERGLASS LAMINATE BOTH SIDES

FINISHED DOUBLE BOTTOM

RESIN-PUTTY FILLET

⑥

STEEL WIRE REMOVED

END FINAL LAM-INATE IN LONG TAPER TO MAKE ENDING LESS APPARENT ~ TYPICAL WHERE APPEARANCE IS IMPORTANT...

⑦ LAMINATE FEATHERING

PLATE 27-A   Sketch #1, #2, and #3 illustrate typical progression of a stitch and glue chine junction when bottom laps side planking, while #4 shows an optional method with side lapping bottom planking. Bottom planking built up from two laminations of plywood, interlocking with side planking, is shown in #5 and #6. Feathering or tapering of the fiberglass laminates to eliminate abrupt changes, typical at tape or fiberglass endings, is shown in #7. As described in the text, resin-putty, tapered from the laminate to the hull surface, is desired to eliminate excessive grinding of structural fiberglass.

working from patterns that give the locations of the stitching holes, drill these only after first backing the underside of the plywood with a block of wood to help prevent splintering. Properly crafted parts are the first key to a properly crafted boat.

In some small boats, the basic shape of the hull is developed using only the planking. This approach involves prejoining flat plywood panels. This may include the side and bottom planking. Then, using a minimum (if any) of interior forms, the panels are "folded" together to form the hull shape. In most hulls, however, some type of frame, form, or spreader is required to shape the planking panels to the hull contour. Seats, bulkheads, and other cross members may be built right into the design, thus eliminating temporary forms.

STITCHING WIRE

Seams where plywood panels join at the keel, chine or stem are held together initially with twisted "stitches" of soft wire. The wires are usually copper, but mild steel can be used. The spacing of the stitches will vary, depending on the severity of the bend. Stitches are typically 2″ to 6″ apart. Distance in from the panel edge should be about 1-½ times the plywood thickness, although ⁵/₁₆″ to ³/₈″ should be considered a practical minimum. Where stitching wire placement is determined by patterns or layouts, holes should be pre-drilled as indicated. Wire of 14 to 16 gauge thickness usually requires a ³/₃₂″ diameter hole. Prebending the wire in the form of a "J" or "U" makes the job of threading stitches through the holes somewhat

easier.

Non-corrosive copper wire can be left in the structure. After the hull seam is taped, stitching wires are snipped off flush with the planking. Wire ends should be set well beneath the surface with a punch, taking care not to damage the resin-putty fillet. Some feel that stitching wire left in the structure can eventually cause problems due to the dissimilarity of resin and metal.

FIG. 27-5—Steel wire stitches are never left in the boat. One method of removal is to heat the wire ends with a propane torch until cherry red.

FIG. 27-6—The heat travels down the wire and softens the epoxy immediately surrounding it, allowing the wire to be pulled free.

 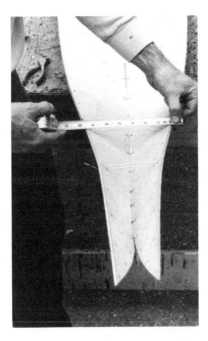 

FIG. 27-7—This 17' sculling skiff is vee bottom and asymmetrical about the ends. Built from two sheets of 4MM thick 4' × 8' plywood panels, the bottom is butt joined at the athwartship centerline.

FIG. 27-8—Thread wire through stitching holes, stretching from one side of boat to the other, and bring the two slit bottom halves together to predetermined dimensions.

FIG. 27-9— The side planking is stitched to bottom planking along the chine seam, with a temporary center form shaping the boat.

FIG. 27-10—Interior seams are filled with resin-putty, filleted and covered with fiberglass laminates. The hull is finished with lightweight fiberglass deck cloth exterior covering, leaving a natural wood finish. Seams and butt blocked areas were painted a contrasting brilliant yellow. The basic hull weighs less than 40 lbs.

Mild steel stitching wire may be used in place of copper, if so desired. Steel wire does provide stronger stitching to bring joints together in larger boats, but steel stitches are never to be left in the boat. The wire can be pre-waxed (with auto paste wax) to facilitate withdrawl. Optionally, use a propane torch and heat the wire ends "cherry red". This will soften the epoxy resin enabling the stitches to be pulled out. Another option is to use resin-putty fillet along the seams between the stitches. Then, after the resin sets, the stitches can be removed and the balance of the filleting finished.

To bring mating parts together, the stitching wires are first tightened by hand, and then twisted firmly with pliers. Perfectly-fitting joints are not required, as the resin-putty will fill minor gaps or imperfections. Usually, a series of wires are threaded through holes, then progressively tightened, alternating from one side of the boat to the other. Mating members not in alignment may be pushed into position or lightly rapped to bring the edges together. Then, the stitching wires are retightened.

After all the stitching wires are in place, align and chock the hull in position, taking care that it is not twisted or racked from alignment. Be sure to retighten the wires before applying the resin-putty fillet. If any junction is not held properly, more stitching wires can be added. At the same time, any unneeded wires may be removed.

FILLETS

Fillets are used to glue and radius stitched inside corners. These are made from resin-putty, which is a mixture of epoxy resin and filler additives. Many types of fillers can be used, although a blend of epoxy resin, microspheres, and silica works well. While microspheres can be used alone, the adding of silica makes the mixture easier to apply. A blend of two parts microspheres to one part silica (by volume) makes a good starting mixture. One part of resin (with hardener added) is then mixed with 2-½ to 3 parts of filler mixture (again by volume). The proportions may be varied slightly, although the resulting mixture should have the consistency of heavy batter.

Warmer ambient temperatures require a stiffer mix. Mix only small batches, at least initially, in order to get the "feel" of the work and to see how well the mixture is suited to the working conditions. Mixtures that are a bit thicker or thinner than noted will have no appreciable effect on bond strength. Mixes that are a little stiff initially may also be "thinned" somewhat by the heat given off during cure ("exotherm"). The best bet is to make a few test runs to determine what consistency is best for your project.

Fillets are applied over a surface primed with epoxy resin. If the epoxy resin has set up, the surface should be lightly sanded before the fillet is applied. The minimum radius of fillets should be specified in the plans, although this may vary slightly, depending on the angle of the joining members. The fillet material should lap onto the joining members at least 1" on each side, and should not exceed the fiberglass tape width. Fillet radius must be adequate to conceal all wire stitches. Forcing the wire down toward joining

FIG. 27-11—Resin-putty, a combination of catalyzed epoxy resin, microspheres and silica, is applied to interior stitch-and-glue seams.

FIG. 27-12—A rounded piece of plastic is used to form a fillet. The putty knife is removing the excess putty on the forward side of the fillet tool.

FIG. 27-13—Fiberglass cloth, in this case strips of bi-axial cloth, are placed over the sanded, resin saturated fillet. Pre-saturating the cloth with resin prior to application is optional.

FIG. 27-14—Excessive resin build up is undesirable. A squeegee (shown) or a brush is used to disperse the resin and force air (white spots) from under the cloth.

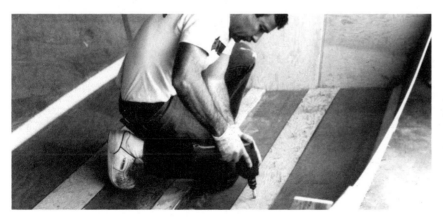

FIG. 27-15—Longitudinal reinforcements are usually installed after the hull shape has been formed. Pan head sheet metal screws are being used to hold the wide plywood batten laminate to the hull, and will be removed after the epoxy adhesive cures.

members with a light tape of a hammer will reduce the required depth.

Filleting need not be a continuous operation. You can stop at will and continue later, if necessary. Fillets can usually be made in one build-up. However, it is possible to make a partial one, allow it to cure, and make another pass to complete the task. When temporary forms are used, it is often necessary to complete the fillet after the form is removed.

Many tools and objects can be used to make fillets, including plastic lids, jar and can edges, back of large spoons, or other round edged object. Try to keep fillets as neat as possible. It not only looks better, but it also helps to minimize clean-up and sanding of the cured resin-putty. Masking tape can be placed on joining members to mark fillet limits. This procedure is highly recommended where a natural wood finish is desired.

Keep an eye on the consistency and texture of the material. Once the resin-putty in the fillet starts to set-up, do not attempt more forming. Clean up any excess putty before the resin sets up, and sand the fillet after it cures. An arced sanding block, made from soft wood or foam, will assure a smooth interior surface for applying the fiberglass laminate.

FIBERGLASS LAMINATES

Standard type fiberglass cloth or tape 7–10 ounce (per square yard) treated "E" glass is frequently used over seams on small non-powered boats. Two laminates, inside and outside, is typical with ¼" or less plywood planking. Some use multiple laminates of this type fiberglass on boats with thicker plywood planking, however when the number of laminates becomes excessive it is preferable to use bi-axial cloth or tape. Standard woven fiberglass strands run vertically and horizontally. If strands parallel a seam much of the strength of resin impregnated fiberglass is lost. Bias cut fiberglass cloth, with fibers oriented 45 degrees either side the seam, are advantageous but if cut from cloth the edges tend to ravel. Weight for weight bi-axial fiberglass is about one and one-half times stronger than regular woven fiberglass. The bi-axial, non-woven, "E" fiberglass has fibers knitted in position oriented 45 degrees either side of a vertical plane. Bi-axial fiberglass is available in heavier weights that are still readily formed around seams. Strips of varying width can be cut from cloth with virtually no ravelling. Two layers of 17 ounce bi-axial cloth over seams can be feathered to the hull surface with resin putty and finished with care are virtually invisible.

The widths of fiberglass covering seams should lap over the plywood surface at least 1". A good fiberglassed seam will tear the veneer from the plywood prior to breaking at the joint. Joints parallel to seams should be staggered and extend over the plywood planking as much as possible. Do not end two fiberglass laminates at the same point. End junctions of fiberglass tape are usually lapped although for appearance exterior surfaces are frequently butted. Grinding or excessive sanding of taped seams should be avoided. Where appearance is important fair fiberglass laminate endings into the plywood planking with resin-putty.

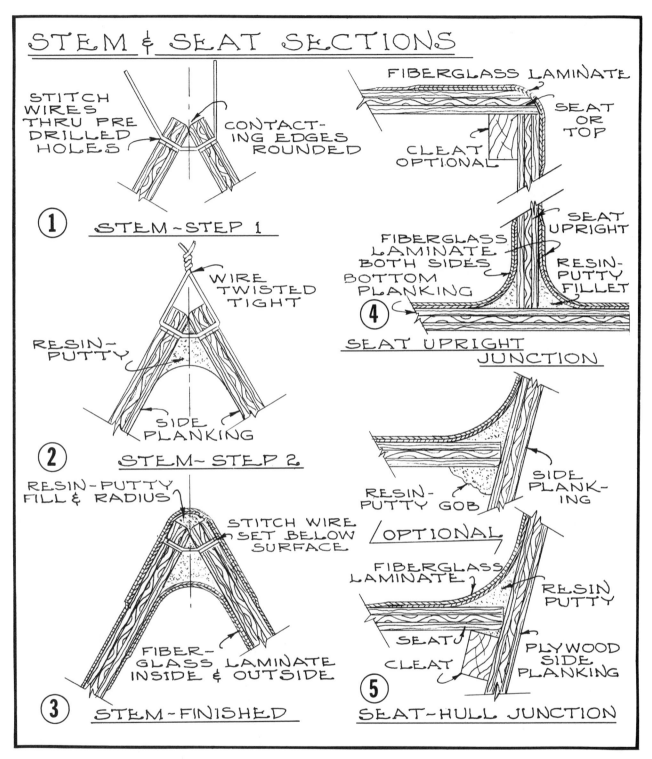

STEM & SEAT SECTIONS

① STEM ~ STEP 1
STITCH WIRES THRU PRE DRILLED HOLES — CONTACTING EDGES ROUNDED

② STEM ~ STEP 2
WIRE TWISTED TIGHT — RESIN-PUTTY — SIDE PLANKING

③ STEM ~ FINISHED
RESIN-PUTTY FILL & RADIUS — STITCH WIRE SET BELOW SURFACE — FIBER-GLASS LAMINATE INSIDE & OUTSIDE

④ SEAT UPRIGHT JUNCTION
FIBERGLASS LAMINATE — SEAT OR TOP — CLEAT OPTIONAL — FIBERGLASS LAMINATE BOTH SIDES BOTTOM PLANKING — SEAT UPRIGHT — RESIN-PUTTY FILLET

⑤ SEAT ~ HULL JUNCTION
RESIN-PUTTY GOB — SIDE PLANKING — OPTIONAL — FIBERGLASS LAMINATE — RESIN PUTTY — SEAT — CLEAT — PLYWOOD SIDE PLANKING

PLATE 27-C Along the stem, and keel, planking is joined with stitch and glue; #1 shows stitching wire threaded through holes in the planking, #2 shows stitch tightened and resin-putty fillet applied, and #3 is a typical finished joint with fiberglass lamination inside and outside. Examples of seats, also typical of any junctions of vertical or horizontal members in the hull, are shown in #4 and #5. Bulkheads or seat uprights may be held to bottom or side planking with wire stitches, small nails or tape until the resin-putty fillet has hardened. Hull side junctions (#5) are supported by cleats, glued or fastened to the hull side, or optionally the top or seat bedded in a gob or heavy bead of resin putty.

289

FIG. 27-19—The transom is inserted and the chine stitched progressively aft. The seams are then filleted with resin putty and covered with fiberglass laminates.

FIG. 27-16—This 12″ power skiff is a good example of a vee bottom boat built with stitch-and-glue methods. The interior is clean without frames and total weight is only 110 lbs.

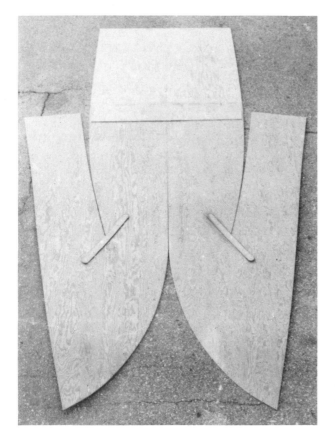

FIG. 27-17—The plywood planking, precut from patterns, is assembled flat on the ground with the two halves stitched together along the keel centerline.

FIG. 27-18—A temporary form is used at midpoint and the side planking gradually bent together and stitched along the stem.

Prior to applying the fiberglass laminates over the interior seams, coat the surface to be covered with a thin coat of epoxy resin and apply tape, add more resin and force it through the cloth weave. Use enough resin to impregnate the cloth so white spots are not present, but avoid using more resin than necessary, brushing, rolling, or using a squeegee to remove any excess. Some prefer to lay fiberglass tape on a plastic covered flat board, and pre-saturate prior to placing over the seam.

Multiple laminates can be done at one time, particularly if a helper is pre-saturating fiberglass tape. Laminations can be added until curing starts. Then the procedure should be stopped until the mixture has cured. If successive layers are to be applied, the process may be resumed after a light sanding of the cured surface.

Exterior hull junctions are treated in similar fashion. All corners must be given a generous radius (a minimum of ⅜″), so that the fiberglass will easily conform to the surface without lifting or forming air bubbles. Use a plane, sanding block, power sander, or other suitable tool to dress the area. Holes, dents, and other imperfections should be filled with resin-putty and sanded smooth. Note, however, that excess sanding on Douglas fir, or other rotary cut plywoods, should be avoided. Then apply the fiberglass tape, using the procedures described above.

If the exterior of the hull is to be fiberglassed (a procedure strongly advised), covering cloth may be substituted for one of the tape layers. You may even replace two layers, if the covering cloth double-laps the seams. The important thing is to have the specified fiberglass laminate over all seams. The foregoing applies primarily to seams taped with standard fiberglass material. Covering cloth should never be substituted for stronger bi-axial or equal fiberglass.

TRANSOMS

The transom of a stitch-and-glue is handled much the same as it would be on a conventional boat, with one major exception. Typically, transoms are framed around the inner perimeter in order to provide solid wood for the fastenings that hold the planking. However, the transom in a smaller stitch-and-glue boat may be thin and therefore not strong enough to accept fastenings. That problem is solved by stitching the transom to the planking panels. Then use resin-putty fillets and fiberglass laminates as described in this chapter.

In some other cases, the plywood may be thick enough to accept fasteners, but these would have to be driven into the weaker end-grain of the panel. The solution here is to use fasteners and add resin-putty fillets and fiberglass tape laminates, in the same mannner as along the chine seam.

SEATS AND FLOATATION COMPARTMENTS

In smaller boats, stitch-and-glue construction lends itself nicely to making lightweight thwarts or seat compartments. Built-in seats and/or flotation chambers can act as formers to help spring the planking around to the point where it can be stitched in place. After

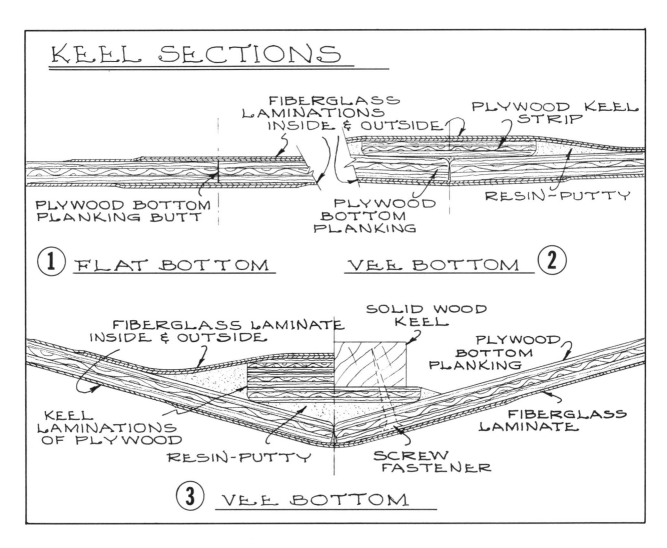

KEEL SECTIONS

FIBERGLASS LAMINATIONS INSIDE & OUTSIDE

PLYWOOD KEEL STRIP

PLYWOOD BOTTOM PLANKING BUTT

PLYWOOD BOTTOM PLANKING

RESIN-PUTTY

① FLAT BOTTOM

VEE BOTTOM ②

FIBERGLASS LAMINATE INSIDE & OUTSIDE

SOLID WOOD KEEL

PLYWOOD BOTTOM PLANKING

KEEL LAMINATIONS OF PLYWOOD

RESIN-PUTTY

SCREW FASTENER

FIBERGLASS LAMINATE

③ VEE BOTTOM

PLATE 27-B If a stitch and glue hull has considerable vee in the bottom, junction of side and bottom planking can be similar to chine junctions. If boat bottom is flat and in two halves joined over the centerline as shown in #1, panels may be butt joined with laminations of fiberglas inside and out. When the bottom has a slight vee, or for flat bottomed craft intended for rough usage, method #2 is used. As a vee becomes progressively severe, keel laminations of plywood, bedded in resin-putty and covered with fiberglass laminates, are used as shown in #3 (left side). Optionally, as shown in #3 (right side), a plywood keel strip bedded in resin-putty topped with a solid wood keel may be used with bottom planking, screw fastened.

the stitches are in the joint is sealed by using resin-putty fillets, with fiberglass laminates over them, to bond the members in place. Note that, since the seat compartments act as braces, held firmly by the resin-putty and fiberglass, only minimal stitches are required.

Vertical bulkheads or horizontal shelves may also be installed by these same methods, in either stitch-and-glue or conventional plywood boats. However, vertical bulkheads crossing the boat and resting on plywood planking can cause a localized stress area and should be avoided, especially if the boat is intended for high speed or rough use.

Closed compartment interior surfaces should be given several coats of epoxy resin prior to closing in. Any closed compartment should have drain plugs or deck plates that can be opened to relieve pressure build-up in hot weather. The compartments can be filled with "pour-in-place" or block foam to provide positive buoyancy.

At the junction of a flat surface or seat to hull side, two options can be used. A cleat can be fastened to the hull side as a seat support, as shown in Plate 27-C-5. It isn't necessary to angle or bevel the cleat (although you certainly can, if you so desire), as the resin-putty will form a gasket/adhesive bond. Another bonding method is to lay a large gob or thick bead of resin-putty along the hull side/seat junction eliminating the cleat.

The seats or tops of compartments rest on uprights. If these uprights are thin plywood, use a cleat at the junction of the upright and the top. This provides additional bearing surface. For additional holding strength, you might also use fasteners. Resin-putty is also needed at seat/upright junctions. Either temporary or permanent fasteners or weights may be used to hold the seat firmly in place until the bond has cured. Interior corners are filleted with resin-putty, followed by laminations of fiberglass.

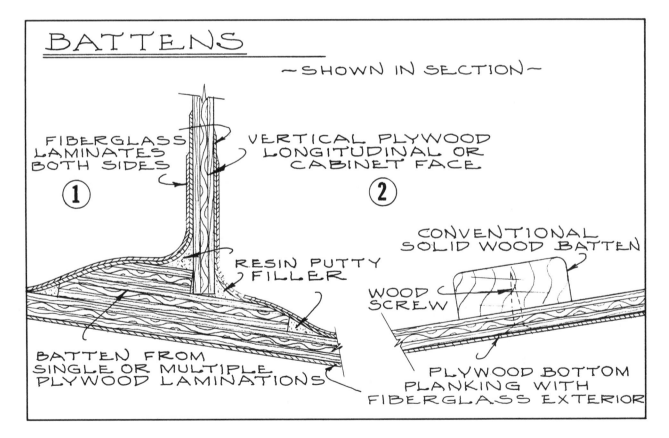

BATTENS

~SHOWN IN SECTION~

FIBERGLASS LAMINATES BOTH SIDES ① VERTICAL PLYWOOD LONGITUDINAL OR CABINET FACE ②

RESIN PUTTY FILLER

CONVENTIONAL SOLID WOOD BATTEN

WOOD SCREW

BATTEN FROM SINGLE OR MULTIPLE PLYWOOD LAMINATIONS

PLYWOOD BOTTOM PLANKING WITH FIBERGLASS EXTERIOR

PLATE 27-D Battens for bottom reinforcing are usually put in after assembly of a stitch and glue hull. Sketch #1 shows using plywood battens, often in multiple laminations, while #2 illustrates a solid wood batten screw fastened through the bottom planking. Vertical members such as bulkheads, or cabinet faces can be used to reinforce the bottom battens and provide additional longitudinal stiffness.

SHEER

The sheer member is usually put in after the stitch-and-glue boat is built. This eliminates fairing the sheer for the side planking, usually a formidable task. Depending on sheer contour and side flare, forcing a sheer to the top edge of the side planking can be a chore. If the sheer is considerably wider than its thickness, bending that requires edge setting becomes difficult. Sheer members with a relatively square cross section will bend easier in such cases. Forcing the sheer in against the planking a little at a time, clamping progressively, will also be helpful.

Unlike conventional construction, the sheer is seldom notched into a transom frame. Blocking, or corner knee, is used to structurally connect the longitudinal sheer with the transom. Plywood aft decks, acting as gussets from transom to sheer, may eliminate the necessity for corner knees. Resin-putty fillets and fiberglass laminates may also be used at sheer-transom junctions.

At the bow, sheers are best notched into a breasthook fitted between the side planking. Elimination of the breasthook is possible on smaller craft with a plywood foredeck lapping over the sheer members. Stitch-and-glue boats with decking have a sheer quite similar to conventional plywood boats.

On open boats, the combined sheer (inner sheer, plus outer sheer or gunwale) is heavier than on conventional craft as the lack of upright side frame members requires additional strength.

FIG. 27-20—Sheer longitudinals are notched into the breasthook on this open skiff.

FIG. 27-21—Corner knees, at sheer-transom junction, reinforce this important junction in an open dinghy.

REINFORCEMENT

Bottom battens, either internal or external, may be required for additional reinforcement. If such supports are in fact needed, they can be added after the stitch-and-glue boat is built.

In many smaller boats, particularly those with fairly thin planking, plywood battens can be used on the interior to increase bottom stiffness. While there are optimal placements in certain cases, battens may be positioned in a number of ways. Such strips can run longitudinally, athwartship, or obliquely on the bottom planking and act as floor cleats to prevent a person from slipping when walking about the boat. Longitudinal battens may also be used as in conventional plywood boats. Such battens can be of solid wood, as described in Chapter 17, and are usually put in after the hull is built.

Bottom battens may also be built up from plywood laminations. These tend to be somewhat wider than conventional battens, and can be quite useful in helping to strengthen the structure. Plywood battens are laminated and glued to the plywood planking (fastenings optional), taking care to follow the proper gluing and bonding practices, as described above.

Vertical plywood longitudinals on battens, as shown in Plate 27-D, provide additional support for soles or cockpit floors. They may also be extended to form longitudinal bulkheads or cabinet faces. Except in smaller boats, arthwartship bulkheads should be fastened to longitudinal battens and not attached directly to plywood planking. In stitch-and-glue boats, an arthwart-ship member in direct contact with plywood planking can create a localized stress area, causing the planking to fracture at some point in the future.

Keels on stitch-and-glue boats are somewhat different than on conventional plywood boats in that they are usually added after the hull is built. Keels may be eliminated in flat-bottomed boats without a centerline planking seam.

In smaller boats which may not have a keel, particularly those with center-joined bottom planking, the center seam should be reinforced with fiberglass laminations, both inside and out, as shown in Plate 27B-1. Small vee-bottom boats may have the center seam backed up with a wide strip of plywood, which can act as a keel. This strip must be glued in place and reinforced with resin-putty and fiberglass laminates, as shown in Plate 27B-2.

As the stitch-and-glue boat becomes larger, with more vee in the bottom, the method shown in Plate 27B-3 may be used. Note that a resin-putty may be used to eliminate fairing the ever-changing keel bevel. Attempting to fit a keel, either of plywood or solid wood, to the inside of the hull would be quite tedious.

Stitch-and-glue methods can also be applied in building boats of conventional construction. Cabins, for example, can be made of sheet plywood with stitched corner junctions. These are then filleted and covered with fiberglass laminate, in lieu of the usual blocking and fastenings. In fact, most permanent junctions can be handled with stitch-and-glue methods. Among its other advantages, this approach can eliminate a lot of hand fitting.

APPENDIX

ADDING FLOTATION

While the addition of flotation in a boat is technically not within the scope of this text, there are cases where flotation material or devices are to be included in the plywood hull. Since it is easier in many cases to install the flotation concurrently during the construction, and because many amateurs know little about the various flotation devices and material options available, it has been included in the text.

Flotation devices or materials may be added to a boat in order to keep it afloat when flooded. The flotation, if provided, should be adequate to support the boat as well as everything aboard, including the motor, tanks, battery, and crew, preferably in a level upright position in the water. A common misconception is that flotation materials added to the boat will make it float HIGHER in the water. This is simply NOT true. In fact, any flotation material added to the boat is an additional weight, and will actually make the boat float deeper in the water in direct proportion to the weight of flotation material added. Since the flotation material weight must be carried around at all times in the boat, it should be kept as light in weight as possible.

There are many make-shift devices and materials that can be used for flotation purposes, both bad and not so bad. For example, some people have used a variety of devices ranging from ping-pong balls in compartments, tethered bleach bottles, and old inner tubes stuffed in place. These devices, however, are not considered reliable or permanent. Air chambers that are integral with the hull would, at first glance, seem to be suitable for flotation. But what if such a chamber is punctured? Obviously such air chambers that are integral with the hull structure could lose their flotation value when needed most in an emergency.

The most suitable methods of providing flotation are by the use of air chambers that are non-integral with the hull structure, and by the addition of flotation materials in the form of various synthetic plastic foams. If non-integral air chambers are used, there should be several chambers provided so that in the event one is punctured, the others will provide sufficient flotation volume to float the boat.

Flotation materials and devices should be correctly located and installed if used. Boats equipped with flotation material only under the floorboards, or low down in the hull, may not float upright when swamped. Flotation added along the sides of a boat, and as far aft and high as possible, will tend to make the boat float upright as well as level in the water (assuming the water is not too

296

rough). The volume of flotation material or air chambers should be greatly increased longitudinally in the area where major weight concentrations, such as tanks, engines, and batteries, will be located, again locating the flotation as high as possible in the hull. Of course, if the boat is swamped, passengers should keep as low in the boat as possible to help keep it upright.

How much flotation should you have in your boat? First off, remember that wood floats, and of course a plywood hulled boat is inherently buoyant as long as it is unballasted. This means that flotation would be provided only to support items which are ADDED to the hull that are NOT inherently buoyant. These would include items like the motor, battery, ballast, tanks and their contents, controls, hardware, crew, etc. From a PRACTICAL and CONSERVATIVE standpoint, notwithstanding any local or Federal regulations to the contrary, flotation can be provided on a 1-to-1 basis; that is, for every pound of non-buoyant material added to the boat, a pound of flotation "value" would be provided.

From a practical standpoint, smaller non-powered plywood boats often have no flotation installed, or may only need a minimal amount since plywood will support about 45% more weight in addition to its own weight before it becomes submerged. The addition of flotation to such craft can use up a considerable amount of space. Consequently, it is common for the crew to wear buoyant life jackets for safety and minimize the volume of flotation. Then too, on larger plywood boats, flotation material is often not used due to the amount of accommodations and storage spaces that would be lost if foam were added. Wa-

tertight self-draining cockpits, sealing of cabin doors and hatches in inclement weather, a good system of powered and manual bilge pumps, buoyant life jackets for all crewmembers, and safe, prudent operation are the usual safeguards provided in larger craft.

What are the various flotation values? Air chambers should be figured as supporting about 62.4 lbs. per cubic foot, while the values of foams will vary somewhat depending on their density. For example, a foam with a density of 2 lbs. per cubic foot will support 60.4 lbs. per cubic foot, and a foam of a higher density would support even less. In other words, the density of the foam per cubic foot must be deducted from the flotation value of air (62.4 lbs. per cubic foot) to find the net flotation value of the foam. From this it can be seen that the less dense the foam is, the lighter in weight and higher in flotation value it will be.

What type of foam should be used for flotation? There is an endless variety of densities with either closed or open celled foams, but not all foams are suitable for flotation use. The foam material must stand up to the combined effects of gasoline, oil, petroleum products, solvents, fresh and salt water. It must also withstand vibration, shock, temperature variations, and exposure to the elements, especially the sun, so that it will be ready to do its job in an emergency. From the standpoint of the amateur builder, the foam should be inexpensive and easy to use as well. Foam purchased in blocks and slabs is usually easy to cut and shape in order to fit into awkward spaces. Various glues and adhesives can be used to secure the foam in place, however, the type of foam must be compatible with the glue or adhesive used. In some cases, the foam can be held in place by various parts of the boat's structure or joinerywork as long as there is no chance that the foam pieces could come adrift in an emergency.

In the following, several types of foams will be described. This listing is not meant to be all-inclusive since the technology of foam plastics is rapidly changing. Since foams tend to resemble one another, and because there are new foams frequently being introduced, some confusion may result with the novice. If in doubt about a type of foam, it is easy to test it to see if it is suitable. Take two small pieces of the foam and immerse one piece in gasoline and the other in water after weighing each one first. If the foam does not deteriorate in the gasoline, and does not weigh more after soaking for many hours, chances are that the foam will provide a suitable flotation material.

Ordinary foamed polystyrene (better known as "Styrofoam" which is a registered trade name) is common and cheap. Densities range from 1 to 5 lbs. per cubic foot. However, it dissolves easily in gasoline and is extremely flammable. Polyester resin will attack and dissolve the foam on contact also. Consequently it is NOT recommended for flotation material. Styrene acrylonitrile is chemically similar to foamed polystyrene, but is specially compounded to be resistant to solvents and is self-extinguishing. It absorbs virtually no water and ranges in density from 1 to 2 lbs. per cubic foot. While suitable for flotation, it may not be as readily available as the polyurethane types to be described.

Polyurethane foams can be either foamed in place or cut to shape from blocks and slabs in the rigid form. Either type is commonly used for flotation and is usually readily available. The foam is very resistant to gasoline and oil, which affect the foam only with a slight swelling after hours of complete immersion in densities of 2 or less lbs. per cubic foot. Over a long period of time, polyurethane foams with densities of less than 2 lbs. per cubic foot will absorb an enormous amount of water, however. Therefore, a high density (say 4 lbs. per cubic foot) should be used for flotation material below the cockpit sole or in the bilges. The foam is combustible but can be made so that it is self-extinguishing, which should be the type selected. This type of foam crumbles easily and can break down if subjected to severe and continual vibration. If using the pour-in-place type, read the label carefully and follow the directions provided. Pour small batches at a time as opposed to filling a void in one pour, as it is difficult to control the material.

Polyethylene foam is a suitable flotation material which is solvent-resistant, tough, and flexible. Although it will ignite, it is slow-burning. The material will swell when immersed in gasoline, but it absorbs virtually no water. Densities range from 2 to 9 lbs. per cubic foot.

Polyvinylchloride (PVC) foam, which is often used as a sandwich core material, is suitable for flotation although quite expensive. It is not combustible but it will melt. The foam is non-absorbent and will not rot or crumble. There are rigid, and rigid-elastic types, the latter being capable of returning to its original shape and size after impact and deflection. Polyester resin will soften the foam somewhat on contact, but the foam will restore itself after the resin cures. Densities range from 2 to 6 lbs. per cubic foot.

ABS foam (better known as "Royalex", a registered trade name) is a thermo plastic foam with a density of about 30 lbs. per cubic foot. It does not absorb water and is not affected by gasoline. While suitable for flotation, its primary use is in the manufacture of small plastic hulls so that flotation can be built in as a part of the hull skin. Hence, it is of limited value to the average amateur boatbuilder.

Foamed epoxy resins are similar to the polyurethane foams and range in density from 2 to 20 lbs. per cubic foot. They absorb only a small amount of water and are quite resistant to solvents. Epoxy foams can be foamed in place or precast in blocks and slabs which can be cut to shape. However, due to high cost at the present, their use is limited, although this could change in the future.

INDEX